#1 *NEW YORK TIMES* BESTSELLING AUTHOR

MIKE EVANS

BORN AGAIN

A NOVEL *of* JERUSALEM'S RESTORATION IN 1967

TIMEWORTHY
BOOKS

P.O. BOX 30000, PHOENIX, AZ 85046

Born Again: A Novel of Jerusalem's Restoration in 1967

Copyright 2014 by Time Worthy Books
P. O. Box 30000
Phoenix, AZ 85046

Design: Peter Gloege | LOOK Design Studio
Cover Photo: www.IsrealImages.com — Chief Rabbi Shlomo Goren
            Blowing Shofar on Temple Mount After Its Capture In 1967

Hardcover: 978-1-62961-024-5
Paperback: 978-1-62961-025-2
   Canada: 978-1-62961-026-9

This book is lovingly dedicated to my great friend,

Lt. Gen. Mordechai "Motta" Gur.

He commanded the Israeli Defense Force division that penetrated the Old City of Jerusalem and broadcast the famous words, "The Temple Mount is in our hands!"

— CHARACTERS AND TERMS —

Mordechai Gur: Colonel in the Israel Defense Force (IDF)

General Broder: Base Commander at Ramat David

David Kovner: Israeli spy living in Syria

Idan Rechter: A supervisor in Mossad's intelligence analysis section

Thomas Nesher: Diplomatic officer at the US Embassy

General Greenberg: IDF commander

Levi Eshkol: Israeli prime minister

Baruch Shatilov: Eshkol's chief of staff

Moshe Dayan: Israeli defense minister

Natan Shahak: Special assistant to Moshe Dayan

Shaul Nissany: Director of Mossad

Mossad: Israel's intelligence agency

Golda Meir: Israeli foreign minister

Rami Segev: An IDF major, in charge of developing plans to execute military strategy

Abba Eban: Career Israeli diplomat, replaces Golda Meir as foreign minister

Lawrence Rosenwald: Senior partner at the New York law firm of Mayer, Meagan & Gottschalk

Yaakov Auerbach: Junior partner at the New York law firm of Mayer, Meagan & Gottschalk

Suheir Hadawi: An Arab girl living in Galilee and former girlfriend of Yaakov Auerbach

Ahmad Hadawi: Suheir's brother

King Hussein: King of Jordan

Haider Raimouny: Hussein's assistant

Marouf Rifai: Footman in Hussein's service and an Israeli spy

Naif bin Talal: Hussein's cousin

FATAH: Palestinian National Liberation Movement

Yasser Arafat: Leader of FATAH

CHAPTER 1

1967—IN THE AIR OVER GALILEE

MORDECHAI GUR SAT ON THE FLOOR of a Douglas DC-3 aircraft, his back braced against the forward bulkhead. Originally built to carry passengers, the plane had been reconfigured for cargo service. Stripped of anything that hinted at civilian accommodation, its frame exposed to the outer skin, it had a steel floor with cleats for securing freight and oversized doors in the back, one of which had been removed.

With Gur that evening was a platoon of young, freshly trained paratroopers about to make their first nighttime jump. They were seated down both sides of the fuselage, backs against the wall, knees against their chest, and their eyes focused on the floor. No one spoke. No one smiled. No one looked around.

Born in Jerusalem, Gur had lived in Israel all his life. At the age of sixteen, he volunteered for service with Haganah, an early pre-independence defense militia. Later, in 1948, he served with the newly formed Israel Defense Forces in the War of Independence. When fighting came to an end he found he enjoyed military life and decided to make it his career. He trained as a paratrooper, worked in counterintelligence, and rose steadily through the ranks, becoming adjutant to the brigade commander. From there he went to Paris where he studied military tactics and the history of warfare. When he returned to Israel, he was promoted to the rank of colonel and placed in charge of the Fifty-Fifth Paratrooper Brigade, a position that gave him battlefield command and one in which he flourished.

As brigade commander, Gur didn't have to be there for the jump that night. He could have remained home with his wife, enjoying dinner and a relaxing moment with her. But trouble was brewing between Israel and its neighbors. War wasn't far off. No one said so explicitly—there'd been no meetings or memos on the topic—but Gur knew it. He sensed it. He felt it. And if war was coming, he wanted his men to be ready at a moment's notice for any eventuality. So he sat with them that evening, full pack on his back, a parachute strapped to his chest, the drone of the plane's engines in his ears, waiting for the signal to jump from the safety of the plane into the cool night air.

Twenty minutes into the flight, the jumpmaster, a tall, rangy soldier from Haifa, rose from his place on the floor near the rear of the plane, attached a tether from a harness at his waist to a hook on the aircraft's frame near the open doorway, and turned to face the men. Above him was a panel of red, yellow, and green lights. As he moved into position, the yellow light came on. "Okay!" he shouted above the noise of the engines. "We're getting close. Everybody up." He gestured with his hands. "Check your gear." The men pushed themselves up from the floor and stood to their feet as he continued, "Remember the drill. Stand up. Hook up. Shuffle to the door. Jump and count to four."

Gur stood with them, watching as the men gathered in a line at the center of the plane. They dutifully attached the rip cord tether from their parachute packs to an overhead line that ran the length of the plane, then turned to face the rear. As they waited, they adjusted their gear, tightened the straps from their packs, and shifted the parachute harness to a comfortable position. *It's the same with every drop,* Gur thought. *Fidgeting. Lots of fidgeting.*

The platoon leader, a lieutenant from Tel Aviv, worked his way past them, checking each one to make certain everything was in place. When he reached the door, he hooked his tether to the overhead line and turned to face the men. "Remember what we talked about in class. Count to four, look up, and straighten your lines. Don't cut away from your main too early, but don't wait too long, either. This is a nighttime jump. It's not much different from a daytime jump except it's dark, which means everything looks different. So pay attention. Drop zone is an open field. You've seen pictures. You all have maps. Find it early, guide yourself toward it. Don't get lost."

While the lieutenant continued to talk, Gur noticed a kid near him fumbling with the shoulder straps of his backpack. His hands trembled and his fingers seemed useless as he tried to untwist a shoulder pad. Gur reached over and straightened it for him, then gave the straps of his parachute harness a tug. "This is the part that matters," he shouted. "Keep it tight." The kid turned toward him with a nod and Gur noticed the name on his shirt. "Strauss? That's your name?"

"Yes, sir," Strauss replied.

"All right, Strauss," Gur pointed. "That parachute harness is the most important part. If it's not tight, it'll pinch you in the wrong place when the chute inflates," he grinned. Strauss nodded nervously and turned to face the rear of the plane with the others.

Seconds later, the green light came on. "This is it," the lieutenant shouted. "See you on the ground." He nodded to the jumpmaster, then turned aside and in two quick steps dove out the door with the practiced ease of one who'd done it many times.

"Here we go!" the jumpmaster shouted. "Remember the drill. Stand up. Hook up. Shuffle to the door. Jump and count to four."

The first man shuffled forward with halting steps, made an awkward turn to the left, and lunged through the doorway into the night. The tether from his rip cord pulled tight against his weight, then jerked free as it snatched the pin from the parachute. Instantly, fabric streamed from the pack, then billowed into the sky as it filled with air.

When he was gone, the jumpmaster pulled the dangling tether inside the plane and held it as others followed, shuffling forward while the next man jumped. They moved with their eyes fixed on the back of the man in front, no one looking up, the tether lines jiggling against their chests as each jump bounced the static line overhead.

Then it was Strauss's turn. He was the last man in the unit and he shuffled forward, made the turn, and froze. "Let's go!" the jumpmaster shouted. When Strauss gave no response, he moved closer, placing his lips near Strauss's ear. "You gotta jump, soldier!" But Strauss didn't move. "Are you listening to me?" the jumpmaster shouted. "Your platoon is waiting for you. You have to—"

Gur waved him off and put a hand on Strauss's shoulder. "First step is the hardest. So never stop at the door to think about it. Just come up here. Acknowledge the jumpmaster and step out. If you stop to think about it, nobody in their right mind would do this. So don't stop."

Strauss nodded his head but remained at the door, unable to take the final step. Gur leaned close once more and said, "I'll make it easy for you, son. Crouch." Gur tapped him on the back of the knee and Strauss bent his legs into a crouching stance. "Are you ready?" Gur asked. Strauss nodded his head. "Count to four. Look up. Make sure your lines are straight." Gur paused a moment longer, then shouted, "Go!" Strauss jumped forward, helped along by a hearty shove from Gur.

When Strauss was safely away, Gur looked over at the jumpmaster. "Reminds me of my first jump."

"Mine too."

Gur gave him a nod. "See you back at the base." Then with two steps he went out the door.

— · —

As Gur plunged toward the ground, he did as all the others and counted to four, then looked up and saw his parachute was open but the lines were twisted. He pumped his legs as if riding a bicycle, creating a gentle up-and-down motion against the lines. Moments later, they came untangled and Gur settled in his harness for the ride.

Off to the north, most of the men from the platoon should already be on the ground, with the last of the jumpers making their final approach. Having jumped much later, Gur was too far south to reach them. Instead of trying, he turned his attention to finding a suitable alternative place to land. That's when he noticed Strauss, drifting aimlessly, apparently unable to steer at all.

Minutes later, Gur dropped to the ground, wrestled the lines under control, and rolled his parachute into a manageable bundle. He stuffed it into his backpack. Strauss was about a hundred meters away, struggling to contain his parachute, which was slowly dragging him across the field. Gur started toward him.

"Didn't they teach you how to do that?"

The sound of Gur's voice startled him and he glanced around, his eyes wide. "Yes," Strauss replied. "But it was daytime."

"You don't like the dark?"

"Not much."

"Well, I'll see that they give you plenty of practice at it." Gur moved past him and took hold of the lines, then walked forward hand over hand and drew them to himself. When they had the parachute under control, Strauss folded it and stowed it inside his pack.

Gur glanced around to get his bearings. "We'd better find the others," he suggested, "or else we'll be hiking back to base."

Strauss looked concerned. "They won't come find us?"

"They should, but you can't always count on it." Gur turned away. "Come on. There's a road over here, I think."

They started across the field toward a tree line about sixty meters away. Gur led the way. Strauss walked to his right, just a few steps behind. They'd gone a short distance when Strauss said, "I was really scared up there."

"Son," Gur replied, "we're all scared."

"You were scared?"

"Jumping out of a perfectly good airplane is an unnatural act. Anybody tells you he isn't scared when he goes out the door, you know one thing for certain."

"What's that?"

"He's lying. Come on." Gur pointed. "I see the road over here."

When they were a few meters from the trees, Gur caught the odor of a cigarette. He raised his hand for Strauss to stop and gestured for silence, then dropped to one knee. Strauss did the same.

Against the shadows beneath the foliage of the trees, the glow of a cigarette was clearly visible and with it the outline of a man's head. Gur watched for a moment, then moved forward on his hands and knees.

Strauss followed. When they were closer, just a few meters away, Gur raised up for a better look. This time he saw the man, clearly visible. He was seated near a clump of bushes on the far side of the tree line, between the trees and road.

As they watched, the headlights of a truck appeared in the distance. It came down the road toward them, then slowed to a stop opposite the bushes where the man sat. Gur listened as the driver leaned out the window and spoke in Arabic. "Has he come by yet?"

"No," the man by the bush replied. "Not yet."

"You are ready?"

"Yes."

"Good."

Then the truck started forward once more. When it was gone, Gur turned away and gestured for Strauss to follow. When they were a few meters up the tree line Strauss whispered, "Who was that?"

"Arabs."

"The guy in the truck was asking whether someone had been by yet—I couldn't quite catch the name. Who was he talking about?"

Gur glanced over at him. "You speak Arabic?"

"Yes, sir. Shouldn't we do something about this?"

"I think we just did all we could do."

As they moved north up the tree line, Gur thought about what they'd just seen. A man hiding by the road. Other men roaming the countryside in a truck. Questions about someone's coming and going. This wasn't good. Something was up and he was certain it wasn't good. He was also certain that he and Strauss were in a vulnerable position—too vulnerable to do anything except watch and listen. The parachute jump that evening was a training exercise. Neither he nor anyone from the plane was armed. Listening, observing, and watching was all they could do. Better to move in the opposite direction and live to report what they'd seen and heard than attempt to intervene and get themselves captured. Or worse, killed.

With Strauss at his side, Gur picked up the pace and continued in the general direction of the original drop zone, following a course that kept them close enough to the tree line to be protected by its shadow but far enough from the road to avoid being seen. Near the northern edge of the field, they came to a fence. Gur helped Strauss across, then waited while Strauss returned the favor. As they cleared it, headlights from a car appeared in the distance, coming down the road toward them. Gur watched and as it drew near a sense of dread swept over him. "This isn't good," he mumbled.

"This is the person those men were asking about?"

"I think so," Gur said slowly.

The car passed opposite their position without incident but when it reached the place where they'd seen the man hiding in the bushes, a violent explosion erupted. Flames shot into the sky, and the car careened from the road into an irrigation ditch. Seconds later came a burst of automatic gunfire and in the glow of the flames they saw two men standing near the car.

Strauss had a look of anger and he shrugged off his backpack. "We have to do something."

"No," Gur took hold of his arm to stop him. "We know what happened."

"What do you mean? Those men we saw earlier attacked that car!"

"Yes, and there is nothing we can do about it."

"Nothing we can do? We are soldiers. We're supposed to do something. We should have done something before."

"We saw one man."

"I know but—"

"And as we watched just now we saw that there were actually two."

"Yes. So what are you saying?"

"I'm saying, if we'd gone in there before, thinking there was only one person, we would have confronted two."

"But we should see about them."

Just then, the gasoline tank on the car exploded. Both men watched as a bright orange fireball rolled into the sky, then Gur said tersely, "Get your pack and come on. We have to get out of here."

— · —

When Gur returned to the base at Ramat David, he filed a report with the watch commander, giving details of what he saw and heard. The next morning, General Broder, the base commander, called Gur to his office to discuss the matter. When Gur arrived, Broder was seated at his desk. Gur saluted and took a seat across from him as they reviewed the incident.

"Do you have any idea who was in that car?" Gur asked.

"Isaac Tikvah," Broder sighed.

"The guy who runs one of the farming settlements?"

"Yes," Broder nodded. "Very influential in the region. Vocally opposed to Arab terrorism and actively engaged with us. Helped with intelligence gathering, response coordination."

"He was part of that action we took against those men from a few weeks ago. The ones in that house outside Karmiel, supposed to be from FATAH."

"Yes."

"So, the people we saw by the road really were Arabs."

"They've been looking for a chance to hit Tikvah." Broder leaned back in his chair. Gur looked away, suddenly uncomfortable with his decision not to intervene the night before. "But tell me something," Broder continued. "How is it that you were in the area? I checked the map. That's a long way from where you were supposed to drop."

Gur had anticipated the question—the location where he'd landed was too far off-course to go unnoticed, but he felt an instinctive need to protect Strauss. "I got separated from the others in the unit. The wind blew me off course."

"There wasn't any wind," Broder countered.

"Then I don't know," Gur shrugged. "Must have been a strange gust. Anyway, sir, there are Arabs out there and judging from what we saw I'd say they have a network in place that's at least as extensive as anything Isaac Tikvah told us about. This isn't groups crossing the border from

Syria or Lebanon, like we were thinking. These are people who live here. Indigenous Arabs."

"I know," Broder nodded. "One of our patrols responded. They got to the scene within a few minutes. Did you see them?"

"No. We didn't stick around."

"Why not?"

"This was a training exercise. Most of the men in that unit were on their first nighttime jump. We weren't armed. We got out of there as quietly as possible."

"We?" Broder asked with a grin.

"One of the men landed near me."

"You both got blown off-course," Broder chuckled, no longer able to contain his humor at Gur's unease.

"He's a trainee, sir." Gur glanced away. "I took care of it."

"Who was it?"

"I took care of it," Gur repeated. "And we need to take care of this situation. We need to put more troops in the field. Form a net across Galilee. A major military operation."

"Don't you think that would just drive the Arabs to another location?"

"Perhaps. But what's the alternative, sir? Wait for them to attack again so we can pick up the dead bodies? If our presence deters them from acting here or anywhere, isn't that enough?"

"I suppose," Broder nodded. "Put your ideas on paper." He scooted closer to his desk. "Write it up. I'll see what they think about it in Tel Aviv."

CHAPTER 2

IN DAMASCUS, DAVID KOVNER left his apartment in an upscale section of the city and walked five blocks to a corner where he boarded a bus. Known to his Syrian friends as Khalid al-Khatib, he'd lived in the city for the past five years posing as an arms supplier and providing the Syrian military with weapons from France, the Soviet Union, and, through connections in Vietnam, surface-to-air missiles manufactured in the United States. With that as his cover, he insinuated himself into the Syrian political structure and developed friendships with high-ranking officials, including Nureddin al-Atassi, the president. He dressed impeccably, enjoyed many of the finer things of life, but refused to hire a personal driver or allow others to shop for him. Food and transportation, he'd learned early in his career, were points of weakness that left him unnecessarily vulnerable to others.

That morning, Kovner rode downtown to a meeting at the apartment of Salah Jadid, a Ba'ath Party leader and one of Kovner's primary connections to the military. Kovner's friend, Daud Masalha, was there also, along with several others. They reclined against cushions on the floor in the living room and sipped coffee while they discussed strategy for the upcoming parliamentary elections. Before long, the conversation turned to the overriding need for regional Arab unity, with Iraq, Syria, Jordan, and Egypt acting as one. And that led to a discussion about Yasser Arafat and the FATAH movement.

"He can be difficult to understand at times," Jadid conceded, "but we are using him to bring the people of Palestine together. I have met with him many times and he is very capable. With our help, he can forge the disparate Palestinian Arab groups into a single identity and that will greatly simplify our efforts to control the region."

"I don't like him," Masalha said with a shake of his head.

Jadid seemed surprised. "Oh? And why not?"

"I just don't trust him."

"You have met him?"

"Yes," Masalha nodded. "Many times. And I have looked into his eyes. They are the eyes of a soulless man."

Jadid laughed. "Perhaps that is the kind of man we need."

"Perhaps," Masalha nodded.

Ibrahim Batatu was seated to Jadid's left. "It doesn't matter whether we can trust him," Batatu offered, "so long as he is working on our side, he is our friend."

"And if not," another suggested, "we can always shoot him and blame it on the Zionists."

"Just so long as he provokes the Zionists into fighting," Kovner added.

"You have doubts?" Jadid asked.

"I don't think Arafat is as concerned about provoking the Zionists as we had hoped."

"Then what is he trying to do?" Batatu asked.

"He's trying to win."

"Ha!" Batatu exclaimed, his eyes wide with laughter. "Defeat the Zionists? By himself?"

"Yes."

"He's crazy," Jadid added, "but he is not that crazy."

"No," Kovner demurred. "He's not crazy. He's a zealot."

"Well, he can be a crazy zealot if he likes," Batatu continued, "just as long as the Zionist soldiers come after us in their frustration."

"I'm not sure Arafat can survive that long," Masalha offered.

"You think the Zionists are that good?"

"No. But Assad hates him. And as defense minister, Assad can have him killed and no one would question it."

"Assad will never kill him," Jadid scoffed.

"Why not?"

"Because Arafat is President al-Atassi's friend," Jadid explained. "And in spite of Atassi's shortcomings, if Assad kills Arafat while Atassi is in office, Assad would be next."

"Maybe Arafat will eliminate Assad," Batatu chortled.

"Oh," they laughed in unison. "You should be careful."

"Talk like that will get you killed by both of them," Masalha jested.

"That is a real threat," Kovner added in a serious tone. "Assassination is a tool of political change our people know how to use."

"And it's always an inside job."

"Yes," Batatu nodded. "Just ask King Hussein."

"How many plots has he survived?"

"Many plots, though only one actual attempt."

"But Hussein may meet his match soon," Jadid said calmly. "And that would be a good thing. A blessing from Allah."

The room fell eerily silent as Kovner and the others exchanged furtive glances. Finally Kovner asked, "What do you mean by that?"

"Just as I said," Jadid replied. "This time, Hussein may be gone for good. And then we can get on with making the dream of Arab unity a reality."

— • —

After the meeting, Kovner and Daud Masalha left the apartment together. As they walked up the sidewalk, Kovner asked, "What was Jadid talking about?"

"He talks about many things," Masalha replied. "Words are his friend."

"But what did he mean about Hussein?" Kovner continued. "What did he mean that this time Hussein might not survive?"

Masalha made a dismissive gesture. "He was just talking."

"It didn't sound like talk. Did you notice the look on his face, and the way everyone reacted? Even you."

"No one in that room knows any more than you or I. Not even Jadid."

"He has great influence in the party."

"Yes."

"Did he hear something?"

"Listen." Masalha glanced over at Kovner. "Jadid is influential, but he is also very dangerous. You should be careful how much you trust him."

"I am aware of his limitations," Kovner responded. "But apparently he has heard something about Hussein. Something more definite than the vague rumors we've heard before."

"Yes," Masalha conceded. "Apparently so."

"Have you heard it?"

Masalha looked perturbed by the questions. "I don't know anything for certain."

"What have you heard?" Kovner insisted.

Masalha's shoulders slumped. "Supposedly," he began reluctantly, "Hussein's cousin is involved. Along with one of the generals." He gestured with his hand in a chopping motion. "But that is all I've heard."

"His cousin?"

"That is what I heard. But I am merely telling you a rumor."

"Which cousin?" Kovner asked. "He must have many."

"That is all I know. And it is only something I heard. I know nothing of fact."

"Is this *our* plan?" Kovner pressed. "Are *we* behind it?"

"I do not know." Masalha shot a look in Kovner's direction. "Why do you ask me all these questions?"

"I want to know. Staying on top of things is how I make a living."

"You are looking to expand your business to Jordan?"

"I would if someone else was there besides Hussein."

Masalha grinned. "That is what they like about you."

"What?"

"Always the opportunist."

"I am merely trying to earn a living."

"Yes," Masalha nodded. "And you are an opportunist. They are opportunists. Jadid. Batatu. All of them. And they see that in you."

"Every situation presents an opportunity for business. For someone. And if there is to be a change in Jordan, I would like to be the one to take advantage of it." They walked a little farther in silence, then Kovner asked with a smile, "So, this plan, it is our plan?"

"I have not been contacted about it. I just know what I have heard."

"Jadid seems to know."

"Yes."

"And if he knows, there could be something to it."

"Perhaps."

"Do we really want Hussein gone? I know it would be good for me," Kovner said in an attempt to keep Masalha talking. "He would not do business with me. Perhaps his successor will. But for the country. Our country. Would it be good for us?"

"Yes. Absolutely."

"Why?"

"We are ready to fight, but we cannot defeat the Zionists by ourselves," Masalha explained. "We need the help of our neighbors. It's in their best interests to help us defeat the Zionists but no one trusts anyone these days, so no one will step forward to act. There is no cooperation. They only give lip service to the notion of Arab unity. So we have to help them cooperate."

"I understand that," Kovner agreed. "We sponsor attacks to provoke the Zionists into responding, hopefully even attacking us directly, so we can use that to pressure Egypt to honor its treaty commitments and attack from the south."

"Right," Masalha nodded.

"But how does that affect Jordan?"

"We need them to participate. Not only for the help of their army but in order to have access to their territory. With our troops and Egyptian troops stationed in Jordan, and in the West Bank that they control, we can easily attack Jerusalem with overwhelming force."

"And Hussein has refused to allow foreign troops in his country," Kovner nodded.

"Exactly. So either he helps or he must be replaced."

"And we are actively working to do that?"

"We are pursuing his removal with many efforts, I know that much. That is why they were talking about Hussein that way. If he will not help us, then he must go. But I know nothing of a specific plan. Just rumor. And if you are smart, you will forget about business for once and say nothing else of this, either."

— · —

Later that afternoon, Kovner took a taxi and rode toward his apartment. When he was still a few blocks away, he passed a car parked near the curb. Two men were seated in front. Both were reading newspapers but it seemed obvious to Kovner that they were watching for someone or something. The sight of it worried Kovner and he began to wonder what they might be doing and whether their presence had any connection to him. With his mind racing, Kovner thought back through his routine the past weeks. Had he been careless? Had he missed something? Was Mukhabarat, the Syrian intelligence agency, on to him?

In the next block Kovner leaned forward from the rear seat. "Pull over up here," he commanded the driver, pointing to a spot on the right side of the street.

"Your address is still two blocks farther," the driver explained.

"I know, but I need to shop and I'll walk from here. Pull over." Reluctantly, the driver steered the car to the side of the street and waited while Kovner counted out the fare, then stepped from the car.

As the taxi drove away, Kovner crossed the street to an open-air market and wandered among the vendors. He purchased vegetables for dinner and made his way to a stall near the back where an elderly man sold meat. Sides of beef hung from hooks that were suspended from the overhang of a building that adjoined the property. Flies buzzed everywhere. A boy with a well-worn stick brushed them from the meat.

Kovner pointed to the side he preferred and told the old man which cut he wanted. Using a long, broad knife, the man cut a slice of flank steak and wrapped it in brown paper. Kovner paid him and tucked the package beneath his arm, then made his way to the street.

At the apartment, Kovner walked to the kitchen and placed the vegetables in the sink, then carefully unwrapped the steak. As he peeled aside the paper, he found a note tucked between the folds. He lifted it to the light and read the single sentence: *Awaiting news of the trees and whether we might expect a crop this year.* Kovner sighed and shook his head.

For the past two years he had provided Mossad, Israel's intelligence service, with information about Syrian artillery placements in the Golan Heights. He'd visited the Heights with General Azmeh, paced off the distances between bunkers, and provided precise information about how to locate each one. Yet his handlers in Tel Aviv wanted more. And that was the thing that worried him most.

Kovner's primary means of communication with Mossad was by encoded transmissions sent with a shortwave radio he kept hidden in a compartment behind the kitchen cabinets. The radio was efficient, simple to operate, and, unlike other forms of communication, it left no trail that could later be found and followed. Its one drawback, however, was the fact that during transmission the signal it produced acted like a beacon announcing its location. Anyone who located the transmission could triangulate off the signal and locate the transmitter. Repeated transmissions made it more likely someone would do just that.

On the other hand, in spite of how vague and uninformed he seemed when talking to Masalha, he had developed hard information about the situation with Hussein that he needed to convey. Jadid was only one source of the assassination rumor and Masalha wasn't the only person he'd asked about it. This rumor came with better sources, better information, and details that lent themselves to outside verification. Transmitting that information was less risky, too, unlike map coordinates for artillery positions, which were easily detected, even if transmitted in code.

Kovner thought about his options as he cooked dinner. He'd ignored Mossad's repeated requests in the weeks before and if he didn't respond soon, they would begin to wonder if he was still alive. The last thing he needed was someone of dubious credentials appearing at his apartment to check on him. The information about Hussein needed to be conveyed and he could send it with minimal risk. And that's what he planned to do.

When he finished eating, he took his plate to the kitchen, opened the kitchen cabinet, and removed the back panel. He lifted the short-wave radio transmitter from its hiding place and with little effort connected the electronic key to the radio. Moments later, he began tapping out a coded message providing information about the plot against King Hussein.

CHAPTER 3

IN NORTHERN GALILEE, Ovadia Shapiro sat at a radio console at a listening station located twenty kilometers east of Nahariya. On the console was an automatic scanner that sampled shortwave signals, methodically moving from frequency to frequency. Shapiro's job was to listen to each frequency for the telltale signature of an agent—a series of numbers and letters tapped out in Morse code on selected days at predetermined times, and were repeated at fifteen-minute intervals until a reply from a listening station signaled reception. Once the identity of the agent was confirmed, the parties were free to exchange coded messages. It was a clumsy system, but one that provided an almost untraceable form of communication.

Originally constructed by the Israel Defense Forces to provide radio communications for military units, the station very quickly proved useful to Mossad analysts and technicians as a tool for eavesdropping on Syrian and Lebanese radio signals. In the years following the 1948 War of Independence, Mossad began sending agents into neighboring countries, and the station became an important communication link in the transmission of surreptitious information.

Listening for the agent's signal was mindless work that required no special technical skill. Consequently, most radio operators lasted only a short time before resigning or seeking other duties. Shapiro, however, didn't mind. Most nights he sat with headphones over his ears, listening while he worked a crossword puzzle.

By seven that evening he'd heard nothing of interest and reached for the switch to put the signal on the intercom so he could listen while he left the console for a restroom break. Just then, a message caught his ear. Instead of pressing the intercom switch, he pressed a button on the console to lock the scanner at that frequency. To his left, reels of a tape machine began to turn as it slowly recorded the transmission. Shapiro jotted down the numbers and letters from the message, then opened a notebook to check it against the list of official identifiers. Halfway down the list he found the sequence was assigned to David Kovner.

Shapiro placed his right hand on the transmission key and tapped out the response—a series of numbers and letters indicating he'd heard the agent's initial transmission and was ready to receive. Seconds later, the message began. Using pencil and note pad, Shapiro transcribed the long and short signals, producing nothing more than a series of letters and numbers that filled a single page. Deciphering it required both an encryption key and a key to the underlying code. For security purposes, Shapiro had neither.

— · —

Two hours later, the message received by the listening station arrived at Mossad headquarters in Tel Aviv where it was promptly delivered to Idan Rechter, a supervisor in Mossad's intelligence analysis section. Working from the Operations Center in the basement of the building, he commanded a staff of analysts charged with evaluating the hundreds of pieces of intelligence gathered every day by Mossad agents. That evening was his turn for overnight duty.

The analysts, most of whom were recent college graduates, represented some of the brightest young men and women Israel had to offer. They were quick and insightful but occasionally brash and temperamental. Rechter, who had taught as an adjunct faculty member at Hebrew University, thought of them as his students, a perspective not undeserved by the analysts but one not always welcomed, either.

By the time Rechter and his team received Kovner's transmission, it had been decoded and deciphered into a legible message. Rechter passed copies of it to his staff and moved to the center of the room. "Okay," he began, "this latest message is from one of our agents in Damascus. It's been marked urgent, which means it's been assigned priority over other work. So let's put aside our other tasks and concentrate on this one."

Ehud Katz called out from the far side of the room, "Does the agent have a name?"

"You know they don't share that information with us," Rechter answered.

"Just thought I'd ask."

"What difference does it make?" someone piped up.

"I don't know," Katz shrugged. "It might make a huge difference but we'll never know because Mossad has a policy of not telling us."

"That's right," Rechter replied, unamused by Katz's sarcasm. "And we aren't going to change that policy tonight. What we *are* going to do is get to work figuring out what this message means and whether the information can be substantiated. So let's work the problem. What do we have?"

Someone spoke up. "A message apparently from an agent."

"This is a man?" Katz asked.

"Yes," Rechter replied. "They tell us that much."

"Where is he located?"

"According to information from the listening post, this transmission came from Damascus. The agent heard several people discussing a supposed attempt on King Hussein's life. The first thing we need to ask is whether this is plausible."

"It says this attempt has the support of unspecified generals and the king's cousin."

"We've already seen the conflicting interests of the generals. They wanted to do more in 1948. Hussein stopped them."

Meir Walder joined the discussion. "In 1948, they only took the West Bank, but that was the area with the heaviest Arab population. We didn't want it. They knew we didn't want it. It was theirs for the taking and they took it to keep it out of the hands of the Egyptians or the Syrians."

"And they didn't even try to take more," someone added.

"I think the generals were all on record as favoring more."

"But is that still true now?"

"Is either version true now—that they don't want more or that they want it all? I mean, since 1948 they've been ambivalent at best."

"They have to act like they want more to prove their Arab bona fides. Otherwise, the Arab League will attack *them* the same as they would attack us."

Walder brought the discussion back on topic. "If a cousin of the king really is behind it, then my guess is that would be Naif bin Talal. He's had his eye on the throne ever since he learned how his grandfather was murdered. If Talal's grandfather had survived, the throne would have come down his line rather than to Hussein and according to our agents in Amman, Talal has had great difficulty accepting Hussein's legitimacy."

"Okay," Rechter said, interested by the last comment. "What do we know about Talal?"

"His father left Jordan and moved to Iraq when Talal was ten. Talal remained with his mother in Amman. Her family owned interests in several construction companies, a couple of food processors, and an import business. When he was twelve he learned about how his grandfather died. This has been a festering problem ever since."

"What about education?"

"Attended madrassa in Amman. Went to Paris for college. Apparently graduated. Spent a few years in Switzerland. Nothing very remarkable."

"Is that it?"

Nathan Shlonsky spoke up. "That's the information we have on him, but the same agents who told us that also tell us that Talal isn't a player in Jordanian politics. He's just a rich guy who never grew up. Prefers to spend his days indulging in luxury. Not really interested in politics except that he's harbored anger toward the Hussein branch of the family over his grandfather. Other than that, he has shown no interest in the political future of Jordan, and the anger about his grandfather is something we only learned recently."

"And what do you make of that?"

downward, he brought his arms over his face and squeezed his hands tight against the back of his head, hoping with all his might that he survived the fall. Then he felt the fabric of the awning against his hips and opened his eyes to find he was wrapped in the sagging canvas as it hung against the frame.

With his fall broken by the awning, Kovner grabbed the metal frame with both hands and rolled, flipping himself off the awning. He dangled over the edge a moment, then let go and dropped safely to the sidewalk, only to find himself face-to-face with the two men he'd seen in the car earlier that day. Then something struck him from behind and everything went black.

CHAPTER 4

THE FOLLOWING DAY, MEIR WALDER traveled across town to a café near the beach where he met Thomas Nesher. They sat at a table in back and talked over coffee.

"Your message sounded important," Nesher began. "What's up?"

"We need to know if you have any recent information on Naif bin Talal."

"Hussein's cousin?"

"Yes."

Nesher had an amused smile. "You have no doubt heard the latest rumors about a plot against Hussein."

"We're trying to determine if there is any truth to the matter."

"We're trying to do the same."

"How long have you known about this?"

"Not long. We only heard it recently as well. From what we know," Nesher continued, "Talal is keeping company with Fayez bin Wahbi."

"The Jordanian businessman?"

"Yes," Nesher nodded.

"Brokers arms for the Soviets, does the same with oil for the Emirates."

"He's very wealthy and has important ties to several high-ranking Syrian government officials."

"But what's the connection to Talal?" Walder asked.

"Our sources say the Syrians want access to Jordan's uranium deposits."

"Ah," Walder nodded. "That would get them interested."

"Very much so," Nesher agreed. "The Syrians see your reactor in Dimona as a threat to their security, but they also see nuclear power as the best way to gain leverage with dominant countries like us and the Soviet Union. And they're certain it would give them an undeniable edge in the region."

"We've heard some of this from our own sources."

"There's one thing you've probably not heard," Nesher offered. "Last year, at a meeting in Istanbul, Syrian representatives approached Hussein about developing the uranium deposits. Hussein turned them down and has refused to discuss the matter further. The Syrians are angry about it, and that is one of the several things driving the Syrian push for war. It's not just about wanting to get rid of you."

Walder had a questioning frown. "They think that a regional war will lead to Hussein's downfall?"

"Not so much that. At least not directly. They aren't sure Hussein would actually join in a regional fight, assuming there is one. But if the Syrians can convince Egypt to join them in attacking Israel, and Jordan *doesn't* join them, then the Syrians would have a reason to invade Jordan as well. For the Syrians, that is becoming the preferred scenario. They would solve the Arab issue in Palestine once and for all, eliminate Israel as a nation, and gain control over Jordan and its uranium."

"But still, how does Talal figure into that?"

"The Syrians are afraid to confront you solely on their own. They don't think they can defeat Israel without help. They have doubts about Jordanian participation, but they also have doubts about Egyptian resolve. To hedge their bets, they are using Wahbi to manipulate Talal in a play to remove Hussein from the throne and put Talal in his place."

"So," Walder continued the thought, "if war doesn't come, they'll just remove Hussein and install a man of their choosing."

"Right," Nesher nodded again. "They really want Israel eliminated, and they really want access to that uranium. But if they can't get both at the same time, they'll take whichever one they can get first, and worry about the other later."

"So, the threat against Hussein is real?"

Nesher arched an eyebrow. "Oh yes. It's real. Talal is Hussein's cousin, but he hates Hussein. And Hussein hates him back."

"Talal sees Hussein as a usurper."

"Yes. And Hussein sees Talal as a snake."

Walder set his cup on the table. "Does Hussein know about the Syrians and Wahbi?"

"Apparently he knows they are after him. But I don't know how much he knows about the plot."

"You have not told him?"

"No," Nesher replied. "The United States has adopted an official position of neutrality toward Jordan. We will neither help nor hinder."

"Washington would like to see him removed?"

"We're neutral."

"But if doing nothing means he is eliminated, you're taking a side."

Nesher glanced away. "Some in Washington think the disruption would be to our advantage."

"But what about the uranium?"

"Washington thinks that if Syria built a nuclear reactor, your prime minister would make sure it never became operational."

"So they don't see a Jordanian coup d'état as a problem."

"Not really."

— • —

David Kovner opened his eyes to find he was sitting in a wooden chair positioned in the center of a cavernous warehouse. From overhead, soft gray light filtered through the dirty panes of a skylight, giving the room a surreal glow. As his eyes adjusted, he saw a table sitting a few meters to one side. From his vantage point, the building appeared abandoned and empty but when he tried to move he discovered his arms were tied to the armrests. His legs were bound to the chair frame. That's when a voice spoke from behind.

"It's no use to try. You aren't going anywhere."

Moments later, the sound of a creaking door came from the shadows, followed by the click of footsteps against the concrete floor as someone approached. As the footsteps drew near, a second voice spoke. "Ah, Mr. Kovner. You are awake." A young man appeared and stood about a meter away. "It is Kovner, isn't it?" He was athletic and handsome, especially when he smiled, but the look in his eyes sent a shiver up Kovner's spine. This was no mere Arab youth. This was a trained interrogator and Kovner knew he was only there for one purpose, to extract information and then kill him.

"You can at least tell me your name," the interrogator continued.

Kovner stared at him but gave no reply. If he was going to die anyway, he might as well make the effort as difficult as possible.

"You are Mossad?" the interrogator continued. "You are spying for the Zionists?" Still Kovner said nothing. "Why do you have a radio? We have intercepted your radio transmissions. Our experts will have them decoded at any moment." He paused as if expecting an answer, then continued. "Tell me something," he said in an offhanded manner. "Why would you do this to us? You had so many friends. So many people placing their confidence in you. Why did you do this?"

All the while, Kovner remained silent.

"You will not speak?" The interrogator stepped closer and leaned over, his hands resting on his knees, his eyes level with Kovner's. "Very well, then. We shall do this the difficult way." He lowered his voice to a whisper. "But you will not like it."

The interrogator backed away and glanced to the left. A big man appeared, moving toward Kovner and as he did, he stripped off his shirt, revealing his large arms and muscular chest. He strode toward Kovner and, without so much as a pause, struck him with a fist against Kovner's jaw. Instantly, the room went black.

Sometime later, Kovner became aware of water dripping off his chin. He lifted his eyelids and saw that he was soaked with water. Fingers touched his jaw and he looked up to see the interrogator standing before him. "You are with us now?" the interrogator smiled. "That is good.

Perhaps now you will give us some answers. You wish to talk now or shall we continue with the…treatments?"

Kovner spit out a loosened tooth. "My name is Khalid al-Khatib," he said as firmly as he could muster. "I am a businessman. I sell—"

"We know what you have been doing," the interrogator interrupted. "Selling useless military hardware to our army." He continued to speak as he moved over to the table. "Making friends with government officials." Now for the first time, Kovner saw the table held a pair of pliers, a knife, and a battery from an automobile. The interrogator smiled back at him. "You were deliberately gaining their confidence. Passing yourself off as a Syrian. And all to gain access to military secrets which you send to your Zionist superiors. But I assure you, Mr. Kovner, you have no friends in Syria now. And your Zionist collaborators are too weak to save you." He turned to the table and attached wire cables to the battery, then looked back in Kovner's direction. "I will ask once more. Who are you working for?"

"I am a businessman. I sell—"

The interrogator snatched up the pliers and with two quick steps crossed the space between them. He grabbed Kovner's wrist with one hand and with the other took hold of the nail of Kovner's little finger in the jaws of the pliers, then jerked the nail out by the root.

Kovner screamed in pain as blood dripped from the tip of his finger. "Okay," he shouted. "Okay. I am an Israeli agent."

"With Mossad?"

"Yes."

The interrogator gestured to the left and a man, different from those he'd seen so far, stepped before him with a bottle of water. He held it to Kovner's lips while Kovner took a long, slow drink. In the meantime, the interrogator returned the pliers to their place on the table and took a pack of cigarettes from the pocket of his shirt. He gestured to Kovner with the pack, as if offering him a cigarette, but Kovner declined with a shake of his head.

When the water bottle was half empty, the man holding it took it away and the interrogator moved closer. "Tell me about the radio," he said casually. "Where did it come from?"

"I don't know."

"Surely you don't expect me to believe that."

"I rented the apartment."

"Yes."

"And when I returned for the first time, it was in the kitchen cabinet."

"It simply appeared?"

"Yes."

"Who made the secret compartment for it?"

"I don't know."

"Then how did you know to use it?"

"They told me."

"Who told you?"

"The people on the radio. In the first broadcast. They told me where it was located."

"Who made that broadcast?"

"I don't know. I listened. They contacted me. And that's what they said."

"That radio operates on many frequencies. How did you know which one to use to hear them?"

"I just knew," Kovner shrugged.

"Because they told you when they sent you here."

Here. The word caught Kovner's attention. *I must still be in Damascus.* Maybe. "Yes," Kovner nodded. "I knew it when I came."

"And what is that frequency?"

Now Kovner realized something else. His captors didn't know which frequencies he used and that left him wondering how they found him if they didn't have those frequencies and weren't listening to his transmission.

"I don't remember."

The interrogator took the cigarette from his mouth. "Surely you remember," he picked the pliers from the table. "You transmitted often. What were the frequencies?"

"I don't remember."

The interrogator dropped his cigarette on the floor and rubbed it out with his foot. "Well," he sighed, "if you don't remember, we'll have to see if we can help."

With slow, deliberate steps, he moved toward Kovner, then grasped his wrist and clamped the pliers on to the nail of his index finger. "Remembering anything now?" he snarled, then jerked the nail free. Without saying more, he extracted the nails from the other three fingers of that hand, and somewhere in the process Kovner fainted.

— • —

Outside on the street, Bashir Kuftaro parked his bicycle in the alley next to three garbage barrels. He checked behind him to make certain no one was watching, then climbed atop the first barrel. An open window was located about a meter above, just close enough for him to grasp the sill. He locked his fingers in place and hoisted himself up, then squeezed through the opening.

Once inside, he made his way to the front of the building and hid behind a stack of shipping crates. From there he had a clear view of Kovner seated in the chair, the interrogator standing in front, with a big man to his left. Several other men stood behind Kovner but Bashir was certain Kovner did not know they were present. One of them held an executioner's sword—short and without a point but very sharp. Bashir knew the end that lay ahead. He watched long enough to confirm the man in the chair was Kovner, then retreated to the window and down to the garbage barrel below.

From the warehouse, Bashir pedaled as fast as he could down the street to a parking lot near the railroad. A red truck was parked there, loaded and ready for the highway. He pulled alongside it, bounded from the bicycle, and up to the driver's door. The driver glanced down at him. "Well, is it him?"

"Yes," Bashir nodded. "It's him." The driver tossed Bashir a handful of coins, put the truck in gear, and drove away.

— • —

Twelve hours later, a courier arrived at Mossad Headquarters in Tel Aviv. A pouch hung over his shoulder with a message from an IDF unit patrolling in the Galilee. The message was delivered to Idan Rechter in the operations center. He read it quickly and sent it upstairs to Ami Rosenblum in the executive services department. Rosenblum took one look at it and ran down the hall to the office of Shaul Nissany, the Mossad director.

"They have Kovner," Rosenblum blurted as he came through the doorway.

"Are we certain?" Nissany asked from his seat behind the desk.

Rosenblum replied. "His identity has been confirmed."

"Where are they holding him?"

"He's in a warehouse on the north side of Damascus."

"The north side," Nissany sighed. "We had hoped for a different location."

"Yes." Nissany glanced away. "That would have been better."

"Should we activate one of the teams?"

Nissany looked up at him. "No, Ami. We can't do it."

"If we leave him there he'll die."

"He's probably already dead."

"We aren't even going to try?"

"A team could probably get to him, but they would never be able to get him out. And our people up there aren't equipped to hide all of them—Kovner and the team."

"You'll pass this on to the prime minister?"

"Leave it to me." Nissany turned away and opened a drawer in the desk. "I'll take care of it."

CHAPTER 5

A FEW DAYS LATER, GENERAL BRODER came to IDF headquarters in Tel Aviv for a regularly scheduled meeting with the general staff. Afterward, Broder met privately for dinner with General Greenberg, IDF commander. The two had known each other since they first became officers during the 1948 war. As they dined that evening, Broder turned the conversation to the subject of Mordechai Gur's report on Arab activity in the Galilee.

"I read the report," Greenberg nodded. "Interesting observations, especially coming from a veteran paratrooper who landed a mile from the drop zone."

"He's one of our best field commanders," Broder defended.

"I know Mordechai," Greenberg acknowledged. "And I agree. He's one of the best. Think there's anything to what he says?"

"He's convinced the Arabs are far more organized than we at first thought and wants a full-scale military operation to deal with them."

"I know what Gur thinks. What do *you* think?"

"If I was going on a hunch, I'd go on his."

"Do you think the men he saw were part of FATAH?"

"I don't know."

"I had some people look into this. Our best information still says the Arabs in Galilee aren't that well organized."

"Maybe they've been improving."

"Maybe so." Greenberg lifted his wineglass and took a sip. "Did you believe the part about Gur getting blown off-course?"

"I checked on that. He was on a training exercise with a platoon of new paratroopers. One of the men had a tough time getting out the door. He and Gur were late jumping."

Greenberg smiled. "Mordechai fought with us in '48, you know."

"Yes," Broder nodded. "I remember that."

"And he was part of the Sinai campaign in '56. He's driven, determined, and goal-oriented. But so far as I know, he's never let that become a detriment to his men. Most of our officers would have simply shoved the kid out the door."

"From what I hear, that's what the jumpmaster wanted to do."

Greenberg gave Broder a knowing look. "I'm guessing Mordechai wouldn't even tell you the kid's name."

"No, sir. I pressed him for it but all he would say was, 'I took care of it.'"

Greenberg grinned. "That's Mordechai. I'll forward the report to Mossad and see if they'll give us something new on Arab activity in the Galilee, but I don't think a major deployment will help, though I admire the sentiment."

"Yes, sir. I'll tell Gur."

Broder placed his hands on the armrests of his chair to stand but Greenberg gestured for him to wait. "Listen. As you know, we've assembled a team for planning. I was thinking Gur might be of help to them."

"Yes. I suppose," Broder mused. "But he's a field commander at heart and I doubt he'd be interested in a desk job."

"We really need someone like him on this," Greenberg explained. "The group we've assembled isn't the typical waste of time. The prime minister has made this a priority. We're all convinced that war is coming. It's just a matter of when. The planning group is figuring out how we can win and I'll be honest with you, it's not all that clear to me that we can survive."

Broder looked concerned. "If all of the neighboring countries attacked at once, they would have an overwhelming advantage."

"By the numbers, even one of them has an overwhelming advantage. They all have armies that outnumber ours. But if they all came at once, in a coordinated attack, we would be outnumbered by an even greater margin. As much as five or six to one."

"Do you think a planning group can do much good? I mean, most of our advantage in the past has come from the willingness of our men to fight and not run."

"If we have to fight, we'll need more than determination this time. The Soviets have armed Syria and they're equipping the Egyptians now. This war will be won by troops in the field but they'll have to fight intelligently. We've gathered the best people we can find to help do that, but very few of them have actual combat experience. They need somebody like Gur to make certain the plans they produce will actually work under combat conditions."

"He'd be good at that. Drives me crazy sometimes in evaluations. Always asking what if. But again, I don't think he has a high regard for planning."

"Sounds like just what the committee needs."

"Our operations can continue without him, but you'll have to be the one to sell him on the job. He won't give up his combat command at my request."

Greenberg smiled. "We'll see what we can do about that."

— • —

That evening, Levi Eshkol, Israel's prime minister, sat aboard a specially equipped Boeing 707 jet as he flew home from the United States where he had met with President Johnson. Their meetings, conducted at the White House, had been unusually cordial, as had conversations with Dean Rusk at the State Department. Moshe Dayan, Israel's defense minister, accompanied Eshkol on the trip and spent time with Robert McNamara, the US secretary of defense. Eshkol's chief of staff, Baruch Shatilov, was with them, too. As they flew home to Israel, Eshkol and Dayan reviewed the results.

"You do realize, don't you," Dayan observed, "the Americans have become friendlier with us only because the Soviets are pursuing a defense pact with Egypt."

"Yes," Eshkol nodded. "Of course."

"This is classic Rusk diplomacy," Dayan continued. "Balancing competing relationships against each other. They need a relationship with us to counterbalance Soviet influence in the region. The Soviets are pouring arms into Egypt. They're sending arms *and* advisers to Syria. If the Americans are to have any influence in the region, they need a partner—and that is what they are looking for in us. That is the reason for their friendly gestures. Not some altruistic or benevolent concern for our well-being and destiny."

"I understand that," Eshkol nodded, "and I don't care. We need their help at least as much as they need us."

"I'm not sure about that, but I understand what you mean. We need them as much as they want us."

"Look," Eshkol reiterated, "they have agreed to an increase in economic cooperation. Our economy needs that. And they have agreed to voice no opposition to our nuclear reactor at Dimona. We need that. And Rusk has privately guaranteed they will veto any attempt to sanction us for it in the UN, which is more support for us at the UN than they've ever shown."

"And," Shatilov, Eshkol's chief of staff, interjected, "they have signed an agreement to sell us their newest surface-to-air missiles."

"Good point," Eshkol added, turning to Dayan. "We need those. Right?"

"Yes," Dayan reluctantly acknowledged. "They will help us greatly."

"And don't forget, General Westmoreland is coming for a visit next year."

"If he doesn't get tangled up in Vietnam."

"I know. I know," Eshkol said with a wave of his hand. "But this visit was a positive step for us."

"Yes, Mr. Prime Minister," Dayan conceded. "This trip was a positive one for us. But if we get in a shooting war with Egypt or Syria, the United States will face some serious choices."

"You think they will abandon us?"

"I think they would like to support us, but our neighbors are backed by the Soviet Union. And that's what Johnson, Rusk, and McNamara will focus on. If we're attacked by our neighbors, the Americans will view support for us as placing them in direct opposition to the Soviets. And that touches their overriding fear of nuclear war."

— • —

When Eshkol's airplane landed at Tel Aviv, Shaul Nissany, the Mossad director, was waiting on the tarmac. He rode in the car with Eshkol for the short trip to the prime minister's residence. "I understand the meetings went well," Nissany offered.

"Yes. You saw the progress reports?"

"Of course."

"We can go over that tomorrow. I'll give you the details if you like. Anything pressing since we talked?"

Nissany quickly caught Eshkol up on the most recent developments in their intelligence efforts regarding Egypt, Jordan, Lebanon, and Syria. Eshkol was already aware that Mossad had agents working throughout the region.

"What about the man we discussed in Damascus? Anything new from him? You were going to contact him about more information on the Golan Heights. He seemed particularly good at that sort of thing."

"Yes," Nissany replied. "Very good."

"Anything new from him?"

"Not yet."

"More information from him would be vital if we were to attempt an assault on the artillery positions. And I think we both know that day is coming."

"Most definitely," Nissany nodded in agreement. For a fleeting moment, he considered telling Eshkol that Kovner had been captured, then thought better of it. There was still the slimmest hope that he might escape.

Thankfully, Eshkol switched to a new topic without pressing the matter further. "Dayan tells me IDF is moving forward with the planning process."

"Yes. They seem to be making progress."

"Are your people participating?"

"We have representatives at the meetings."

"I know that," Eshkol frowned. "But are they participating?"

"I'm certain they are."

"Find out, would you? We need this process to work. I don't want them just sitting in on someone else's discussion. I want them taking part in the planning process. You guys can't always take the safe position."

"Begging your pardon, Mr. Prime Minister, but we have agents in the field risking their lives for this country."

"And the rest of you won't even risk your reputations," Eshkol retorted. "Spend all of your time protecting your image and your policy portfolios." He cut his eyes in Nissany's direction. "You'll get them in this process, and you'll change the culture at Mossad, or I'll find someone who will." Eshkol took a deep breath. "Now, what else is there?"

"No much."

"Then there must be something, so out with it."

"In his latest transmission, our agent in Damascus provided details of a new plot against King Hussein."

"Any different from the others?"

"This one has greater specificity and it supposedly involves the king's cousin."

"His cousin?"

"Our analysts think there may be something to it." Again, Nissany knew more—the Syrian connection to Talal and the American theory that this latest threat was a play for Jordanian uranium deposits—but he had learned it was better to give Eshkol information in small portions, allowing the prime minister time to process it rather than overwhelm him with details that might not be of immediate importance. Especially when he was in a testy mood.

"What's the downside if the plot is successful?" Eshkol asked.

"As we discussed before, we know this king and have a history of a more-or-less workable relationship. Anyone who is a likely successor would be much worse. The cousin in particular."

"Perhaps we could use this to our advantage."

"Yes," Nissany nodded. "That is a possibility."

"Your people are on top of the situation?"

"Of course."

"Anything we need to do about it at the moment?"

"No, sir."

"Good. I've been looking forward to sleeping in my own bed. Is that everything for now?"

"Those are the most recent developments."

"Are you prepared to brief us thoroughly on these matters?"

"Yes."

"Good. Let's do that tomorrow. Are we sharing our intelligence with the troops on the ground?"

"As much as possible."

"What does that mean?"

"We provide them with a truncated version of our reports."

"Truncated? You mean sanitized."

Nissany bristled at the comment. "We are funneling as much information as possible to them," he said with an edge to his voice, "but in a way that protects our sources."

"Shaul, having information doesn't do us much good if our troops aren't able to use it. And they can't use it if they don't know about it."

"Yes, Mr. Prime Minister. I understand."

CHAPTER 6

AN HOUR BEFORE SUNRISE the next morning, Golda Meir lay wide
awake in bed. She held a report from Isaac Valero, her personal physi-
cian. She'd received the report the day before and read it now for the
third time.

Golda had come to Israel at the age of twenty-three with her hus-
band, Morris. Their first years were spent on a kibbutz at Merhavia, but
the work there was difficult and when Morris's health made manual
labor no longer an option, they moved to Jerusalem where they both
found jobs in the offices of Solel Boneh, a construction and development
firm. Several years later, Golda was recruited by the Jewish Agency in Tel
Aviv, where she held key positions in the agency's political department.
After Israel obtained its independence, she was appointed minister to
the Soviet Union by the newly formed government and went on to hold
numerous offices. When Eshkol became prime minister, he appointed her
to continue as Israel's foreign minister, a position she held in the previous administration. Her long and productive career had been successful
and rewarding, but it had not come easily or without personal expense.
Morris was gone, having died ten years earlier and their children were
grown, all of them living elsewhere. Now, approaching seventy years of
age, her health bore the marks of a life lived to the fullest and she was
left to face those consequences alone.

For the past several months she'd been unusually tired, then she
noticed a low-grade fever accompanied by night sweats. Golda knew

something was wrong but she dreaded doctor visits and put off seeking treatment as long as possible. The report in her hand was not a complete surprise even if the diagnosis, lymphoma, was unwelcome.

Dr. Valero wanted to schedule a visit for her with a specialist in New York for further analysis. She hesitated but he insisted and began arranging an appointment. She knew he was right—immediate treatment could force the disease into remission——but with tensions rising in the region, a trip like that seemed out of the question.

As she scanned the report once more, the telephone on the nightstand rang. She rolled on her side and lifted the receiver. The call was from her assistant. "The prime minister returned in the night. He wants you to attend the morning security briefing so he can review his trip with you."

"Will anyone else be in attendance?"

"The defense minister. Mossad director. And I suppose Baruch Shatilov will be there. Doesn't he attend all of these meetings?"

"Usually. Have the staff put together some information for me. I'll come by the office before I go."

Golda hung up the phone, leaned back in bed with her head resting on the pillow and stared at the ceiling. Her body felt tired, bone tired. "I could lie right here and not move a muscle all day," she said to herself. The doctor's report lay on her lap and she glanced at it once more. A trip to New York would give her time to rest, away from the telephone and the endless meetings. A reason to do it, too…or maybe just an excuse. Others had their troubles and they didn't let them interfere with their duties. Why should she be any different? She breathed a heavy sigh. There was no use thinking about it right now. She wasn't going to New York anytime soon.

After a moment, she laid the doctor's report on the nightstand and picked up a book entitled *Night*, an account of a Holocaust survivor named Elie Wiesel. Part of a trilogy, the three books described Wiesel's journey from the destruction of his faith in God during Nazi captivity to recovery and spiritual renewal afterward. She'd been reading it off and on for the past several weeks, now she took it in hand once more.

Whatever awaited her at the office would be there whether she arrived ten minutes early or ten minutes late. She could spare the time to read a few pages before rolling out of bed. She owed herself that much.

— • —

Later that morning, Nissany, Dayan, and Golda met with Eshkol at the prime minister's office. Eshkol gave a detailed report of his trip to Washington and the discussion he had with President Johnson. "The Americans appear to be moving in our favor, but they still are reluctant to supply us with arms. Although they are selling us surface-to-air missiles."

"But not the airplanes we need," Dayan noted, "and not the cruisers for our navy."

"They are concerned about what will happen to those weapons if we are attacked by our neighbors," Golda replied.

"They should be worrying about what would happen if *we* lose," Dayan said. "And doing everything they can to prevent that from happening. They need us to win."

"We talked about that," Eshkol explained. "Johnson is not unsympathetic to our situation, but Rusk and McNamara think that if they sell us the armaments we really want, it will only force the nations around us to escalate their arms buildup."

"They're already escalating their buildup," Golda noted.

"And doing so purely out of hatred for us," Dayan added. "Not to keep up with our modernization efforts."

"The latest figures on continued Syrian and Egyptian arms purchases bear that out," Nissany suggested. "And on top of what they've bought, the Soviets recently provided a shipload of tanks to the Egyptians as an outright gift."

"The T-55," Dayan nodded.

"And they've sent missiles, artillery, and hundreds of aircraft to Cairo on credit."

"Which is why we must continue with our preparation efforts,"

Dayan offered. "Even with only what is on hand now, our neighbors could attack at any moment."

Eshkol glanced over at him. "We are on schedule with our tank modifications?"

"Yes," Dayan answered.

"And it is going well?"

"The new cannon fits perfectly. Much better than the one they came with. When we finish with the modification program, our Sherman tanks will be at least as good as any of the Russian tanks, including the T-55."

They continued to talk about regional military issues, then gradually the conversation shifted to the plot against King Hussein.

"According to our source in Damascus," Nissany reported, "this latest attempt on Hussein involves several Jordanian generals and Hussein's cousin, Naif bin Talal."

"We've heard bits and pieces about this already," Golda observed. "Are we certain this report is credible and not just an evolving rumor?"

"Our verification section is working on that right now," Nissany answered, but once again he refrained from telling them Kovner had been captured.

"What about the Americans?" Golda wondered. "Have you consulted with them about this? They have better access to Hussein than we do."

"We have talked with them," Nissany nodded. "Their sources in Jordan tell them the generals behind the plot have sympathetic ties to Syria."

"Do we know the names of these generals?" Eshkol asked.

"No. Apparently no one does. But the Americans have suggested that Talal is being handled by Fayez bin Wahbi, a Jordanian businessman who supplies arms to Syria."

"He also brokers oil for the Arab nations," Dayan added.

"That's correct," Nissany agreed. "The Americans think Wahbi is involved because the real driving force behind this plot lies with a Syrian desire for access to Jordanian uranium deposits."

Golda leaned back in her chair. "That makes sense. So the Americans think Syria is developing a nuclear program?"

"Not yet. They haven't begun constructing facilities. But according to the Americans, Syrian officials see our nuclear program as a threat. But they also see nuclear power as the key to their domination of the region."

"If they had nuclear capability," Dayan suggested, "they would gain the upper hand over all of their neighbors."

"And that, so say the Americans, is what's really driving the unrest."

"We can never let Syria gain nuclear weapons," Golda replied.

"The Americans know that," Nissany responded. "In fact, they appear to be relying on us to make certain it doesn't happen."

Eshkol looked puzzled. "What leads you to that conclusion?"

"They have heard of this latest threat to Hussein, and they think it is not only plausible but very much a reality. Yet they have done nothing about it because they would not mind seeing him removed."

"They prefer Talal?"

"In theory," Nissany nodded.

"They haven't informed him of this threat?"

"No. While they think Syrian access to the uranium would be bad in the long term, the disruption of murdering Hussein would be good for the short term."

Eshkol's brow wrinkled in a contemplative frown. "Can our operatives in Syria provide more information about the effort to obtain uranium?"

Nissany shifted positions in the chair. "We are working with them, as well as with operatives in Jordan and Egypt. We just don't have a way to quickly verify this information. And frankly, I'm not certain we can find anything to corroborate either the plot or the matter of the uranium."

"So where does that leave us?" Dayan asked.

"We've heard similar threats in the past." Nissany moved the conversation sideways, hoping to avoid a direct answer. He abhorred taking an overt policy position. Past experience had taught him that bold initiative left Mossad at risk to ridicule in the event of failure. He'd vowed never to let that happen on his watch. "But prior threats," he continued, "were nothing like this one, especially if the American version is correct. This one is more specific and it includes a reference to the king's family. None of the other threats sounded quite like this one."

"So, what do you propose we do with it?" Eshkol asked, pressing for options.

Nissany answered slowly, "Well, one possibility would be to do as we've done in the past…" His voice trailed away, and Golda stepped in to complete the thought. "You mean forward this to the Jordanians and let them worry about whether it is true or not?"

Eshkol seemed dissatisfied with that option. "I think we should use this information a little more creatively."

Nissany frowned. "How do you mean?" Hoping to maintain the illusion of substantive discussion while preserving his own deniability.

"I'm wondering if we couldn't use this to establish a better relationship with Hussein."

Dayan and Golda exchanged questioning glances. "Relationship?" Dayan asked. "You are suggesting we *have* an existing relationship with Hussein?"

"Yes," Eshkol insisted. "It's not a good relationship, but I think we do have some sort of understanding between us. He's been less than enthusiastic in following the lead of his fellow Arab League members, and he's been cooperative with us on issues not directly related to the general Arab question."

"But he can't cooperate with us now," Golda explained. "Not overtly. Are you thinking we can establish some kind of back-channel relationship?"

"I'm thinking strategy." Eshkol glanced in Dayan's direction. "When war comes, and I'm certain it will, we cannot fight simultaneously on three fronts. Correct?"

"Against Egypt, Jordan, and Syria?"

"Yes. We can't fight all three at once, can we?"

"No. You're correct," Dayan nodded. "Ideally, we need to fight them one at a time."

"But to defeat the Egyptians," Eshkol continued his argument, "we would have to concentrate our power to the south and that would leave us vulnerable to everyone else."

"That's true," Dayan nodded once more.

"I'm sure our neighbors know this and I'm equally certain they are confident we cannot hold the other two at bay long enough to defeat one before the other overwhelms us. So," Eshkol continued, "perhaps we could find a way to send this information about the plot to Hussein and do so in a manner that lets him know we are serious about our relationship with him and that we think the information may be more credible than our previous warnings. Let's hope that he is grateful for our unsolicited assistance and perhaps will think twice about attacking us should the others attempt to invade."

"That would be a good idea if we had a way to contact him directly, but I don't see how we can do that," Golda argued. "It's not likely Hussein would agree to see me and certainly not on a formal visit. If he did, it could place him in serious peril."

Eshkol propped his elbows on the armrests of his chair and crossed his legs. "How would it place him in jeopardy?"

"If the other Arab leaders find out Hussein met with an official from Israel, or if one of the Jordanian opposition groups finds out, they will use it against him to portray him as soft on Jews."

"That he's not really Muslim," Dayan chimed in. "That he's nothing more than an agent of imperialist forces, a pawn of the colonialists, and on and on."

"And then," Golda added, "the message we took to him would very likely become a self-fulfilling prophecy, simply by me being there."

Eshkol sighed and looked away. "Well, when you put it like that, it sounds like doing anything with the information would be a bad idea."

"Maybe not," Dayan spoke up. "Perhaps Abba Eban could help."

"You think so?"

"He's a diplomat. Knows lots of people. And he might know a way to get this information to Hussein that would allow it to be received in the way we intend it—a friendly acquaintance giving a friend a heads up. I mean, telling Hussein isn't a bad idea. We just can't do it directly."

Eshkol looked over at Golda. "Could the Americans help?"

"I'm sure the Americans could get a message to Hussein if they wanted to, but they have proved unreliable and inefficient in that regard. And if what they've told Shaul is really how they feel, they might agree to forward it and then simply do nothing with it."

"Besides," Dayan suggested, "we can't really afford to be seen as beholden to the Americans, though we really need their help. If we want to do this—and the more I think about it the more I think we should—then going through Abba in New York would be the best way. That would remove us from direct linkage to the issue, give everyone room to deny everything—us, Abba, King Hussein—and still get the information to him."

Eshkol seemed to warm to the idea. "Okay," he nodded at Golda. "Give it a try, but make sure you give Abba explicit instructions about what you're asking him to do."

"Certainly," Golda responded.

"We don't need any mistakes with this."

"I'll get right on it."

— · —

After the meeting, Golda returned to her office and prepared a memo to send by cable to Abba Eban in New York. When the text of that communication was finalized, she dispatched a courier to New York with a report giving Eban the latest information on the plot against Hussein, the Syrian desire for access to Jordanian uranium, the meeting in Istanbul as reported by the Americans, and the involvement of Hussein's cousin.

Finally, late that afternoon, Golda left the office for an appointment with Dr. Valero and one more round with him about the need to see a specialist.

"It's all arranged," Valero told her. "All you have to do is make the call to set a time, and get yourself to New York."

"He has agreed to see me?"

"Yes. Oscar Jordan is a friend of mine." Valero looked at her with kindly eyes. "You have to let him help you, Golda. Phone him and arrange time for an appointment."

Golda looked away. "I'm not sure I can do that now."

"Why not?"

"Things are happening and I—"

"Things will always happen. If you wait for a convenient time you'll never find it."

"I know, but—"

"This looks like a low-grade version of the disease," Valero said, ignoring her arguments. "If we treat it now, it may lie dormant for a long time. You can come back, serve again, do something else—some of those things you've always wanted to do. But the fact that you are chronically tired and your blood counts are out of alignment leaves me wondering precisely what we're dealing with. And it leaves me worried."

Golda looked over at him. "Don't you think the fatigue might have something to do with my job?"

"Yes, it could. But you're not deficient in vitamins and minerals, which is usually a factor with fatigue and something I initially expected to find. But that's not your problem. Those levels are right where they should be. Which is why we need to find out for certain what is happening with your body. Besides," he said, his tone softening, "the trip will give you a chance to rest, away from everything."

Golda nodded. "I've thought about that."

"Good," Valero smiled. "You should think about it while you're calling Oscar."

"The chance to sleep would be worth the flight."

"Call for the appointment. He's waiting to hear from you."

"I'll do my best to arrange a time."

"Good." Valero stepped toward the door to see her out. "And I will do my best not to nag you about it...too much."

CHAPTER 7

TWO DAYS LATER A LETTER from the French ambassador arrived at the foreign ministry. It was delivered by hand. An assistant brought it to Golda. The letter informed her that French contacts in Damascus had indicated an Israeli named David Kovner was dead. The French ambassador wanted to know how Israel would like to proceed with the matter. It was a cryptic message and seemed to assume Golda knew something about Kovner. She, however, knew nothing of him and wondered why the French government felt compelled to notify her about his death. "They don't do that with private citizens," she mused to her assistant. "Why did they feel compelled to tell me about this one?"

"Do you want me to have someone find out?"

"Yes, please."

A few hours later, Rivka Chaiter, a member of the assistant's staff, came to the office with the results. Golda was seated at her desk. Chaiter stood while she gave the information. "We checked with as many sources as we could contact without raising too much attention," she began. "According to them, David Kovner's real name is Yoram Laron. He was born in Lebanon, grew up in Galilee, but for the past several years has been living in Damascus. Supposedly he's a businessman engaged in the shipping business, but from what we could find we think he's really an arms dealer. That's a new venture for him, though. A background check through legitimate sources suggests he was never engaged in any kind of business prior to moving to Syria."

That information struck Golda as odd—someone using an assumed name, posing as a businessman, working as an arms dealer. This sounded like a cover story for something else. "What did he do before he went to Syria?"

"Immediately prior to leaving for Syria he had spent a career in IDF."

"Career?"

"Fifteen years."

Golda was angry. "A Mossad agent?"

"That seems to fit."

"Working in Damascus."

"It would appear so," Chaiter replied.

Golda was livid. A dead Mossad agent in Damascus. She was sure this was no ordinary agent and certain Nissany knew about Kovner when they had met with Eshkol just after his return from America. If this agent was Nissany's source for the Hussein plot, he'd deliberately withheld information from her and, worst of all, from the prime minister. "I'd fire him on the spot," she grumbled.

Chaiter had a puzzled expression. "I beg your pardon, ma'am?"

"Nothing," Golda retorted as she stood from behind her desk. "Just tell them to bring my car around."

"Certainly," Chaiter replied and scurried from the room.

— • —

Within the hour, Golda rode to Tel Aviv and arrived at Nissany's office unannounced. He hastily rearranged his schedule and ushered her into his office. He moved around his desk and took a seat. She sat across from him.

"I didn't realize you were coming today," he began. "What's this about?"

Golda tossed the letter on his desk. "Take a look at that."

"What's this about?"

"David Kovner."

Nissany read the letter and handed it back to her. "I have no idea who or what that's about."

"Well, the French think he's important enough to contact me and from the tone of that letter they seem to assume we think he's important, too."

"The French are free to assume anything they like."

"Our citizens die quite frequently in other lands," Golda continued, "and I assure you no one contacts my office about them. Yet for some reason the French ambassador felt compelled to notify me about Kovner." She looked Nissany in the eye. "Perhaps you'd like to try your explanation again."

"Golda, what are you getting at?"

"I'm sure they know what I know and that is Kovner—or Laron, or whatever his name might have been—was someone who worked for you."

"That's preposterous," Nissany scoffed.

"We checked, Shaul. The relationship is obvious. He went to work for Mossad right after one of your recruiters lured him away from IDF. He's been living in Damascus posing as an arms dealer, even though he was never in business prior to going there. He's one of yours. That much is obvious, but what I want to know is whether he was your source for the Hussein plot."

"What difference does that make?"

"If he was dead when we met with Eshkol the other day, and you knew it, then you've put yourself in a serious situation."

"By not telling you about it?"

"Withholding information from me isn't your problem."

"What's my problem?"

"You knew he was dead when we met with Eshkol and Dayan the other day, after they returned from America, but you sat right there in the prime minister's office and kept quiet about it—even after the prime minister asked pointed questions about operations in Damascus." She gestured with the letter. "Questions that should have elicited a response from you about this."

"Secrets," Nissany replied coolly, "are only secrets when they are kept." His eyes darted away. "Once told to others, they become mere gossip for a women's tea."

The sexist implication was obvious, and a sense of rage flew over Golda. "How dare you minimize me? I've given my life, my marriage, my family in the service of this country." She gestured with her index finger for emphasis, jabbing the air as she spoke. "And you, with your smug arrogance, make a mockery of it—of me and everyone else who sacrificed to see this country become a reality."

"All right," Nissany said with a wave of his hand. "Calm down."

"And don't tell me to calm down! I'm not the one who lied to the prime minister."

"I didn't lie," Nissany retorted. "And lower your voice. Someone might hear you and misunderstand."

"Not telling the prime minister something of substance, in response to a direct question, is just as deceitful as overtly lying."

"Okay," Nissany began again. "Look...Kovner was one of ours. He worked for Mossad. I knew he'd been captured when we met with the prime minister, but I didn't know he was dead."

"When did you find out he was dead?"

"Several days ago."

You knew he'd been captured when we briefed Eshkol?"

"Yes. But as far as we knew, he was still alive. There was still hope."

"No, no, no," Golda shook her head. "Don't try that with me. You never intended to rescue him and you know it. You thought you could get this past us and we'd never know what happened to him. But you lost an agent. How much did he tell the Syrians before he died?"

Nissany shrugged, "Who knows?"

"You don't know?"

"Golda," he answered with frustration, "there is no way to know what he said."

"You must have had someone on the inside. How did you know he'd been captured and that he was dead, without knowing what he told them?"

"We have a network of informants operating throughout Syria. They told us."

She paused a moment, shaking her head, then looked over at him. "You have to tell Eshkol."

"In due time," Nissany said with a dismissive tone.

"The time is due now." Golda stood. "You can come with me and tell him now, or I'll do it myself."

— • —

Reluctantly, Nissany accompanied Golda to Eshkol's office. They joined him in a seating area to the left of Eshkol's desk, Golda on the sofa, Nissany and Eshkol in armchairs at right angles to her. Nissany was obviously uncomfortable as Golda described the message from the French, then handed Eshkol the letter. He scanned it quickly, then looked at them both with a frown. "What's this about?"

Nissany cleared his throat, then began slowly. "The man they refer to in that letter—David Kovner—was one of our agents. He was working for us in Damascus."

Golda caught Eshkol's eye and gave him a knowing look. Eshkol turned back to Nissany. "He was in Damascus. This was our source?"

"Yes," Nissany nodded.

"He's the one who told us about the artillery positions on the Golan Heights?"

"Yes."

"And the one who told us about the plot against Hussein?"

"Yes."

"Okay." Eshkol laid the letter on his lap and leaned back in the chair. "He's dead now. But that doesn't explain the obvious tension between you two. So what's the rest of the story?"

"He was captured several days ago," Nissany explained.

"How many days ago?"

"A week. Ten days," Nissany sighed and turned sideways in the chair. "Maybe more."

The expression on Eshkol's face turned solemn. "You knew about this when you saw me at the airport. When I returned from the United States."

"Yes, sir," Nissany nodded.

"But you let me think he was still alive and able to help us."

"He was still alive," Nissany insisted. "But, yes, we knew he had been captured."

"And you thought it was a good idea for me to set policy and make decisions assuming something was true when, in fact, that assumption was false?"

"I was in the room," Nissany replied. "I was there when we were making those decisions. Nothing we decided would have been affected by whether he was alive or not."

"But that's not your decision to make," Eshkol snapped. "That's my decision. I'm the prime minister. Not you."

"Yes, sir."

"Did you try to retrieve him?"

"Your agent. An agent being held by people who mean to destroy us!" Eshkol's voice was loud and he paused a moment to regain control. "Did you attempt to rescue him?"

"We did not think it was worth the risk to our other agents, and Kovner—"

"Wait a minute," Eshkol snapped, cutting him off. "How would retrieving this man put your other agents at risk? Did Kovner know who those agents were?"

"No, sir," Nissany shook his head. "He knew only about the things that affected his work, his area of responsibility. He knew nothing about others we'd sent into the area or recruited to help us."

"You assume."

"We're fairly certain of it," Nissany insisted. "He had no contact with them."

"That you are aware of."

"Yes, sir. As far as we can determine, he knew nothing of our ongoing operations. He's been in Syria several years, far removed from the scope of Mossad's other activities. Anything he might have told them would relate solely to what he was doing. Not to any of our other operations. He didn't know any of that."

"Then back to my question, how would rescuing him put others at risk?"

"We have a network of nationals. Syrian nationals. Some of them Jewish. Some of them not. They help us gather information, keep tabs on people, that sort of thing. They can get into places none of our people can reach. They are the ones who told us about Kovner. If we tried to rescue Kovner and failed, the Syrians would know, obviously, that we had information about his location. They might be able to work backwards from those few facts and determine how we knew where he was being held and the identities of those who furnished the information. Kovner was vitally important to our effort, but once he'd been captured the question of rescuing him had to be weighed against risks to the entire network and all of our other operations in that area."

Nissany gave a good explanation, the logic of which Eshkol seemed to recognize, but it did little to mollify Eshkol's anger. "That might be so, but it still doesn't change things between us. Telling me about him wouldn't risk anyone."

"No, sir."

"You have a moral and legal obligation to give me the best advice possible. I have clearance to hear anything you know and the authority to receive all the information available to you that relates to the areas of my responsibility. For the love of everything, Shaul, my decisions are only as good as the information I receive!"

"Yes, sir."

"Are you trying to deliberately set me up to fail?!"

"No, sir. Not at all. And I resent—"

"Resent whatever you like, Shaul. I don't give a—" Eshkol caught himself and paused. "I ought to fire you on the spot. Right now. This moment. I ought to dismiss you from your position."

"Yes, sir."

"And if it happens again, I will."

"Yes, sir. It won't happen again."

"Is this the way you're forwarding information to the troops on the ground?"

Nissany countered, "What could that possibly have to do with this?"

"You kept things from me," Eshkol gestured with the letter. "And I'm the prime minister. What are you keeping from the troops?"

"That's an entirely different situation."

"No. It's not," Eshkol insisted. "And from now on I want copies of everything you send to the field."

Nissany had an ironic smile. "Sir, that's a lot of—"

"I don't care what it's a lot of. If you want to keep your job, you'll see that I'm copied on every intelligence briefing you give to IDF, written or oral."

"Yes, sir."

Eshkol took a deep breath and glanced down at the letter. "Now," he turned to Golda and lowered his voice. "I suggest we contact the French and ask them to confirm the information they sent. See if they can give us more detail."

"I should be the one to do that," Nissany interrupted.

"You've done enough to make a mess of this already," Eshkol responded. "We'll let Golda take care of it."

"But I—"

"Shaul!" Eshkol shouted. "Stop trying to protect your turf and think about what's at stake."

"I'm not protecting—"

"That's exactly what you're doing," Eshkol boomed. "You're doing it today. You do it in every meeting I've attended with you. I see it. All the other ministers see it." He paused again and took a moment to collect himself. "As foreign minister," he explained, once again in an even tone, "Golda can contact the French as a matter of course, one diplomat to another, raising no suspicions. If you contact them, it will look like an admission from the director of Mossad that Mossad had an agent working in Syria. Do you want to admit to that?"

Nissany raised his chin in an aloof posture. "I have always assumed everyone knew we had people there."

"I'm sure they do, but we don't want to admit it."

"But I—"

"Shaul," Eshkol's tone was cold and emotionless, "I'm directing you to stay out of the response. That's an order, not a request."

"Yes, sir."

"Golda will respond on our behalf and she'll tell us what they have to say about it."

"Yes, Mr. Prime Minister," Golda replied. "I'll take care of it."

— • —

That afternoon, Golda sent a message to the French Embassy asking them to confirm Kovner's death and provide such details as they might find. The following day the French ambassador responded that Kovner's body was discovered in a garbage barrel behind a Damascus hotel and was being held at a morgue in the city under an assumed name. The ambassador offered to recover the body. The following morning, she met with Nissany at his office to discuss the matter.

"Do you want to have the body returned to us?"

"You and Eshkol can decide, I've been directed to stay out of it."

"You know that's not what he meant."

"It's certainly what he said."

She smiled at him. "Do you like working for Mossad?"

"Yes. Of course. I was born for this job."

"Exactly. And I was born for mine. Now, what do you want to do with the body? Shall I ask them to return it?"

"No," Nissany sighed. "Eshkol is right, as much as it pains me to admit it. We can't risk acknowledging that Kovner worked for us."

"He has family—two brothers," Golda offered. "And we have an obligation to see that he's properly buried."

"We all have family." Nissany seemed unsettled at the mention of Kovner's personal details. "All of our agents know the risk of working for us. They and their families know what service in Mossad entails. We have other agents operating in Syria and throughout the region. We mustn't do anything that puts them in greater danger than they're already in. So thank the French and respectfully decline."

"Very well, I'll run that past Eshkol, but I think he'll agree." Golda stood to leave, then turned to ask, "Do you think his information was accurate?"

"His information?" Nissany frowned. "From the French?"

"No. From Kovner. About the plot against King Hussein."

"He's never been wrong before. And I think his death confirms the accuracy of his work."

"You believe the threat is real?"

"I try never to believe anything until the facts prove it. But I think this one has a higher probability than the others."

"Sixty percent?"

"Eighty."

"Have you taken steps to confirm it?"

"Yes," he was clearly angered by her question. "That's our job, Golda."

"I'm only asking because—"

"We are confirming it," he said, interrupting her. "As is our standard policy. We are working to confirm it. Have we ever given you bad information before?"

Golda arched an eyebrow. "Do you really want to get into that now?"

"No," he mumbled. "I suppose not."

CHAPTER 8

MORDECHAI GUR STARED OUT the window of the car as they sped down the coastal road from Haifa. Patches of bright blue Mediterranean Sea zipped past, appearing as brief interludes between the long, low grass-covered dunes. He saw this but paid it no particular attention as his mind ran back to the events of past few weeks.

The report he'd prepared about Arab activity in Galilee had attracted more attention than he'd expected. Not long after he submitted it, General Greenberg, a friend and colleague, and now IDF Commander, summoned him to an evening meeting in Nazareth. They ate a pleasant dinner together and engaged in friendly conversation, then Greenberg turned their talk to the topic of strategic planning. It seemed odd, two fighting men discussing supply—the bane of any army man worth his rank—but Greenberg seemed bent on reviewing it and so they talked. "War is coming and it won't be like it used to be," Greenberg said, waxing eloquent on the subject. "Can't just grab your rifle and go now, like we could before. Today's war requires logistics, procurement, and timing. Planes fly faster, farther, higher. Bombs are bigger and missiles put everything within reach."

"That's true. Things are more sophisticated than before. But we still have to put soldiers on the ground. Can't win a war without occupying the enemy's turf."

"I'm glad you see things that way, Mordechai. Because I need your help."

"How's that?"

"War's coming. You know it. I know it. Folks in Jerusalem know it, too, when something tragic happens and they're forced to think about it. Otherwise, they have the luxury of ignoring it. We don't."

"No, sir." Mordechai knew Greenberg had something to say and he decided to wait for him to say it rather than push the issue. He didn't have to wait long.

"We've put together a planning group to help us get ready. Not one of those waste-of-time committees like we used to have. This one is actually tasked with figuring out how to win the war. I need you in that group."

"I'd be happy to meet with them, sir. We aren't due to return to field training for a few weeks."

"I'm not talking about dropping in on them once in a while, Mordechai. I need you to take this as a full-time assignment. Move to Tel Aviv. Work out of an office in the headquarters building."

Gur looked stunned. "You're asking me to move over to supply?"

"Not supply," Greenberg scowled. "Planning."

"Planning."

"Strategic planning." Greenberg laid aside his fork. "Look, you have combat experience, serious academic training, and a keen understanding of how things work on the battlefield. We need your help to get this right."

"But, supply?"

"I'm not asking you to become a clerk, Mordechai." Greenberg struggled to control his frustration. "War is coming. Syria's pushing for it. Egypt is preparing for it. The Soviets are dumping shiploads of weapons on our neighbors every day. They mean to attack us and they intend to destroy us. I'm telling you, I need you to get down to Tel Aviv, wrangle the Planning Group members into shape, and figure out how to win the war!"

They talked into the night, but Greenberg had a history of getting his way and sometime before sunrise Gur reluctantly agreed. He really didn't have much choice. When the commander of the army asked, it really wasn't a question. Just a polite way to issue an order.

In spite of his outward resistance to the assignment, Gur realized participation in the planning process could give him the opportunity to influence policy, something he very much wanted to do. He had ideas about how the army should function and suggestions about ways it could do so more efficiently, but the move from field commander to planning had been difficult to accept. He'd consoled himself by convincing General Broder to make the change a temporary assignment, under the assumption he would return to the base at Ramat David after his stint in Tel Aviv came to a conclusion. But as he rode south that day he wondered if he would ever again lead men into battle, or if he'd reached a turning point in his career.

When he reached Tel Aviv, Gur settled into temporary quarters and prepared to begin with the planning group first thing the following morning. His wife would make the move later, after he'd made sure the new position would work. Early the next morning, he attended his first meeting. Whatever hopes he had about influencing policy and change in the army met with serious misgivings the moment he entered the room.

For one thing, a quick count of the participants told him the group was far too large to be effective. With thirty-six men and twelve women, all they would do was talk. Not only that, the group included civilians, who from Gur's experience were almost always curious about army life but uninformed about the rigors of combat to the point of being useless in making military decisions. But most disturbing to him was the fact that, other than the group's commander, no IDF participant held a rank higher than captain. Rami Segev, a major, who looked to be about ten years younger than Gur, led the group but he was the highest-ranking member of the group and Gur was certain he had little or no combat experience. True enough, the presence of general officers tended to dampen innovation, but lack of their involvement seriously hampered implementation of new recommendations. Generals did not take kindly to lieutenants telling them how to run their units. They could develop brilliant plans but if the generals weren't part of the process those plans would get no further than the shelf.

Gur made the obligatory tour of the room, shaking hands and

introducing himself, then took a seat in the corner and waited. To his surprise the gathering that morning came quickly to order and lasted only about twenty minutes. The group was divided into teams of three or four, which were each assigned to specific segments of the process—defense of the southern border, protecting the Jordanian flank, security of infrastructure, bridges and railways, and the like. Segev asked for progress reports from each team but team leaders kept them short and to the point. Discussion was held to a minimum. Gur began to have second thoughts about his initial assessment.

When the meeting concluded, the teams departed for their respective work areas. Gur lingered behind, unsure what to do next. Segev called him over.

"Colonel, I'm assigning you to the team planning for the defense of Government House in Jerusalem."

"Okay," Gur replied with a puzzled frown. "But I didn't hear a report from them just now."

"That's because the team doesn't exist," Segev noted. "You'll be a one-man team for now. I'll consult with you as the work progresses and we'll decide together whether to add more people."

"Okay," Gur nodded. "I can do that."

"Good. I thought you'd like it. I understand you grew up in Jerusalem."

"Yes. I did."

"Then you should find great pleasure in figuring out how to defend part of it."

"I shall."

"Your office is down the hall." Segev started toward the door. "Come on, I'll show you." Segev continued to talk as he led the way. "Feel free to avail yourself of whatever resources you need. If you can't find what you want, ask. Our group has been established at the request of the prime minister, so they've layered our work over the top of the command structure. For planning purposes, we outrank everyone but General Greenberg. I report directly to him."

Gur was impressed. "They mean to get a result."

"General Greenberg has insisted this won't be a waste of anyone's time, which means whatever we draw up has to work. I'm hoping you can help us stay relevant to actual combat conditions."

"I'll do my best."

— • —

Gur spent his first morning in Tel Aviv getting acclimated to the IDF headquarters building and setting up his office. That afternoon, he located the map room and spent the remainder of the day pouring over maps of Jerusalem, refreshing his recollection about key sites, and familiarizing himself with the terrain.

The following day, Gur avoided the office altogether. Instead, he requisitioned a car from the motor pool and drove to Jerusalem. Dressed like a tourist, complete with camera and map, he roamed the city, soaking up the smells and listening to the sounds. Before long, he found himself in front of Beit El Synagogue on Rashi Street, just a few blocks from the house where he grew up. He sat in the car and stared up at the building, thinking of all the times he'd been there with his family as a child. He'd had lots of questions about scripture, particularly about the ones promising the restoration of Jerusalem.

"Some say Jerusalem will be restored to us," Gur remembered telling his father. "Some say the city is being restored to us now and that the things we see happening around us are part of that restoration."

His father tried to supply an answer but finally gave up and in frustration said, "Go see the Rabbi."

The following day, Gur stopped at Beit El Synagogue to see Rabbi Breslov. They sat in the sanctuary and talked. "Here is the answer you are seeking," Breslov explained patiently. "In order to understand the text of the prophets, to find its truest meaning, we must look behind the words to the events of history. Jerusalem has been destroyed and restored many times. It was destroyed by the Babylonians and it was rebuilt by Nehemiah. It was destroyed by the Romans and it was rebuilt by the Romans themselves. Then it was taken by the Arabs, the Turks, and now by the British. Others in faraway lands try to decide our fate, but God will have His way."

"Again?" Gur asked eagerly. "Now?"

"Men of the world have shown they can take the city from us and from each other, but God has shown that they cannot take the city from Him. This is a holy city and no matter what men do to it, this city will always belong to God. He has restored the city in the past. He is restoring it in the present. He will restore it in the future. It will always be His city, and He will always return it to us."

Many years had passed since that conversation, but Gur had lived long enough to see some of what they'd discussed actually come to pass. After the war for Israel's independence, most of Jerusalem came under Jewish control, but an eastern portion, including the Temple Mount, remained in Jordanian hands, a fact that deeply troubled Gur—much the same as the questions he'd asked Rabbi Breslov as a boy.

Why had God allowed the city to remain in Muslim hands? Why had He not restored the entire city at once to Israel? Had they gotten in the way of God's plan? Was that even possible? Could a generation, consumed by the desire for one thing, trade away the future destined to another?

As a young boy he continued to think of these things, even after that day with Rabbi Breslov. Back then, he was certain if he prayed long enough and thought hard enough, he could find an answer. Now all he found were questions—unanswered questions lingering from the past and new ones arising from the present.

After a few minutes Gur put the car in gear and continued from the synagogue to Nafha Street. A little way down the block he came to an empty lot where his childhood home once stood. He'd been long gone from there when, in 1948, an artillery shell landed squarely in the center of the house. His parents were at home when it hit and were killed. His mother's skeletal remains were found on the remnants of the dining room floor, an arm severed at the shoulder, a leg gone at the hip, and a large chunk of metal casing buried in her skull. His father was found atop her, one arm under the back of her neck, the other draped over her shoulder, his fingers clutching the severed arm. But no one was certain exactly how they died. The house caught fire with the explosion and by the time it was extinguished not much was left.

Gur parked the car at the curb and stepped out. The lot, overgrown with weeds, had been in their family for generations. It belonged to him now even though he hadn't been there in years. Three steps of the old walkway led up from the street to the front door. He sat down there and for the first time in a long time let his mind recall the scenes of his childhood. Some people remember little of their past, and Gur always thought that was best. He, however, seemed to recall everything. The sound of the stick against the rag ball as they played in the street, the day the girl two houses up kissed him on the cheek, the sound of his mother's voice calling him in at night, and all of it in vivid detail. So vivid it was almost as if he were there again, at home, on the street, with the neighbors on the sidewalk, or watching from the front steps. And tears flowed down his cheeks. "This is why I don't come here. This is why I stay away."

After a while, he pushed himself up from the steps and returned to the car. From the empty lot on Nafha Street he drove through the old neighborhood and turned to his assigned task. Government House was situated atop a hill on the southern edge of Jerusalem, a location that afforded a commanding view of the city. It also provided a strategic advantage to anyone who occupied it. Capturing the site and holding it would be critical to any defense of the city, a strategy that now seemed implicit in Segev's direction to him.

Positioned along the Armistice Line of 1948, the facility was home to the United Nations Truce Supervision Organization, which was charged with keeping the peace between Israel and its neighbors. Though the name implied great authority, in reality the UN presence was quite anemic. The hill could be easily captured by Israeli troops and, in fact, depended on IDF protection to ensure its neutrality. It could almost as easily be overrun by Jordanian army units if they attacked first and in overwhelming numbers, which Gur thought quite probable.

To the south, along the western bank of the Jordan River, lay territory that was controlled by Jordan and to the east lay Jordan itself, leaving the hill and Government House exposed to attack from two sides.

The terrain in both directions, however, was steep and rough, which severely limited any military action. Circling around to attack from the west would permit a full-scale assault, but that would require the Jordanians to pass through territory that was firmly within Israeli control. Negotiating their way through those neighborhoods would make surprise an impossibility.

Gur studied the scene from the top of the hill, then made his way down to the bottom where he surveyed the approaches in detail. Protecting the obvious, conventional access point from the west was a first priority, but enemies and necessity often combined to invent new conventions. Gur had no intention of ignoring the potential for an attack by the more difficult routes and supplemented his photographs with a hand-drawn map and pencil sketches of the area.

As sunset approached, he went back to the top of the hill for one final look. Off to the north, he caught the fading streaks of sunlight against the roof of the Dome of the Rock, the mosque situated atop the Temple Mount on a raised plaza where the Jewish temple once stood. He had many religious doubts as an adult, but one thing he held from childhood and believed with all his heart—the presence of a mosque on that site was a sacrilege God of the Torah would not leave unpunished, and he wondered how long it would remain.

Beyond the Temple Mount lay Mount Scopus, the site of Hebrew University and another large section of no-man's-land carved out by the 1948 armistice. Isolated in an area held by Jordan, it was connected to western Jerusalem by a single roadway. Gur hadn't thought much about it before, but standing there that evening he realized for the first time how important Mount Scopus really was. Strategically, the three hilltops—Government House to the south, Mount Scopus to the north, and the Temple Mount in between—formed the three dominant points of the city. Control of any two would give an army control of the city. "We can't just defend Government House," Gur said to himself. "We have to defend Scopus, too." He wheeled around to scan the city to the west. "In fact," he whispered, "to defend any of this, we must take it all." With the

Temple Mount already in Jordanian hands, the fate of either of the other two points would determine the fate of the city.

As the sun dipped below the horizon, Gur hastily scribbled a note to himself, then started toward the car. He would prepare a plan for securing and defending Government Hill. But he would do more than that. He would create a strategy to capture and hold the entire city.

CHAPTER 9

IN NEW YORK, ABBA EBAN reviewed the cable from Golda Meir and studied the report he'd received from the courier. As Israel's representative to the United Nations, he'd come to know many diplomats and officials from countries throughout the world. Representatives of countries whose leaders would never send an official delegation to Jerusalem were readily agreeable to talk in the halls and conference rooms of the UN facilities. Eban took full advantage of that access, solving problems and opening opportunities with all the tact and finesse of a career diplomat. Yet for all those relationships, official and unofficial, there still were issues and circumstances that could only be addressed by someone outside the diplomatic system. The threat to King Hussein seemed like just such an occasion.

Eban spent the better part of two days pouring over pages of research material on Hussein, his family, and their rise to power, then let the matter lie for a day, giving himself time to thoroughly digest the situation. Finally, he settled on the one person he was certain could deliver the message in a way Golda and Eshkol intended. That person was a lawyer, not a diplomat.

Later that week, Eban arranged an appointment with Lawrence Rosenwald, a senior partner at Mayer, Meagan & Gottschalk. A law firm with more than seventy-five attorneys, it counted among its clients many influential celebrities, multinational corporations, and a handful of important ministries and agencies of government. Rosenwald, now in his eighties, worked exclusively on matters relating to the state of Israel. He had contacts worldwide and was a personal friend of heads of state on every continent, which made him the go-to person on a wide variety of issues. Eban was anxious to enlist his help. They met at Rosenwald's office.

For the first twenty minutes, Eban outlined the plot to assassinate King Hussein, the supposed Syrian connection, and the play for control of Jordan's uranium deposits. He gave Rosenwald enough information to permit an informed decision but refrained from divulging everything he knew about the situation. "The stakes are high," Eban commented when he finished. "We need to handle this situation with the greatest of care." Eban avoided making a direct request for assistance. He knew what he wanted from the meeting but after years of dealing with the firm he'd learned it was better to let Rosenwald react, rather than give him directions.

"Have you informed King Hussein of this plot?"

"That's why I came to see you. We want to tell him but we can't really do that ourselves. And we were hoping for some advice about how to proceed."

Rosenwald had a satisfied smile. "I knew Hussein's father."

"Yes," Eban nodded. "I know."

"Knew him well, actually. I've only met Hussein a few times, though. Worked with him on a project for Bechtel Corporation in Aqaba. We got along well enough but neither of us was particularly warm to the other."

"I read our files on him and his father. You had quite a relationship."

"You have to tell him, no question about it. He's your best hope among the Arab nations."

"But we can't approach him directly."

Rosenwald shook his head slowly from side to side. "No, that would put him in a very vulnerable position."

"Yes."

"You need an intermediary."

"That's exactly what we need."

"But I'm not sure I should be the one to do this," Rosenwald added with another shake of his head.

Eban was confident Rosenwald really wanted the job but etiquette required him to feign humility. It was a familiar dance. Eban had seen it before and often played along, but not this time. "I'm not sure you're right for it, either." Rosenwald was taken aback by the comment but Eban continued without giving him time to respond. "I think this should be given to someone of lesser stature in your firm." Rosenwald's expression softened. Eban continued. "Someone who is capable of handling it properly but can get in and out of Jordan without drawing a lot of attention."

"Hmm," Rosenwald nodded, picking up on Eban's reasoning. "That was my concern, too."

"A lesser-known member of your firm won't have those recognition issues."

"Someone who can create an additional degree of separation without any added attention."

"If this thing falls apart," Eban added, "we will all need space in which to maneuver. Someone who can get in without much fanfare would give us that room."

"Did you have someone in mind?"

"Yes, I was thinking about Yaakov Auerbach. He and I worked together in the past. He seems like just the man."

Rosenwald nodded in agreement. "He might be a good fit. Lived in Israel a couple of years. Seems to know the region. Young, but not too young. Does good work."

"But there can be no mistakes on this one," Eban cautioned.

"You want to talk to him?"

Eban laid a copy of the report on the desk. "I think you should be the one to tell him."

"Very well," Rosenwald sighed. "But I don't think we want to give him the actual report," he said with a gesture of his hand.

"No. Read it. Summarize it verbally for him. Then destroy the copy."

"Right."

— • —

Yaakov Auerbach grew up in Chicago, but just before his twentieth birthday he left the United States and traveled to Palestine. A family friend had moved there and, with his help, Auerbach landed a job at a farming community near Degania, not far from the Sea of Galilee.

Auerbach came to Degania with lofty dreams that he couched in even loftier rhetoric—telling anyone who'd listen about the wonder and beauty of a collective lifestyle, the regenerative effects of an agricultural environment, and the reward of hard labor. Then he met Suheir Hadawi, an Arab girl who lived with her family on a neighboring farm. After that, he no longer talked of the communal dream, he only talked of her. But that was a long time ago, before that day in a Jerusalem alley, with Suheir on the pavement, blood oozing from a gunshot wound, her life slowly ebbing away.

Now, at the age of forty-five, he was living in New York, an attorney and junior partner with Mayer, Meagan & Gottschalk. He spent long days in a windowless office and nights alone in a Manhattan apartment. Work was the object of his attention and when he wasn't in the office he was thinking of his clients, their cases, the issues waiting on his desk. Memories of Suheir almost never came to mind, but he'd never married and rarely even dated.

That afternoon he was seated at his desk, files stacked to the left, papers and note pads to the right, his head hunched over a document that lay open before him. Sometime around two, Louise Landau appeared at the door.

Though no one knew Mrs. Landau's exact age, she'd been with the firm longer than any of the associates. She'd been hired by Mr. Gottschalk, so the story went, and at his death went to work for Mayer, then Meagan, and finally Rosenwald. Her word carried more weight than all but the most senior members and, according to office legend, no one who crossed her had ever made partner.

"Mr. Rosenwald would like to see you," she announced.

Auerbach laid his pen aside, pushed back from the desk, and stood. "I just saw him this morning. Has something happened?"

"You know he never tells me anything," she said with a dour expression. "Come on. He's waiting."

Auerbach slipped on his jacket, grabbed a legal pad from the desk, and followed her down the hall. When they reached the door to Rosenwald's office she paused to let him pass, then closed the door behind him. Auerbach crossed the room and stood at the desk.

A file lay open on the desktop and Rosenwald was bent over it. Auerbach assumed he was reading and hesitated to interrupt, but the longer he stood there the more convinced he became that Rosenwald was asleep. After a moment he cleared his throat and when that got no response he said, "Mrs. Landau told me you wanted to see me."

Still Rosenwald did not look up but spoke in a coldly detached tone. "You have some experience in Israel?"

"I lived there for a while."

"What about Jordan? Ever get to Amman?"

"I passed through there once," Auerbach was now standing in front of the desk.

"Yes," Rosenwald said slowly. "I seem to remember something about that from your story." He looked up, finally, and his face softened. His tone became more engaging. "You enjoy working here?"

"Very much."

"Good." His cheeks rose in what Auerbach had come to believe was a smile, though Rosenwald rarely showed delight of any kind. "I think you have potential," he continued. "Unlike some of our lawyers." Rosenwald gestured with a flick of his wrist. "Pull that chair over here and take a seat." Auerbach was caught off-guard by the warmth of the gesture; he'd never been offered a chair in this office before, but he did as he was told and took a seat. Rosenwald continued. "As you know, I have a longstanding relationship with David Ben-Gurion. He and I attended law school together in Istanbul. Ben-Gurion didn't graduate. I did."

"Yes, sir."

"I've been to Israel many times."

"Yes, sir."

"Abba Eban ..." Rosenwald paused abruptly, a blank look on his face. "You know who he is?"

"Yes, sir," Auerbach nodded. "I've assisted on several of his UN projects."

"He has received word of a plot to kill King Hussein of Jordan." Rosenwald paused a moment as if waiting to judge Auerbach's reaction before continuing. "Mossad has confirmed several of the elements are, in fact, plausible and feels there's a high probability this is a real threat."

Auerbach was unsure how to respond. Some in Israel, he knew, would cheer Hussein's death but others thought well of him. Rosenwald, however, seemed always at odds with popular opinion and had little tolerance for idle chatter on serious topics. Auerbach chose to avoid taking sides. "They really think it's true?" he asked.

"It seems so," Rosenwald nodded. "A couple of generals said to be involved along with the king's cousin." He opened a drawer and took out the report he'd received from Eban. He glanced at it, then tossed it in Auerbach's direction. "Read that while you're sitting there, but give it back. I told them I wouldn't show it to you, but if you're going to do this there's no reason you can't read the memo for yourself." He swiveled his chair and stared out the window as if waiting while Auerbach read.

The suggestion he might have some involvement in the matter left Auerbach apprehensive, but he pushed those concerns aside and quickly scanned the report. When he finished, he laid the paper on the desktop. "Rather brutal, being betrayed by your own cousin."

Rosenwald spun back to face him. "Arabs like to portray themselves as the only civilized people on the planet, but they are really quite the opposite." He leaned back in the chair, elbows propped on the armrests, fingers clasped together. "I checked with Washington. They're concerned about the Syrians."

"The report mentions uranium."

"Yes," Rosenwald nodded. "We've known about it for some time. Oil company engineers discovered the deposits but withheld the information from the Jordanians." Rosenwald chuckled. "Bedouins have known about those deposits for years, they just didn't know the potential. Jordan could become more powerful than all the oil-rich sheiks combined. An agent from Aramco finally told Hussein about it. I'm not sure how the Syrians found out. But the big question on Washington's mind is how the Israelis learned about it."

"About the deposits?"

"Yes. The whole thing. The plot, the deposits, the Syrian interest in controlling it."

"We aren't concerned about the Syrians?"

"We?"

"The United States."

"Who can tell?" Rosenwald shrugged. "The Syrians are of no consequence to McNamara. Rusk understands the importance of the region but I'm not sure he has the influence with Johnson to do anything about it."

"Surely President Johnson has no intention of allowing them to gain control of it."

"I don't know," Rosenwald sighed. He pushed himself upright in the chair. "Anyway," the detached tone returning to his voice, "Abba Eban and the Israeli Foreign Office would like to tell King Hussein about that plot. They're convinced war with Egypt is just a matter of time and think that if they warn Hussein he might be less inclined to join the fight against them. But Eshkol—" Rosenwald paused, once more a puzzled look on his face. "Do you know him?"

"Only from the newspapers. I've never met the prime minister."

"Yes, well, if this turns out well for you, we'll have to see what we can do about that." Rosenwald cleared his throat. "Anyway, Eshkol and Golda Meir are concerned that any attempt by them to pass this information directly to Hussein might have difficulty getting through and perhaps would not be treated with the seriousness it demands. They are also worried that if news of their contact, or even attempted contact, became public Hussein might be placed in further danger—viewed as sympathetic to the Jews, that sort of thing. So Abba Eban has asked us to get the message to the king and do so in a way that allows the king to take that message seriously. That's where you come in."

"I would be glad to help," Auerbach replied, at a loss as to what Rosenwald intended, "but I'm afraid I wouldn't know what to do or who to call to get a message through to them."

"That's what I expected you'd say, so here's how we'll handle it. You will travel to Amman and check into a hotel. Next morning, you will go downstairs. A car will be waiting for you and someone will approach you. You won't know them but they will know who you are. That person will take you to the palace, where you will meet with King Hussein. Officially you will be there to discuss an oil pipeline. That's your cover story. During the course of your meeting you will tell the king that two men on the general staff of his army are cooperating with the Syrians in a plot to assassinate him and install his cousin in his place." Rosenwald reached in the top drawer once more and took out a file, which he dropped on the desktop. "Background information on all the players is in here. Read it, digest it, but leave it in your desk. Don't take it with you."

Auerbach was perplexed. "You want me to go?"

"Yes," Rosenwald replied with a hint of frustration. "That's why I asked you. I'd go myself but it's too far and I'm too old. The trip is arranged. All the details have been put in place. The only thing left is for you to do as I've instructed and deliver the message."

"And what shall I say when King Hussein asks how I know about the plot to kill him?"

"Tell him I told you so."

Auerbach had a questioning frown. "You told me?"

"Yes."

"And that will be enough for him?"

"It will be more than enough." Rosenwald gave a dismissive wave of his hand. "Your plane leaves in the morning. Mrs. Landau has your itinerary."

Auerbach rose from his chair, picked up the file from the desk, and turned toward the door. As he opened it to leave he glanced back to see Rosenwald, his chair turned sideways, gazing out the window. He thought for a moment about mentioning the conversation to Mrs. Landau—the odd shifts in Rosenwald's voice and changes in his demeanor were becoming more pronounced—then he thought better of it. She probably knew it already anyway. Instead, he stepped from the office and pulled the door quietly closed behind him.

— • —

Back in his own office, Auerbach tossed the note pad and file on his desk and took a seat. He opened the bottom drawer, took out a cardboard cigar box, and set it atop the file. Inside were newspaper clippings, three lapel pins, four Palestinian coins minted during the British mandate, and half a dozen black-and-white photographs. He sorted through the photos until he came to one with dog-eared corners and a crease across the bottom. He held it with both hands and leaned back in the chair, his eyes absorbing every detail.

The picture showed the view looking north from the barn at the Degania compound, across neatly cultivated fields toward a clump of trees in the distance. Barely visible through the foliage was the clay-tiled roof of a house. As he focused on the house, Auerbach was transported back in time and suddenly all those memories he'd kept locked inside came rushing out. He thought of the time he and Suheir had spent beneath those trees, nestled in the shadows just beyond the edge of the field—out of sight from the compound and unnoticed by Suheir's father. The smell of her soft dark hair, the mystery deep in those beautiful almond eyes, the taste of her lips against his.

And just as quickly, he saw her lifeless body lying in the alley in Jerusalem. It had been a horrible ending to a wonderful adventure and as he thought of it his eyes grew moist. "This is why I never open that drawer," he whispered as a single tear trickled down his cheek. "This is why I never think of her."

CHAPTER 10

TWO DAYS LATER, KING HUSSEIN came from his second-floor residence in the Nadwa Palace and made his way downstairs to his study. Using a phone on the credenza, he placed a call to his assistant, Haider Raimouny, summoning him to a meeting, then took a seat at the desk and waited.

Raimouny had been selected from among a host of candidates to fill the position left vacant by Hussein's longtime aide, Ali Al-Sharyri. The choice had been difficult, but for the past five years Raimouny had served well, though he sometimes seemed unduly petulant for a king's servant. Recently, however, Hussein had come to doubt Raimouny's loyalty. He couldn't say why, exactly, but he was certain something was amiss and equally confident that if he kept quiet and paid attention, the nature of Raimouny's misdeeds would eventually be exposed.

To protect himself, Hussein redoubled his personal-security retinue and imposed closer scrutiny of his daily routine. Many things he wished to do were disguised in a way that not even Raimouny knew precisely what occurred. Those measures and others gave Hussein added confidence in the safety of the palace and the royal family but often resulted in meetings similar to the one he was about to have.

Hussein was seated at his desk when the door opened and Raimouny appeared. "You called, Your Majesty?" Raimouny took his place a few feet away.

"I have a meeting today," Hussein began. "We need to talk about it."

"Your Excellency," Raimouny replied, "your morning is clear. There is nothing on the schedule."

"The schedule is clear, but my morning is full."

Raimouny looked perplexed. "I don't understand."

"Yaakov Auerbach arrived from New York yesterday. He is staying at the Imperial Hotel."

Raimouny frowned. "He is here for a meeting?"

"Yes," Hussein nodded. "He is coming here."

"But I do not understand." Raimouny grew increasingly bewildered. "The meeting is not on the schedule. This is the first I have heard of it."

"I made the arrangements myself," Hussein replied.

Raimouny's eyes opened wide in a look of surprise. "You arranged the meeting?"

"Yes."

"And Mr. Auerbach is coming here because …?"

"He is here to discuss a pipeline," Hussein explained.

"Which pipeline?"

"The one Bechtel wants to build." Hussein had no intention of telling him the real intent of the visit. "We have issues to discuss and he is here to address them."

"Bechtel?" Raimouny shook his head slowly. "I do not understand. I have heard nothing of such a project. Will others join you?"

"No."

"He is an engineer?"

"No. An attorney."

Raimouny was flabbergasted. "Why are you conducting a meeting with a lawyer by yourself? Wouldn't you like someone to assist you? Especially with the technical details."

"Samer Hattab from the interior ministry will join us," Hussein assured. "If the discussion becomes too technical, I am sure he will know someone to call."

"Very well," Raimouny said, apparently satisfied that Hattab would attend. He bowed politely. "How may I be of assistance?"

"I want you to send Bahjat Mousa to pick up Hattab. He will be waiting at the Ministry of Interior building."

"Yes, Your Excellency. Shall he bring Hattab here?"

"Tell him to take Hattab to the hotel, pick up Mr. Auerbach, and bring them both here."

Raimouny seemed unsure. "They are to travel together?"

"Yes."

"With your personal driver?"

Hussein was growing frustrated. "Is that a problem?"

"Auerbach is a Jew, is he not?"

"Perhaps. But he is also an American."

Raimouny's eyes opened wide again. "We would do business with an American Jew?"

"Americans buy much oil these days," Hussein explained, doing his best to keep the truth from Raimouny. "Our experts say they will continue to purchase oil in ever-increasing amounts into the foreseeable future. Arab states are the world's dominant producers. America is the dominant consumer. We in Jordan have no oil but we have access and facilities that can be used to our advantage. We need the Americans as much as they need us. And we need this pipeline."

Raimouny shook his head. "I do not like making friends with the Americans. And least of all American Jews. It is dangerous."

"In this world, making friends with anyone is a risk, but we have no choice in this matter. We need the revenue." Hussein scooted his chair closer to the desk. "Go now," he directed. "They will be waiting."

— • —

Auerbach was standing in the lobby when King Hussein's car and driver arrived. Hattab from the Ministry of Interior met him near the front desk and escorted him to the car. They rode together to the palace seated side by side in the back.

As the car came to a stop in the driveway outside the palace entrance, Raimouny came down the steps to greet them and led the way to Hussein's office. The king was seated in an overstuffed armchair when they entered.

Raimouny announced Hattab and introduced Auerbach, then backed away and disappeared down the hall. A footman closed the door behind him, leaving the king alone with Hattab and Auerbach.

"Your Excellency," Hattab said with a bow, "I shall take my leave." He, too, backed away from the king's presence, crossed the room to the garden door near the desk, and disappeared. When he was gone, Hussein gestured to a chair beside him. "Please, have a seat. I am sure you must be tired from your long trip." He lifted his hands chest high, clapped them twice, and smiled politely. "We shall have some tea in a moment. And then we will talk."

— · —

In the hallway outside Hussein's study, a footman, Marouf Rifai, heard Hussein's clap. He rose from his place on a bench by the door and scurried down the hall toward the kitchen. The cook was standing near the stove when he entered the room and went to work assembling items on a tray. When it was ready, Rifai hoisted it to his shoulder, turned toward the door, and started back to the hall.

Moments later he was back at the door to the king's study. He rapped lightly on it with his knuckle, then pushed it open and stepped inside. The two men were seated side by side and seemed to pay him no attention as he set the tray on a low table near them and put out the cups, honey, milk, and spoons, then added a plate of sweet breads. Hussein and Auerbach continued to chat and Rifai listened intently as he filled their cups with tea.

Auerbach had an accent, Rifai noticed. An American. From the East Coast. New York, probably. But he wasn't a white European and the accent wasn't quite distinct. A hint of something else. Midwestern, perhaps. He was all but certain their visitor was Jewish.

When the cups were filled, Rifai bowed politely, then stepped from the room to the hallway. He closed the door behind him and returned to his place on a bench near the wall. Sitting quietly, he listened as voices from the office drifted through an open transom window.

— • —

Alone again with the king, Auerbach at last delivered the message about the assassination plot—key generals, backed by the Syrians, wanted to remove Hussein and replace him with the king's cousin, Naif bin Talal, in the hope of allowing Syria access to Jordanian uranium deposits. Hussein listened patiently, then asked, "Which of my generals do you suppose is involved with this plot?"

"Tareq Ayasrah," Auerbach replied.

Hussein laughed out loud. "General Ayasrah is my most trusted ally."

Auerbach did not flinch. "Then he knows you well," he nodded with quiet confidence.

"Yes," Hussein replied, no longer laughing.

"And he knows where you are most vulnerable."

The smile was gone from Hussein. "And tell me," he had a serious tone. "How is it that you have come to have this knowledge of my generals?"

Auerbach squared his shoulders. "I know because Lawrence Rosenwald told me."

Hussein threw back his head and laughed even louder than before. "Lawrence knows, and he sent you?"

"Yes."

Hussein daubed the corners of his eyes as he struggled to stop laughing. "How is Lawrence these days?"

"Mr. Rosenwald is well." Auerbach was unsettled by Hussein's reaction. "You know him?"

"Yes," Hussein nodded, still chuckling. "Of course."

"I wasn't aware you knew each other. You don't seem quite his age."

"He and my father were friends."

"Mr. Rosenwald and your father?"

"He didn't tell you?"

"No," Auerbach shook his head.

"Just sent you over here with a message?"

"Yes."

"He and my father were good friends. He and I...not so much, but that is to be expected with the acquaintances of one's parents. The age difference. We just never were that close. But he and my father were good friends. My father met Lawrence when he was in Istanbul."

"Ah," Auerbach nodded with a knowing expression. "Law school."

"Yes. They were in law school. Lawrence and David Ben-Gurion. My father was simply living there. I'm not sure of the details exactly. One of those youthful accounts that gets bigger and bigger each time it's told. Lawrence used to come to Amman to visit my father. They would sit together late into the night reminding each other of the things they did when they were young men. Always something about a girl and a bottle of wine." Hussein laughed again, though not as hard as before. "Maybe it was two bottles." He pushed himself up from the chair and stood. "Come." He reached down to offer Auerbach a hand. "Let us have some lunch and I will tell you why you are really here."

— • —

Meanwhile, after leaving the palace, Samer Hattab traveled across town to the home of Fayez bin Wahbi, a wealthy merchant. Naif bin Talal was there along with several others. They'd been waiting for Hattab to arrive.

"What happened?" Wahbi asked.

"The American is with the king now," Hattab answered.

"Do you know why he is here?"

"No. The story we were told and the story we were given to tell others who ask is that the lawyer from America came here to discuss details of a pipeline to be constructed from Saudi Arabia."

"And that story is false?"

"There is no pipeline under construction and none under consideration," Hattab explained. "But as to the real purpose, I do not know and I don't think anyone else does, either."

Talal spoke up. "Haider Raimouny did not know?"

"No."

Abdullah al-Majali, a friend who was with them, shook his head. "King Hussein's assistant doesn't know. What can that mean?"

"What was this man's name?" Wahbi asked.

"Yaakov Auerbach."

Abdel Eleyan, a minor investor in several of Wahbi's business deals, had an astonished look. "Auerbach is a Jewish name."

Al-Majali arched an eyebrow. "Hussein is meeting with one of the Zionists?"

Talal spoke up again. "I know this man, this Auerbach. I know him," he repeated calmly. "He is a lawyer from New York. He works for a friend of Hussein's father. Let us make some calls." He nodded to an assistant who then left the room while the conversation continued.

"I do not like this," Wahbi had a worried look.

"Hussein is a traitor," Eleyan snarled.

"It is not so much even that," Wahbi lamented. "But the Americans."

"Ah, yes," Al-Majali nodded thoughtfully. "The Americans. Do you think he will involve them in our dispute?"

"I do not know," Wahbi replied. "But their presence here would not be good."

A few minutes later, Talal's assistant returned and whispered something in Talal's ear. Talal smiled and glanced up at the others. "It is as I first thought. Auerbach is a lawyer, and he is from New York." He looked over at Hattab. "The story you heard is the same one they are telling in New York, too—that he is here to negotiate a deal for a pipeline from Saudi Arabia to be constructed by the American company named Bechtel."

Eleyan asked, "Which law firm is he with?"

"Mayer, Meagan & Gottschalk," Talal replied. "Lawrence Rosenwald is a partner, and a friend of both Hussein's father and David Ben-Gurion."

"First the Zionists put the Americans under their spell," Al-Majali said. "Now they are doing the same with Hussein."

"Part of the Jews' grand scheme to control the world."

"This business about a rebirth of Israel is just a front. What they want is control of the oil."

"*Our* oil."

"First they will gain control of Palestine, then little by little they will creep across the Middle East. And when they are finished, they will have the world by the throat."

Talal's assistant held up a copy of a book entitled *Protocols of the Elders of Zion*. "It is all written in here. Everything you are saying about them right now was written many years ago in this book."

"They are condemned by their own words," Wahbi pointed to the book.

"We must do something."

"But what?"

Talal smiled once more, "Leave it to me. I will take care of everything."

Wahbi grinned. "You have a plan?"

"One that is already in motion."

"This is why the Syrians will support you."

"And why parliament must make you king after Hussein is gone," Al-Majali added.

"But first we must eliminate his source of strength. His generals. And when the generals are gone, there will be no one left to stand in our way."

"But will he do it? Will he kill his own generals?"

Talal again turned to his assistant, who handed him an envelope. Talal gestured with it as he spoke. "In this envelope are documents and photographs few people have ever seen. With them, Allah will deliver this moment to us. When my cousin reads these documents and sees these photographs, he will remember his father, the mistakes he made in ignoring threats to his life, and the end those mistakes brought to him. And Hussein will sense he has no choice but to act." Talal handed the envelope to Samer Hattab. "You can get these to Haider Raimouny?"

"Yes."

"And he will present them to the king?"

"Most certainly."

"Very well," Talal grinned. "If Hussein reads those documents and acts upon what is written there, it will not matter what Auerbach from New York tells him or whether the Americans come. We will be in control."

CHAPTER 11

AUERBACH AND KING HUSSEIN sat across from each other in the dining room and waited while Marouf Rifai served the first course of lunch. When he was gone, Auerbach said, "So, tell me, why am I really here?"

"You are here for two reasons," Hussein explained. "First, because Israel intends to launch an attack against Egypt and they would like for me to avoid intervening on Egypt's side."

Auerbach was aware of the growing tension in the region but knew nothing of pending military operations. He decided to play along and see what he could learn. "Why would Israel attack Egypt?" he asked, feigning ignorance.

"In order to annex the Sinai Peninsula."

Auerbach had a genuine frown. "That sounds a bit ..."

"Absurd?"

"I wouldn't use that word," Auerbach replied, suddenly feeling he'd become too familiar with the king. "It's just a little difficult to believe they would do such a thing."

"Ben-Gurion said as much himself. With words from his own lips."

"When did he say that?" Auerbach had read all of Ben-Gurion's speeches and knew of several that might have been construed this way but he wanted to know what Hussein knew.

"The final year he was in office," Hussein explained. "In a speech to

97

the Knesset. It was his words but they all feel the same way. The current prime minister, Levi Eshkol, is merely following Ben-Gurion's policies."

Hussein was correct that Ben-Gurion had set the country on a path from which others were not likely to soon deviate. "But assuming all that is true, how does that affect you?"

"When Eshkol launches his attack, Syria and Iraq will respond by attacking Israel from the north. In order to have any hope of success against Egypt, Israel must commit the bulk of its forces to the Sinai. When Iraq and Syria start across the northern border, there will be no one there to stop them. And if we join with an attack from the east, Israel will be finished as a nation."

"You think Eshkol and the others are trying to convince you not to do that?"

"That is what they hope," Hussein replied with a smile. "They hope that if they give me a tip that saves my life, I will think twice before entering the coming conflict. And I might oblige them if the threat were true."

"You don't think there is a threat to your life?"

"The only threat to my life comes from the temptation to show leniency to Israel."

"So to protect your life you must plunge your country into war?"

"It is a terrible choice, I know," Hussein nodded. "My country needs peace. We have no oil reserves as our neighbors do and must rely on the ingenuity of our people for economic resources. We need time to develop our economy. War would sap us of needed improvements. But if I avoid a conflict between Egypt and Israel while others from the Arab League join the fight, I will be a dead man. That is one of the many lessons I learned from my father. He attempted a path of cooperation with the Jews. Instead of anti-Zionist rhetoric, he tried to focus on sustained economic development for our people, and his fellow countrymen killed him for it. They will kill me, too, if they think I am employing that same tactic."

"Interesting observation," Auerbach mused as he paused to take a drink. "You said there were two reasons I'm here. What's the other one?"

"The other reason you are here is because Lawrence Rosenwald and Abba Eban know that delivering this message to me is a fool's errand."

"A waste of time?"

"A very dangerous waste of time. Abba Eban suggested it because Eshkol and Golda Meir told him to. Rosenwald agreed to deliver it because the State of Israel is his client and he wants to keep their business. But if you had proposed this on your own, he would have fired you on the spot."

"Then why did you agree to see me?"

"Because the request came from Lawrence Rosenwald." Hussein gave him an indulgent smile. "And I will tell you, even Golda Meir does not believe your effort will work."

"You think they made it up?"

"The assassination plot?"

"Yes."

"No," Hussein shook his head. "I don't think they are lying, if that's what you're asking. I think they heard a rumor from a Mossad contact and hope that it's true. I think they are good people and understand my predicament. And I think they are offering me this gesture as a way of acknowledging our common situation. But I suspect they are as skeptical about the underlying plot as I am."

"You seem to understand the region very well."

"Anyone in this region of the world would tell you the same."

"So you think Mr. Rosenwald stayed home because he did not want to be associated with a failed effort?"

"Lawrence Rosenwald is many things but afraid is not one of them. He sent you knowing that if telling me has the desired effect, and I refuse to join the others in war, that would be a good thing and everyone will know that you were merely the messenger. That others were behind the effort. And perhaps he is thinking of the future of his firm and that you might be able to one day pick up where he must leave off. But if your trip does not produce a positive result, or if something awkward happens as a result of your visit, they can deny any connection to this whole affair. Rosenwald can yell at you in front of Abba Eban to smooth things over with his client. Israel can deny any connection to the affair. Rosenwald looks good. Israel looks good. And everything works out right. They will probably give you a raise, too."

"You're certain of that?"

"If it had been otherwise, Lawrence Rosenwald would be here and you would be sitting in your office in Manhattan."

Auerbach realized Hussein was correct and shifted the conversation back to the point of the visit. "You really don't think the threat is real?"

Hussein's eyes darted to the left toward the door. "There are always men looking for a reason to kill me. That is the nature of this country." He looked over at Auerbach. "But I cannot give Eshkol what he wants."

"I understand," Auerbach nodded, convinced more than ever that regional war was inevitable.

"If this was a matter between myself and Eshkol," Hussein continued, "or between myself and the Israeli people, we would have no dispute. But that is not the world in which I live. As I said, if the other Arab nations join Egypt in a war against Israel, and I do not send the army of Jordan into battle with them, I will be forever labeled a Zionist sympathizer, a tool of imperialist forces, and a pawn of colonial interests. And I will have to contend with far more serious threats than the bungled attempts of junior officers." Hussein smiled and his face softened. "But I will give you something to help you out. Something you can take back to New York that may help you with your employer."

"I would be glad to relay any message you might have," Auerbach acceded.

"You are aware that President Nasser and his Egyptian generals have created the Palestine Liberation Organization."

"Yes."

"Nasser intends to use that organization to gather all the disparate Arab groups of Palestine and form them into a single militant force. Nasser's friend Ahmad Shukeiri is the PLO president and through him Nasser intends to exert control over the entire region. In his mind, the PLO, not the war Syria demands, will be his vehicle for Israel's undoing."

"It seems rather obvious that he means to use them as a disruptive force."

"Yes," Hussein acknowledged. "But what is not so obvious is that the Syrians hate him for it."

Auerbach was aware that leaders of the two countries were not personally close but he didn't realize their disdain for each other ran that
deep. "The Syrians hate Nasser?"

Yes, they act like friends because neither wants the other to know
how much they dislike each other. Their hatred of the Jews is the only
reason they attempt to cooperate. Otherwise, all the anger that they direct
toward the Zionists would be directed at each other," he laughed.

"Why do the Syrians hate him?"

"They see Nasser as weak and always beholden to non-Muslim
nations—first the British and now the Russians. And because of that,
they have no intention of letting him control Palestine. To counter his
influence in the region they have recruited their own organization—the
Palestinian National Liberation Movement—which they call FATAH—and
which they intend to use as their own version of a unifying Palestinian
apparatus. And they have chosen Yasser Arafat to lead it. You have heard
of him?"

"Yes."

"You should study him closely. Arafat is a dangerous man. He will
cause the Zionists much trouble because, unlike Shukeiri, who is merely
a politician, Arafat is a true rebel. The Jews should watch out for him. He
already had a large underground organization when the Syrians recruited
him. They were the ones behind many of the attacks in the past, but no
one knew who they were back then. Now he is continuing those same
attacks but with the blessing and assistance of the Syrian government."

"So the attacks we have read about in the news are all at the behest
of the Syrians?"

"Yes. That is what I am trying to tell you. And they are doing this in
an attempt to provoke the Zionists into striking Syrian targets. When that
happens, Syria will use the Zionist response as a pretext for war. This is
very important. Many more attacks are planned, including one against
Israel's National Water Carrier project in the Galilee. You are aware of
that project?"

"Diverting water from the north to deserts in the south," Auerbach
responded.

"Taking it from the Sea of Galilee and sending it all the way down to the Negev." Hussein beamed with pride as he spoke of it. "Fascinating project. I have tried many times to convince our engineers to undertake similar projects in our own country." His countenance turned dark. "But Arafat plans to attack that project and he intends to strike at the heart of Israel."

"The Israelis will destroy him if he does."

Hussein nodded again. "Arafat and his Syrian supporters are hoping for just such a response. If Israeli leaders wish to avoid a full-scale regional war, they must refrain from attacking Syrian positions, even if Arafat is successful against targets of intense national pride."

Auerbach had been listening closely and wondering if Hussein was attempting to tell him something even more explicit than their frank conversation. "I will pass that information on."

"See that you do," Hussein urged. "One small mistake by the Israelis could be their undoing."

— • —

After lunch, King Hussein's assistant, appeared in the hall outside the study. He and Hussein escorted Auerbach to the front of the palace, then Raimouny accompanied him to the airport in King Hussein's car.

At the airport, Bahjat Mousa, Hussein's driver, steered the car around the terminal building and drove across the tarmac. A Lockheed Electra four-engine prop plane from Trans World Airlines was parked on the runway apron. Mousa brought the car to a stop near the plane's door. He and Raimouny exchanged a final good-bye, then Auerbach came from the car, climbed the steps to the fuselage door, and stepped inside the airplane.

At first, everything seemed normal. The airplane lifted off the runway, turned to the south, and began to slowly climb. Out the window, Auerbach watched as the Jordanian landscape moved slowly past. Thirty minutes into the flight, they banked to the west and continued to climb. The landscape below, now only rolling desert sand, became a tan sea. Auerbach watched for a moment, then settled back in his seat, folded his hands in his lap, and closed his eyes.

During a restless slumber Auerbach became aware of a commotion about him and opened his eyes to see everyone staring out the windows on the right side of the plane. Smoke belched from the outboard engine followed by a burst of flame that caused many of the passengers to gasp. Auerbach was worried but by the time he was fully awake the engine's propeller stopped turning and a voice came over the loudspeaker. "This is the captain. We had a little trouble with one of the engines but we've extinguished the fire and should be fine for the remainder of the flight." Passengers watched a moment longer, then returned to their seats. Auerbach closed his eyes once more.

Just as he drifted off to sleep, the plane shook violently. Auerbach glanced to the left and saw a gaping hole in the wing where once an engine had been. The airplane rocked from side to side, then plunged downward at a steep angle only to level off for a moment before beginning a steady descent.

Attendants hurried through the cabin, moving from row to row. "Remove all sharp objects from your clothes and prepare for a hard landing." Others demonstrated the proper position for impact—lean forward as low toward your knees as possible, clasp your hands over your head. Auerbach found that word—*impact*—as disconcerting as the missing engine.

Twenty minutes later, much longer than he'd expected, the plane settled down on a flat stretch of desert sand. At first it seemed it would skid to a gentle stop on its belly. Propeller blades on the functioning engines sliced through the sand, sending sandy showers into the air. Finally, the plane turned sideways and rose up on one side as if to flip over, before slamming down to a hard stop.

"Out! Out! Out!" an attendant shouted. "Get out now!"

Passengers rose at once, elbowing their way past each other to reach the aisle, then shoving others ahead of them toward the door. Auerbach, seated near a window, waited while the others went ahead, then rose from his seat and walked quickly to the door.

CHAPTER 12

IN THE NEGEV SOUTH OF JERUSALEM near the Egyptian border, a farm worker driving a truck to Bir Hadaj, a Jewish settlement near Beersheba, saw the plane go down and came to assist. With the help of the crew and some of the passengers, including Auerbach, the seriously injured passengers were loaded onto the truck and taken to the settlement. Auerbach and the others were left to wait in the shade of the disabled aircraft.

A few hours later, a caravan of buses and trucks arrived and all the remaining passengers were ferried to Bir Hadaj. At the settlement, they received first aid and a comfortable place to rest. Meanwhile, the settlement director radioed government authorities in Jerusalem.

"We've notified the defense ministry," the director told them. "They're arranging for your safe passage to Jerusalem. I'm sure someone will help you continue to your destination from there."

Auerbach spoke up. "Will we be leaving here today?"

"I assume so," the director replied. "But we'll have to wait and see. If not, we have plenty of space for you to remain overnight." A grin turned up his cheeks. "And plenty of work to help you forget your troubles."

Troubles, Auerbach thought as he turned toward the window. He had no troubles. In fact, sitting there, gazing out at the neatly arranged farming plots and the desert beyond, he felt right at home. Bir Hadaj was nicer and newer than the facilities at Degania, but the sense of the place was the same. Everything communal. Clothing, shoes, even the underwear, washed in a central laundry, dispensed from a central storeroom. Very little personal property solely for oneself. Everyone working to grow and harvest a crop. He liked the feel of the place, and the nostalgia that welled up inside seemed all but overpowering.

But before long his thoughts turned to Suheir and what might have been. Memories of her filled his thoughts and he returned in his mind to the day he was with her near their home in Degania when her father found them together. He wasn't scared at the time, but looking back now he wondered why he wasn't. He should have been. "That man could have killed me," he chuckled to himself. Still, if he'd died that day he would have died a happy man. She was the most beautiful woman he'd ever known and even now, after all the years, the image of her in his mind caused him to smile.

— • —

Hours after the crash, an IDF patrol located the aircraft crash site. They secured the area and called for assistance. Shortly after that, a recovery team reached the location and began sorting through the wreckage. Right away, Chaim Sharett, an expert with the team, focused on the engines. Colonel Epstein, the recovery team commander, followed Sharett through the site.

"I see no evidence the plane was hit by gunfire," Sharett observed. "No bullet holes in the wings or fuselage that we can see."

"Of course, the bottom of the plane is buried in the sand," Epstein noted.

"True, but I don't think we'll find any evidence of gunfire," Sharett continued. "If it had been a missile, the damage would be far more extensive. Even a clean hit to the engine would do more than what we have here." He pointed to the engine that had caught fire. "This is damage from an internal problem. Something happened inside the engine. This is actually rather common among propeller-driven aircraft."

"So what do you think caused the crash?"

"I think we're looking at an internal engine problem."

"With both of them?"

"Yes." Sharett backed away from the damaged engine and started toward the opposite side of the plane. "Something happened inside that engine," he said, gesturing over his shoulder.

"Could that problem have been related to the other one?"

"Perhaps, but contrary to what you might see in American movies, the probability of two engines failing at the same time on the same aircraft is extremely remote."

"It had four engines," Epstein noted. "Couldn't it continue to fly on just two?"

"Yes," Sharett nodded. They were on the opposite side of the plane by then and he stood at the empty mounting bracket. "But with the engine on this side missing and the one on the other wing on fire, they could have encountered other problems." He pointed to the bracket. "Perhaps the loss of this engine disabled the control surfaces or rendered them ineffective. Weight of the aircraft is also an issue."

"You mean weight at takeoff?"

"I mean, if it was already flying heavy—at or near the limit—the redundancy of the engines might not have been enough to overcome the added load of flying with only two." Sharett turned to face Epstein. "That's my initial assessment. It'll take a few days to sort through everything and reach a definitive conclusion. But even then I think we'll come back to the same hunch I have right now."

"Which is?"

"That the engines failed due to internal issues."

"Well," Epstein sighed, "we need to know whether this was sabotage or simply poor maintenance."

"Then we should remove the aircraft intact and transport it to a warehouse where we can examine it in a clean, secure facility." Sharett glanced down at the ground with disgust. "This sand has a way of getting into everything."

"I think that's out of the question, at least for now," Epstein replied. "How difficult is it to pull the engines?"

"Not very difficult at all. We can unbolt them from the wings and they'll come right off. The problem here, though, is the plane is sitting on the ground. The engines have dug into the sand. To get them out we would have to excavate beneath them in order to drop them from beneath the wings."

"They'll unbolt, though?"

"Yes. Very easy to detach them under normal conditions."

"Then we could unbolt them, and drag the plane forward to get it out of the way."

"Ahh," Sharett nodded. "A good idea. That would leave the engines where they are and we could simply hoist them onto a truck." He smiled at Epstein. "You can do that?"

"That won't be a problem. We can get a couple of bulldozers in here to move it."

Sharett glanced up at the sky. "It'll be dark soon."

"We'll set up lights. We need to get busy. People are asking what brought this aircraft down and they want an answer as quickly as possible."

— • —

In Amman, Jordan, Haider Raimouny, King Hussein's assistant, found the king in the garden behind the palace. He approached Hussein tentatively, bringing the envelope he received from Talal. Hussein saw him, then noticed the envelope. "You have something you wish to discuss?" he asked.

"There has been an accident, Your Excellency."

A frown wrinkled Hussein's brow. "What sort of accident?"

"The airplane on which your American visitor traveled has crashed in the Negev."

Hussein was startled. "Mr. Auerbach?"

"Yes," Raimouny said. He bowed reverently. "I am very sorry."

Hussein moved closer. "What caused this tragedy?"

"It appears that it might have been the result of sabotage."

"An act of war, we would recognize immediately. But sabotage, we would only uncover upon investigation. How could anyone know that was the cause, so soon after it has occurred?"

"I am only reporting what others are saying."

Hussein thought for a moment, then asked, "If it was sabotage, who would want to do such a thing?"

"Perhaps this will shed some light on the matter." Raimouny offered Hussein the envelope. Hussein took it from him and opened it to find the documents and photographs Raimouny received earlier from Talal. Hussein scanned them quickly.

One of the documents was a memo from Syrian intelligence summarizing a meeting with Jordanian General Tareq Ayasrah in which he discussed the possibility of stationing Syrian troops on Jordanian soil, particularly the West Bank. According to the memo, when asked about whether this would be possible, those who attended the meeting quoted Ayasrah as saying, "You would have to replace the current regime first."

A second document included a list of potential locations in Jordan that might be suitable for stationing Syrian troops. The list bore Ayasrah's signature. Photographs accompanying the documents showed Ayasrah with Syrian army officers.

Hussein glared at Raimouny. "Summon General Ayasrah at once," he demanded.

"Certainly," Raimouny was barely able to contain his delight at Hussein's reaction.

— • —

Within the hour, General Ayasrah arrived at the palace. Hussein was seated at his desk in the study. Ayasrah stood before him. "I understand a TWA aircraft that flew from our airport crashed a few hours ago in the Negev," Hussein began.

"Yes, Your Majesty. That is correct."

"What happened to it?"

"First reports indicate it was shot down by the Zionists."

"Why would they shoot down the plane?"

"You would have to ask them."

"Could it have been the result of sabotage?"

"Perhaps," Ayasrah conceded, "but one could not determine that without investigating the wreckage."

"You have not seen the wreckage?"

"No, the aircraft went down in an area controlled by the Zionists. We have no way of gaining access to it."

Hussein stared at him a moment, then asked bluntly, "Do you wish to kill me?"

Ayasrah was astounded. "Begging your pardon, Your Excellency?"

Hussein repeated the question. "Do you wish to kill me?"

"Of course not," Ayasrah said nervously. "Have I not shown my loyalty?"

"On many occasions," Hussein nodded.

"Then why do you question me in this manner?"

Hussein handed him the documents and photographs, then gestured for silence with a finger to his lips as he rose from behind his desk and crossed the room to the door. While Ayasrah read, Hussein took a long stick from behind one of the chairs and used it to push the transom window shut above the door.

Ayasrah gestured with the memo. "This is from our meeting last year." Hussein moved to his side and gestured for him to lower his voice. Ayasrah continued at a whisper. "I reported this to you after the meeting. They asked me if I thought it was feasible to station Syrian troops on Jordanian soil. And I told them for that to be possible they would need a different king, but they left out the rest of my statement."

"Which was?"

"That such a change would be impossible and that they would have to kill me first. I told you all of these things when I returned from the trip and you said to explore the idea of staging Syrian troops here anyway, that as long as we were talking to them they wouldn't try anything else. So we went through an elaborate process of evaluating potential sites for stationing their troops." The general gestured with the papers in his hand. "And that is where this came from." Ayasrah sighed and shook his head. "How is it that you have these documents?" He flipped through the photographs. "And these pictures. Where did this come from?"

"Haider Raimouny gave them to me. Right after he told me the civilian airplane was forced to the ground by an act of sabotage."

"Your Excellency," Ayasrah fumed, "I know you have enjoyed the assistance of Haider Raimouny and are well acquainted with members of his family, but I must say, I do not trust him."

"I know," Hussein nodded, "and neither do I."

"Then what is going on?"

Hussein gestured for him to follow and led the way to the far side of the room, near the door behind the desk. "There is a plot to assassinate me," he whispered.

"We have faced this many times before."

"This one comes from deep inside our ranks."

Ayasrah had a troubled look. "From the military?"

"Perhaps," Hussein said. "But most of the leadership comes from one of the departments. I think it is from the Ministry of Interior."

Ayasrah was skeptical. "What makes you think that?"

"I believe Naif bin Talal is with them."

Ayasrah looked startled. "Your cousin? How can that be?"

"He is friends with Fayez bin Wahbi." Hussein pointed to the documents in Ayasrah's hand. "That is where those documents came from."

Ayasrah seemed satisfied Hussein's assessment was correct, but he was troubled by it. "Why would Talal do such a thing?"

"Talal has longed for the throne since my father's death," Hussein explained, "and Wahbi has always been loyal to Assad of Syria. Assad has made no secret he would like to see me replaced. I am certain he has promised both Talal and Wahbi many things in exchange for their cooperation."

"But Assad is only the Syrian defense minister. Nureddin al-Atassi is head of state."

"Come now," Hussein chided. "You and I both know Assad is the one with the power, even if he lacks the title. He calls the shots."

"You are right about that," Ayasrah agreed. "But what should we do?"

"Talal and his friends are attempting to goad me into removing all of my best generals, all of whom are loyal to me. Then when I have done that, they will use that very act against me as an indication that I am not fit to be king and should be removed. Parliament is weak. There are some who would resist such an attempt, but eventually Talal and his friends would prevail and I would be removed. Then, when I am gone, Talal will be appointed king, the generals who were loyal to me will be gone, and those who remain will have undying devotion to him."

"This is preposterous."

"Indeed," Hussein agreed. "Which is yet another reason why I'm sure my cousin is behind it. And also why it could very well succeed. Key leaders in the interior ministry are committed to this plan. They know the vast mineral riches that we possess. Not oil like our neighbors, but phosphate, and most of all uranium. They want to exploit those resources for personal profit and see the Syrians as their best option for doing so."

Ayasrah looked stricken. "We would become a Syrian vassal state."

"Yes."

"Then I ask again, what should we do?"

"I have a plan, but I will need your help."

"Certainly, Your Excellency." Ayasrah bowed. "I serve at the pleasure of the king."

CHAPTER 13

BACK IN TEL AVIV, MORDECHAI GUR was hard at work creating a plan for the defense of Government House and the hill on which it sat. He was also at work on a much larger plan to seize control of the city—not merely to defend the western half, which Israel controlled, but to seize all of Jerusalem.

As he worked that day at his desk, Rami Segev, the major in charge of the planning group, appeared at Gur's office door. "Just stopping by to see what progress you're making."

Gur glanced up without a second thought. "Trying to figure out how the Jordanians would come up the difficult side of Government House hill."

"Yes," Segev said in a distracted voice. "That would be good to know." By then he was standing at Gur's desk, sorting through the documents and maps that cluttered it. "What's this?" he asked, pointing to one of the maps.

"A map of Jerusalem."

"I can see that," Segev replied. "But it doesn't look like a defense of Government House. It looks like something else."

"That," Gur sighed, "is a plan for taking control of Jerusalem."

Segev had a stern look on his face. "Taking control of the city," he repeated.

"Yes," Gur nodded.

"We're supposed to be defending it," Segev noted.

"I know, but—"

Segev cut him off. "We've offered this option to Dayan in the past but he has refused to consider it."

"Dayan. Eshkol. Other members of the cabinet think Egypt is our strongest opponent. Too strong to ignore. Defeating Egypt will require all of our resources. We cannot win a multi-front war."

"How about you?" Gur asked. "What do you think?"

"I think, given our current state of readiness and troop levels, they are correct about the two-front issue. We cannot win a two-front war."

"And these officials think if we are attacked by Egypt that will be the extent of it? Jordan, or Syria, or Lebanon will not attack, too?"

"They hope Jordan will not attack."

"And what if that hope proves incorrect?"

"Then we may lose the city," Segev conceded.

"And with it the entire country."

"But if we divert part of our forces from an engagement against the Egyptians," Segev offered, "we will lose the Negev. That's not speculation. That's a fact. And if we lose there, we could lose the entire country that way, too."

"Perhaps. But if we lose Jerusalem, the middle of the country will be exposed. There won't be much to stop the Jordanian army from driving straight across to the sea."

"That's true, but there's only so much we can do. We don't have unlimited resources."

"No," Gur acknowledged. "But what we do have are plenty of assumptions. And I've been looking at those. I think we've got some of this wrong."

Segev frowned. "Like what?"

"The key to any defense of our nation is the elimination of the enemy's air force. Regardless of which country attacks us, that's the key. Syria and Jordan might not pose much of a threat, by the numbers, but we still must eliminate their air force in order to defeat them. The Egyptians, however, outnumber us in every category. The only way we can minimize that advantage is by obtaining air superiority."

"They outnumber us in aircraft, too," Segev pointed out.

"But that is one area I think we can easily address," Gur suggested.

"You have a supplier who'll give us a thousand more on credit?"

"We don't need more planes. We need more flights."

"What do you mean?"

"If we hit Egyptian airfields in two waves, the first one concentrating on destroying their runways, the second on destroying their planes while they are still on the ground, we can eliminate a prime source of Egypt's strength."

"You mean if we attack first?"

"Yes. Of course. Under any strategy, we must attack first."

"But they outnumber us in planes and in bases. We can't possibly destroy all their runways."

"Why not?" Gur wondered.

"It would take too many sorties. We've already modeled this from every angle," Segev added. "It would be impossible to eliminate even a significant number of their planes before they have destroyed all of ours."

"But," Gur countered, "that estimate of sorties is based on a turn-around time of three flights per twenty-four hours."

"That's the generally accepted guideline," Segev said defensively. "Even the U.S. follows that guideline."

"But the Americans have so many planes and aircraft carriers that they don't have to concern themselves with whether turnaround operations could be done faster. They have an insurmountable numerical advantage."

"Yeah," Segev agreed. "And that is precisely what we face with Egypt. An insurmountable advantage."

"Look," Gur argued, "just because others calculate this on three flights a day doesn't mean it can't be done another way. If we could reduce our turnaround time we could increase our number of flights from three per day to...perhaps five. That would greatly increase the number of targets we could hit."

Segev had a skeptical frown. "Three per day is doable. Anything above that is pure speculation. Planning on five flights would be just a shot in the dark."

"I'm not talking about speculation," Gur responded. "I'm talking about finding out how quickly crews can actually do the tasks. Fuel the planes. Reload them. Send them out."

In spite of himself, Segev was intrigued. "Well...IAF conducts training runs every day. I suppose I could see if they can arrange for us to observe a crew arming a plane." He gestured to the documents on Gur's desk. "But your job isn't to reorganize the Israeli Air Force or set policy regarding Jerusalem. Your primary task is to plan for defense of the city. Defense of it," he reiterated. "Not the taking of it."

"That's what I was trying to explain earlier. We can't defend Jerusalem."

Segev frowned. "What do you mean?"

Gur slid a map from the desktop clutter and laid it where they could see. "Look right here," he pointed. "This is Mount Scopus. And just below it is Temple Mount. And down here is the hill with Government House."

Segev nodded. "What about it?"

"These three hills are the highest in Jerusalem. Two of them are already in Jordanian hands."

"Well," Segev hedged, "technically Mount Scopus is neutral ground."

"But it's situated within the area controlled by Jordan. When the fighting starts it would be very easy for them to take the hill. And if they do that, they will begin the fighting with two of the highest points in the city under their control. They would dominate the city from the start. We wouldn't have a chance. If we want to defend our half, we have to take it all."

"And as I said earlier," Segev reiterated, "we don't have the forces for it."

"But if we can decrease the turnaround time for our aircraft, attack Egyptian airfields before they attack us, we can eliminate their air force and take control of the skies. Then we would free up planes from having to defend us and could use those extra airplanes to attack Egyptian positions in the field. That would allow us to pull enough troops out of action in the south to enable us to take the city."

"That's a convoluted plan," Segev said with a wry smile.

"But it will work," Gur insisted.

"Yes, it might. But I don't think Dayan will go for it."

"He won't have any choice."

Segev thought for a moment. "Okay," he said finally, "I'll arrange for us to view an IAF ground crew in operation. That will allow us to determine whether this idea is as feasible as you think. But in the meantime, don't spend much time on this." He turned away and started toward the door. "Defense of Jerusalem," he said with emphasis. "That is our focus right now. And your part is keeping Government House in our hands."

"Right," Gur agreed.

Segev paused at the door and turned back to Gur. "You know, we discussed defense of Jerusalem with General Narkiss several months ago."

Narkiss was legendary among IDF officers for his opinionated views regarding the use of military force, especially when it came to Jerusalem. Gur was curious about his views on the rapidly deteriorating situation. "What did General Narkiss say?"

"Pretty much the same thing you just did." Segev pointed again to the documents on the desk. "Get busy on a plan to defend the city. That's our primary job."

— • —

Three days later, Gur and Segev traveled to Hatzor IAF Base. The executive officer met them at the gate and took them by jeep to the flight line. He parked a few meters away and they climbed out. "We have the planes out here that you can see up close, but if you go up in the tower you can watch them take off and land."

Gur and Segev walked with him as they made their way down a row of fighter jets. "We weren't interested in the flying part," Gur pointed out. "We want to see the crews on the ground."

The executive officer frowned. "The ground crews?"

"Yes," Segev added. "We want to see how long it takes them to turn around a flight."

"Oh. Well. We can do that." The executive officer motioned for an aide who was standing behind them. The aide came quickly to his side. The executive officer said something to him, then turned back to Gur and Segev. "The ground crews are working at one of the hangars." He gestured to the jeep. "We'll ride over there."

A few minutes later, they arrived outside a large hangar. A fighter jet was parked in front and several crewmen were busy arming it with ammunition for the machine guns. Gur and Segev stepped from the jeep and watched.

After a moment, Gur turned to the executive officer. "They're working at a leisurely pace. How fast can they do it when they try?"

The executive officer had a questioning look. "How fast?"

"Yeah," Gur explained. "A plane pulls in here empty. How fast can they rearm and refuel it?"

Again, the executive officer called an aide to his side, then sent him off with an order. When the aide was gone, he turned to the ground crew. "Listen up!" he called. "These men are with the planning group in Tel Aviv. They're doing a few tests of readiness and want to see how quickly you can rearm one of these fighters. Get your gear ready. Another plane is on its way."

The ground crew scrambled into action, using a towing tractor to move the fighter out of the way. About the time it was parked safely to one side, a second fighter touched down on the runway, turned onto the apron, and made its way toward them. It came to a stop near the hangar door where the other one had been. Gur checked his wristwatch and noted the moment it was chocked in place. Fifteen minutes later, the plane was rearmed and ready.

"Good job," the executive officer said with pride. Then he turned to Gur. "Was that fast enough for you?"

"They're quick," Gur agreed. "But that's just the munitions. How long does it take to refuel it?"

"Depends on how much fuel it needs."

"Suppose it's empty."

"A full load takes about ten minutes, maybe a little less, but," the executive officer pointed down the way, "the refueling pad is down there. Getting the plane from here to there takes another four or five minutes. So you're looking at fifteen minutes to rearm, plus another twenty minutes to refuel, depending on how busy the tarmac is."

Gur was all business. "Show me where they do the refueling."

The three men climbed back into the jeep and rode down to the far side of the next hangar. "This is the refueling pad," the executive officer pointed as they came to a stop in front of two large tanks.

Gur looked dissatisfied. "That won't work."

"What do you mean? We've been refueling here since I've been stationed at the base."

"It takes too much time," Gur explained. "We have to get the turn-around time down to ten minutes total."

"Only way to do that is to put these two operations in the same location."

Segev spoke up. "Why aren't they done in the same location now?"

"Safety," the executive officer replied. "The two operations are separated to minimize the risk of fire."

"Okay," Segev said. "We'll talk to someone about working on that."

The executive officer glanced over at him. "Need to see anything else?"

"How long can a crew sustain the fifteen-minute rearming rate?"

"I don't know," the executive officer shrugged. "No one's ever tried it. Today was the first time I've known how long it takes."

"We'll come up with some training exercises to see," Segev offered. "We need to know if that rate is sustainable."

The executive officer gave Segev and Gur a ride back to the front gate. From there they drove toward Tel Aviv.

"If we can combine fueling and arming in the same location," Gur suggested, "we can make this work."

"But we'll have to convince IAF to actually do it. And that won't be easy."

"This is vital to our survival. We have to strike first and we have to achieve total destruction of their air capabilities."

"Think we can get the turnaround rate up to four flights per day per pilot?"

"We need five," Gur answered. "That will give us an air force two-thirds larger than we already have, just by conducting more flights. And without buying a single new aircraft."

— • —

Shortly after they returned to headquarters, Segev received a call from General Greenberg, IDF Commander, who wanted to know what he and Gur were doing at the base in Hatzor. Segev did his best to explain.

"We cleared it through their executive officer," Segev said when he was finished.

"He didn't have the authority to give that approval," Greenberg objected. "I need a thorough briefing on exactly what you did. The commander from Hatzor is on his way to see me and I need to know what I'm talking about before he gets here."

Segev found Gur and the two of them hurried upstairs to Greenberg's office. When they arrived, General Bentov, the air force commander, was there. Greenberg introduced them and then Gur took the lead. "Any scenario we face from our neighbors would almost certainly include an attack by Egypt."

"I'm not concerned about that right now," Bentov retorted. "I want to know why you were on the base at Hatzor without the base commander's representative."

"We cleared it through the executive officer. We thought he was authorized to grant us permission. We asked. He said yes."

"Continue with your presentation," Greenberg suggested. "I'd like to hear the rest of what you were saying."

Bentov shook his head in disapproval. Gur continued. "Under any scenario, we would almost certainly face an attack by Egypt. If we can't defeat them, our strategy against other neighboring countries won't matter. But in a head-to-head war of attrition—ground or air—the Egyptians win. We have three hundred fifty planes, they have nine hundred fifty. We have eight hundred tanks, they have more than two thousand. To prevail against odds like that, we would need a three-to-one kill ratio and that's assuming we strike first. If they attack us first, we're finished. We can't survive a first strike from their air force. In order to win, we have to attack first and disable their entire air force on the first day."

"Impossible," Bentov growled.

"Not if we concentrate on the runways."

Bentov looked over at Greenberg. "I have no idea what he's talking about. So far all I've heard are theories, to which everyone agrees, and a lot of nonsense."

Greenberg nodded to Gur, who tried again. "If we disable their runways—"

"All of them?" Bentov interrupted.

"Yes, if we disable their runways, the airplanes are useless."

"The Egyptians alone have twenty-five or thirty bases. How would you disable all of them?" Bentov once again looked over at Greenberg. "This is why I say planning is a waste of time. They never give us anything we can use."

"The Egyptians have thirty-one bases," Gur pointed out. "Twenty-six of them are of strategic importance. The others don't relate to what we face. If we strike the dozen closest ones first, half their air force will be on the ground at once. Unable to fly. Then we hit the other fourteen."

"But while you are hitting those first twelve, won't airplanes from the other fourteen take to the air?"

"Yes," Gur conceded. "They would no doubt attempt a counterattack. I didn't say this would be easy. I said it is doable. We already have runway crater bombs that will render the runways inoperable. We just need to deliver the ordnance to locations where it will have the greatest overall effect, and do it in a single first strike."

"And that's the problem," Bentov said emphatically. "We have three hundred planes. That's all. Not three hundred one. Not three hundred ten. Just three hundred. Which limits the number of targets we can strike." He shook his head at Greenberg again. "This is a waste of time."

"And that's why Major Segev and I were at the air force base," Gur said with a smile.

"Doing what?" Bentov demanded. "I've been sitting here all this time waiting for someone to tell me. Why were you on that base?"

"We wanted to see how quickly ground crews could turn around an airplane."

"Turn it around?"

"Rearm and refuel it."

"What difference does that make? We don't fly our sorties close enough for that to matter."

"Current modeling uses a three-sortie-per-day rate."

"Yes," Bentov nodded impatiently. "This is standard in the defense world. Everyone knows this."

"We want to get that up to five."

Deep furrows wrinkled Bentov's brow in a look of disbelief. "Five?"

"Each aircraft making five sorties per twenty-four hours," Gur explained.

"That's preposterous," Bentov scoffed. "It can never be done."

"I've seen your crews," Gur said quietly. "They could handle up to six sorties per day if the pilots could hold up."

Bentov slid forward in the chair as if to stand. "My pilots can hold up just fine and I don't need you—"

Greenberg interrupted. "Isn't it worth a try?" he asked in an encouraging voice.

"It won't work."

"How do you know?"

"No one's ever flown that many missions in a single day."

"Has anyone tried?"

"Not that I know of."

"You would like to do that if you could, wouldn't you?"

"Fly six missions per day?"

"Yes. I suppose so."

"If we'd had air support at Tiberias in '48, how many men would still be alive?"

Bentov softened. "We would need to conduct some studies. Under conditions that simulated a combat pace."

"You could work up a plan for that?"

"Perhaps a dozen planes," Bentov continued. "Not too many. Just the right number to work with one of the ground crews."

"We wouldn't have to do the entire twenty-four-hour run," Segev suggested. "Twelve hours would give us enough information to project the drop-off rate. We could use that to calculate the total number of sorties possible in a day."

Bentov shook his head. "No, the drop-off rate might accelerate the longer they work. We need to know that before we factor this into our strategy. And some of this will vary based on distance to target and a hundred other variables. Not to mention pilot and aircraft stress."

"It will be stressful," Gur agreed with a nod. "But it will be much less stressful than being a prisoner of the Egyptians, which is what will happen if we don't succeed."

CHAPTER 14

WHEN AUERBACH DID NOT RETURN to New York as scheduled, Mrs. Landau notified Rosenwald. "Find out where he is and why he's delayed," he ordered. "If something went wrong we need to be in a position to handle it at once."

Mrs. Landau checked with the State Department and learned that the airplane on which Auerbach was flying had crashed in the Negev. She rushed into Rosenwald's office to tell him.

"Was he injured?" Rosenwald asked.

"He appears to be unharmed."

"Well," Rosenwald stroked his chin. "At least he got out of Jordan without creating a problem."

"Do you think we should notify his family?"

Rosenwald looked surprised. "He has a family?"

"A brother."

Rosenwald thought for a moment then asked, "We're certain Auerbach was unharmed?"

"Yes," Mrs. Landau replied. "Both the State Department and the airline say he is fine. And he's safe."

"Then this is merely a delay."

"Well," she shrugged. "I think it's a little more than that."

"Let me talk to Eban first. He's the client. We need to find out what he has to say about it before we make any more calls."

Rosenwald contacted Abba Eban who in turn sent a cable to the

Israeli Foreign Office asking for information about Auerbach's condition. He came to Rosenwald's office with the response.

"Our Foreign Office has confirmed that the plane on which Auerbach was traveling was forced to land due to engine failure."

"Where did it go down?"

"In the Negev. South of Beersheba."

"Any information about how it happened?"

"No one is certain yet of the cause. The matter is still under investigation."

"But Auerbach got out of Jordan without creating an incident?"

"There is no report of trouble."

"Your Foreign Office has sources in Jordan that can confirm that?"

"Yes, but the Foreign Office does not know what Auerbach was doing."

Rosenwald was surprised. "You didn't tell them?"

"Based on their earlier communication with me," Eban explained, "I thought it best if they had a level of deniability."

"Maybe so." Rosenwald glanced out the window. "But you're certain Auerbach is okay?"

"He was retrieved from the Negev, examined at a Jerusalem hospital, and sent to a room in the King David Hotel. They expect him to return to New York on a flight from Tel Aviv in a few days."

— · —

After meeting with Rosenwald, Eban had second thoughts about his earlier decision to withhold Auerbach's identity from the Foreign Office. Later that afternoon he sent a cable to Golda Meir disclosing Auerbach's mission.

When Golda Meir received the cable from Eban, and learned Auerbach was delivering the message to Hussein about the assassination plot, she dispatched security agents to find him. They located him in the bar at the King David Hotel and brought him to Golda's office.

"I understand you traveled to Jordan to meet with King Hussein."

"As...an attorney," Auerbach began hesitantly, "I'm not sure I can discuss my trip with you."

"You work for this country?"

"Yes."

"And I am a cabinet member in this country's government."

"I understand that. But you aren't the person who...you aren't the client."

Golda retrieved a copy of Eban's cable message from the corner of her desk and tossed it across to him. "Maybe this will help."

Auerbach read the message detailing his mission to Hussein, then laid it on the desk. "I suppose ..."

"I suppose you should tell me what happened. Abba Eban came to you at my direction. What happened in Amman?"

"I told King Hussein about the plot, but he didn't believe the threat is real."

"Hmm," Golda leaned back in her chair. "I was afraid of that."

"He thinks there are always people who want him dead, but didn't think this particular threat was real."

"He thinks we're lying?"

"No. He thinks an operative from Mossad overheard a rumor about a plot and you want to believe it's real. He also thinks I was sent to tell him about it hoping he would be beholden to you for saving his life and refrain from participating in any upcoming conflict with Egypt."

"He thinks there will be conflict with Egypt?"

"I don't know how certain he is of Egypt's plans but he's very certain of yours."

"What do you mean?"

"He's convinced Israel plans to invade the Sinai."

Golda seemed unfazed by the news. "For what purpose?" she asked.

"To annex it. Make it a part of Israel. Extend your border all the way to the Suez Canal."

"What gave him that idea?"

"He said David Ben-Gurion announced it in a speech to the Knesset."

Golda sighed and shook her head. "I told Ben-Gurion he said too much," she muttered.

Auerbach arched an eyebrow. "He actually gave the speech?"

"Yes."

"I thought Hussein was making it up."

"No, it wasn't a recent speech. One Ben-Gurion made several years ago. But none of our Arab neighbors have forgotten it."

"Apparently it made a big impression."

"Yes," she smiled. "Quite an impression even among our own people. That speech is at least part of the reason Ben-Gurion is out of office."

"Well, for whatever reason," Auerbach continued, "Hussein sees himself as more vulnerable to his Arab neighbors than to you."

"He's probably right," Golda acknowledged.

"But he gave me a message for you."

Golda's eyes brightened. "What message was that?"

"Hussein says the Syrians have recruited Yasser Arafat and FATAH to help them put pressure on you from within. Using indigenous Arab groups here in Israel. They're the ones behind most of the terrorist attacks you've experienced the past twelve months."

"This isn't new information. We've known this for quite some time."

"According to Hussein, they plan to attack the water project in Galilee."

Golda looked concerned. "Did he say when the attack might occur?"

Auerbach shook his head. "Just that they were going to attack it. According to him, the Syrians are hoping to use FATAH as a way of provoking your forces to attack positions inside Syria's borders."

Golda nodded. "That has been their strategy since the 1948 cease-fire." She switched topics. "So, Hussein really thinks we want to attack Egypt?"

"Yes."

"And he thinks the Syrians want us to attack Syria."

"Hussein says the Syrians could attack you on their own, but they don't think they can win by themselves. They need help. Egypt is the strongest Arab country in the region and an obvious ally for Syria against you. But the Syrians believe that, left to their own choices, the Egyptians won't attack you under almost any scenario. So they are trying to create a situation that puts pressure on Egypt.

"We attack Syria, then they can press Egypt to come to their defense."

"Yes."

"An example of Middle Eastern logic at work," Golda smirked.

"I would also say—and this is just my observation—unlike Hussein, the Syrians don't believe you intend to annex Sinai or take any other unprovoked action."

Golda had a quizzical look. "Why do you say that?"

"Because if you did annex the Sinai Peninsula, wouldn't that be enough to provoke a regional war anyway?"

"Yes," she nodded. "I suppose it would."

"And if you did that, then Syria apparently wouldn't need to lure you into the illusion of conflict. They would have one that was open and obvious."

"Right."

"So if the Syrians are trying to lure you into the illusion of a fight, maybe they're convinced you won't create a real one on your own. That you won't invade the Sinai, or take any other provocative action solely on your own."

"Hmm," Golda mused. "I see what you mean."

CHAPTER 15

WHEN AUERBACH LEFT, Golda called Moshe Dayan, the defense minister, and arranged to meet with him in her office. She got right to the point. "You remember we asked Abba Eban about passing our information to King Hussein."

"About the plot to assassinate him?" Dayan asked. "Whatever happened with that?"

"Abba contacted a lawyer in New York," Golda explained.

"That firm that does a lot for us...Mayer ..."

"Mayer, Meagan & Gottschalk."

"Yes."

"They sent one of their lawyers," Golda continued. "A man named Yaakov Auerbach."

"He was able to meet with Hussein?"

"Yes."

"How did Hussein react to the message?"

"Apparently," Golda sighed, "the king dismissed it as just another rumor. But he told Auerbach about Syrian involvement with Yasser Arafat."

"Everyone knows about that," Dayan waved dismissively. "FATAH is nothing but an extension of Syrian intelligence operations."

"According to Hussein, they plan to attack the National Water Carrier project."

Dayan frowned. "Arafat? Think there's anything to it?"

"I don't know," Golda shrugged. "But why would he tell us if it wasn't true?"

Dayan grinned. "Do you know how ridiculous that sounds?"

"I don't mean everything Hussein says is true. I mean, given the context, why make the suggestion if there was no basis in fact for it. Was he merely being courteous? We tell him about a plot, he feels compelled to tell us about one, even if it's a manufactured story? Or is he telling us something more?"

"Like what?"

"Like there really is a plot. Or a way of saying I'd really like to help but I'm in an awkward position. Please don't hold it against me."

"I don't know," Dayan said with a gesture of his hands. "He doesn't have much to lose either way. It's an obvious target, something anyone could suggest. Hussein knows about it. Even tried to get his own people interested in a similar project."

"This is also consistent with what Mossad has been telling us. They've heard this same story about an attack on the water project."

"I still think information we receive, from any of these sources, about supposed specific targets is prone to be false, or at best conjecture based on circumstance. I don't think any of the Arab groups are that well organized."

"Perhaps. But we should redouble our security along the carrier and have someone check into it."

"Did Abba have any other information from this lawyer?"

"That's the interesting part and the reason I asked to see you. When Auerbach concluded his meeting with Hussein, he boarded a flight in Amman headed for New York. The plane on which he was riding is the one that went down in the Negev."

Dayan's mouth fell open and his eyes were wide in a look of surprise. "He was on the TWA flight? Why didn't you tell me that from the beginning?"

"You didn't give me a chance."

"How did you find out about him?"

"When the plane went down and he didn't return to New York on schedule, someone at his law firm tried to locate him. They knew who he was and what he was doing, so their first call was to Abba Eban. Abba cabled me."

"We should have known about this earlier. Why didn't he tell us he was sending someone?"

"I think we were rather clear about the need to keep that effort separate from us."

"Still, it would have been good to know what was happening."

Golda looked over at Dayan. "Any possibility we shot down that airplane?"

"No. Initial indications are that the engines failed due to internal issues. The airline denies the plane was in poor condition and has furnished maintenance documents that back their claim. But a crew removed the engines from the airplane and brought them to a facility in Tel Aviv for further examination. They'll figure out what happened."

"Any possibility it was sabotage?"

"No one has ruled that out yet."

"And you're certain we didn't shoot it down?" Golda asked once more.

"No." Dayan made a slicing gesture with his hand. "Absolutely not. We have no record of anyone firing on it. Evidence at the scene indicates it was not fired on by anyone. No bullet holes. No damage that would have come from a missile. And I'm not sure we even had units in a position to fire on it if we'd wanted to."

"That's a little unsettling in itself," Golda observed.

"Yes, it is."

"The plane took off from Amman," Golda said, moving on with the discussion. "An act of sabotage would involve the Jordanians."

"That would seem so," Dayan nodded.

"Do you suppose the Jordanians knew what Auerbach was doing?"

"I have no idea," Dayan shrugged. "Have you told Eshkol about him?"

"Not yet. I wanted to speak with you first, to make certain we have everything in order on our side of the matter, before I talk to him."

Dayan had an amused grin. "He always asks you one more question, doesn't he?"

"Drives me crazy." One corner of Golda's mouth turned up in a disapproving look. "No matter how hard I try, he always asks one question more than I'm prepared to answer."

"Maybe he does that on purpose."

"To aggravate me?"

"No, to keep you constantly looking for more."

"Keeps me constantly pulling at my hair."

"Well, about the Water Carrier," Dayan said. "I'll instruct IDF to redouble their security. But I'd also like to have someone go up there and look around, see if he can tell what Arafat and FATAH are doing. Find out if they're really that organized. We've heard some reports from officers stationed in Galilee that indicate things might be different from what we're hearing through official channels."

"You don't trust Mossad?"

"Sometimes, but it's better if we develop our own sources."

"I prefer to have information move through the usual channels," Golda countered. "So that everyone who needs the information gets it."

"If this goes to Mossad, it will take weeks to get an answer," Dayan groused. "And the information we get from them will come to us with *perspective*."

Golda had a puzzled look. "Perspective?"

"Analyst's opinions," Dayan explained. "Our troops in the field prefer raw information."

"Do they have the capacity to analyze it and figure out what it means?"

"Probably not in the larger political context, but in terms of the tactical situation on the ground, yes. They do better with raw, unprocessed information." Dayan paused. "This is happening in Galilee. It's my home. I grew up there. I need to send one of my own men up there to find out what's going on."

"Well, you certainly don't need my permission," Golda conceded.

"But I have to brief Eshkol on these latest developments and neither of us can control what happens after that."

Dayan stood to leave. "You want me to do the briefing with you?"

"No, I can handle it. But listen, if you send someone up there, just make sure whoever you send doesn't end up causing more trouble."

"Like the man you sent to Jordan?" Dayan quipped.

"He didn't cause the plane to crash," Golda huffed. "But yes, like that." Dayan turned toward the door but before he reached it Golda said, "There is one more thing."

Dayan turned back to face her. "Yes?"

"How well do you get along with Abba Eban?"

"Rather well. You've seen us together. I think we do all right. As well as anyone can when working with a genius. Why do you ask?"

"Just wondering."

Dayan was curious. "What are you not telling me?"

Golda had a thin, tight smile. "If I could tell you, Moshe, I wouldn't need to be so circumspect, would I?"

— • —

Late that afternoon, Golda met Eshkol in his office and briefed him on the interview with Auerbach. When she came to the part about how Hussein thought they intended to annex the Sinai, Eshkol shook his head. "Ben-Gurion said too much in that speech," he groused.

"Yes, he did," Golda acknowledged. "And he paid a price for it, too."

"And we are paying a price for it as well."

Golda ignored the urge to defend Ben-Gurion and continued. "Hussein knows we want him to stay out of any potential conflict, but he says if the others fight he will be forced to join because of internal politics. He's very much aware of why his father was killed."

"He would avoid a war with us otherwise?"

"He told Auerbach that if this were a matter between us and Jordan, there would be no conflict."

"So this isn't about us, or the Arabs. It's about him remaining as king."

"Yes," Golda nodded. "And staying alive. And consistent with our analysis, Hussein did say that FATAH is working on behalf of the Syrians and indicated that the National Water Carrier was their next target."

"So, was he trying to tell us something?"

"Other than about the threat to the Water Carrier?"

"He can't stay out of the conflict, yet he tips us about a supposed attack sponsored by one of his fellow Arab countries. Is he saying something by that?" There was a hint of frustration in Eshkol's voice. "Why tell us? Why not just keep quiet? Let them blow it up."

"I don't know," Golda shrugged. "I agree it's a curious response. We give him an assassination plot, he gives us a plot against one of our vital facilities. But I don't know if he's trying to tell us something other than that."

"He knew the information about the threat to his life came from us?"

"Yes."

"So why tell us anything?"

"I can't answer that."

Eshkol shot her a look. "Why not?"

Golda was frustrated by the question and the suggestion that she wasn't doing her job. "Because I don't know," she snapped. "I don't have all the answers. Perhaps he was offering it to us as a consolation. Perhaps he offered us that information because he hates Arafat and FATAH and distrusts the Syrians. I don't know. I'm just trying to assist you in making the best decision for each of the situations we face."

Eshkol pressed the issue. "Have you told Dayan?"

"Yes."

Eshkol was clearly displeased. "Before you told me."

"I vet most things of a noncritical nature before I tell you. That's what we're supposed to do. No one has a corner on intelligence. None of us can fully understand everything. We all talk to each other before we come to you. It would be a waste of your time to include you on preliminary discussions. If you are going to be the one who processes everything, then you wouldn't need a cabinet at all."

"And Mossad?" Eshkol continued the line of questioning. "You already told them what Auerbach had to say?"

"No. Do you want me to?"

Eshkol shook his head. "I'll see that the information gets to Mossad. Maybe they can determine the extent of FATAH's organization. But if you told Dayan before coming to me, why not also discuss it with Mossad?"

"I have a good working relationship with Moshe."

"From the old days."

"We go back a ways."

"But not so much with Shaul Nissany."

"When I want to talk, I usually need someone who won't take what I say and dash right over here to tell you about it." Golda shrugged. "We need to increase our security for the Water Carrier."

"Yes," Eshkol agreed, apparently grateful for the change of subject. "I'll discuss it with Dayan."

— • —

When Golda arrived at home that evening, she put on a kettle for tea. A few minutes later there was a knock at the back door. Golda knew without looking the caller was her neighbor, Aliza Begin. Over the past several years, the two had become good friends, meeting in the evening two or three times a week after Golda came home from a day at the office.

They sat at the kitchen table and talked over a cup of hot tea.

"You look tired," Aliza observed.

"I am tired."

"You've been working for Israel a long time."

"Yes," Golda nodded between sips. "And sometimes I wonder if it's been worth it, or if we'd been better off staying in America."

"You miss Morris?"

"Only when I think about him."

"I'm sure there are days it seems like you aren't accomplishing much."

"But as soon as I think that, I realize the deeper truth. Israel would survive without me, but I would not survive without Israel."

"Another stressful day?"

Golda nodded. "I wish I could tell you about it."

"I do, too."

"The worst part is the constant internal political turmoil. Everyone protecting his own territory. Always on guard, thinking someone is out to get them."

"Menachem can't stand being on the outside. Not for a minute. He's in the Knesset and takes his responsibility seriously, but not being in the cabinet is rough on him."

"I can understand how he might feel that way, but being *in* the cabinet isn't any easier." For most of her life, Golda kept her health concerns to herself. Not even her family knew the most recent developments. But now, facing the diagnosis of cancer, a possible extended trip to New York for treatment, and the mortality issues it brought to mind, she wanted to talk about it. To process it. So she looked across the table at Aliza and said quietly, "I have a problem."

Aliza had a worried frown. "What is it?" She set her teacup on the saucer. "Are you all right?"

"The doctor says I have lymphoma."

Aliza looked stricken. "When did you find out?"

"A few days ago."

"All this time and you didn't tell me?"

"I needed time to think."

"I knew something was wrong. I knew something wasn't right. What can the doctors do?"

"They think it's a low-grade version but they aren't sure. They want me to go to New York for some tests."

"Yes," Aliza insisted. "Absolutely. Can they treat it?"

"If it is the less dangerous kind, they think there's nothing to do right now but watch and see. If it's the more aggressive kind, they'll start treatment right away."

"Well, if they say watch and wait, it must be good."

"Yes. I suppose." Golda couldn't repress a chuckle. "On the other hand, it could mean I'm too far gone."

"I don't think that's what they mean."

"No, I don't, either. But it would be good to take the trip and get some rest."

"When are you going?"

"I don't know," Golda shrugged in a diffident manner. "It seems like such a fuss."

Aliza reached across the table and took Golda's hand. "You have to go."

"I know, but I just can't seem to get away."

"There will always be something waiting on your desk. You have to put that aside and take care of yourself." Aliza withdrew her hand. "You've been at this a long time."

"You've been here longer than I."

"It seems like we just got here."

"But now we're almost twenty years past independence."

"Hard to believe we've come this far."

Golda looked away. "And still we have so far to go."

CHAPTER 16

MOSHE DAYAN RETURNED TO HIS OFFICE that evening to find a memo from Eshkol directing an increase in security along the Water Carrier. He forwarded the directive to General Greenberg and then called his assistant, Natan Shahak, back to the office for a late meeting.

Shahak had been born in Palestine to an Austrian couple who moved there in 1935. When he turned nineteen, he left home to make his own way. A childhood friend told him about a farming commune at Degania in Galilee and he applied for admission. The kibbutz admitted him because he had farming experience and he knew how to repair the farm's equipment.

Dayan was from Degania also, and in 1948, during the War for Independence, he was sent there to coordinate defense of the settlement against the Syrian army. The battle for Degania was a serious fight and, despite his lack of formal training, Shahak proved a capable soldier. When Dayan organized an army to take the Galilee, Shahak went with him. In the closing months of the war, when Dayan was given command of the army in the Negev, Shahak went along, too. After the war, Shahak remained on Dayan's staff and when Dayan was elevated to defense minister, Shahak became his special assistant.

Though it was late when Shahak received Dayan's call, he came to the office immediately. Dayan showed him two IDF reports on FATAH suggesting that they and other Arab groups operating in Galilee might be far better organized than first thought. Dayan refrained, however, from telling Shahak about the supposed plot to assassinate Hussein or Auerbach's trip to Jordan.

"This could be serious," Shahak said after reading the report.

"Very much so. Did you see who wrote that second memo?"

Shahak glanced at it once more. "Mordechai Gur."

"*Colonel* Mordechai Gur," Dayan corrected. "Do you know him?"

"I've heard of him. A paratrooper, isn't he?"

"At the time he wrote that," Dayan noted, "he was in command of the Fifty-Fifth Paratrooper Brigade."

"Where is he now?"

"He's in the planning group."

"Planning?" Shahak frowned. "Sounds like a fighting soldier to me. Not a desk guy."

"That's why he's there. We need someone with experience to keep the planning on track."

"Still, it seems like a waste of his talent and experience."

"That's what Gur thought until Greenberg explained it to him. We need this planning group to provide useable work. For that, we need someone like Gur." Dayan pointed to the report. "What do you think we should do about that?"

"The situation in Galilee?"

"Yes."

"Well," Shahak began, "we could pass the information on to Mossad and let them handle it." He was thinking while he talked. "But we'd have to wait a couple of months to get a response. By then, whatever's going to happen up there will have developed beyond our control. So," he looked up at Dayan, "what if we sent someone ourselves? Someone from IDF or one of the special sections. Get our own man up there to find out if any of what Gur says is true."

"That's exactly what I was thinking," Dayan grinned.

"Want me to see who's available to do it?"

"No." Dayan shook his head. "I've already found someone."

Shahak had a perplexed look. "Who?"

"I'm sending you."

Shahak's eyes opened wide. "Me?"

"Yes. You."

"But I'm not a field operative."

"Nonsense. You're from the region. You know the people. You are perfect for the job."

Shahak was flattered that Dayan would ask, and excited about the prospect of returning to Galilee, but still skeptical. "You really want me to do this?"

"Yes," Dayan insisted.

"Very well, then," Shahak said reluctantly. "I shall do it."

— • —

The following day, Auerbach wandered the streets of Jerusalem, remembering the day, years before, when he was with Suheir at her father's house in Degania, the confrontation that ensued when her father discovered them, and her father's decision to separate them by sending her to Jerusalem to live with her uncle. That had worked only until Auerbach discovered where she was, then he left Degania to find her. He located the uncle's house and watched her from a safe distance, then came out to meet her when she was on her way to fill the water jar at the neighborhood well. He could still feel the touch of her lips.

After a while, wandering the streets and thinking of her was no longer enough. Curiosity got the best of him and he attempted to retrace the path he remembered Suheir taking from her uncle's house to the well. He found the well but had trouble remembering which alley was the correct one. So much had changed since then.

Finally, he gave up figuring out her route and began asking about the Hadawi family. At first, people ignored him, passing by without an answer. But a shop owner overheard him asking and told him the location. Auerbach arrived at the house to find an old man seated on a wooden chair near the front door, whittling on a stick with a pocket knife.

Auerbach knew very little Arabic, and the old man knew very little Hebrew. But between their limited vocabulary and hand gestures, he learned that the man was Suheir's uncle.

"I knew her," Auerbach attempted to explain. "A long time ago."

"She remembers all her friends," the old man replied. "You should go see her."

"Suheir?"

"Yes," he nodded with a smile. "Suheir Hadawi. Lives near Degania now."

Auerbach was stunned. "Degania?"

"Yes," the old man nodded once more. "With her brother."

"Ahmad?"

The old man smiled. "You know Ahmad?"

"He was my friend, too. I knew them both."

"He is a good boy."

"Suheir is alive?"

"Yes. You thought she was dead?"

"She was shot. In the alley."

An angry look came over him. "Suleiman got what he deserved. He was bad. Very bad."

Auerbach talked with the old man awhile longer, then started back to the hotel, trying with each step to make sense of what he'd heard. Suheir was alive! The old man had insisted it was true. But how? She was lying in the alley. He saw blood oozing from her body. "But she's alive," he whispered.

As Auerbach entered the lobby at the King David Hotel, a clerk at the front desk waved him over. "We have a message for you," she handed him a note.

The message was from Golda Meir's office. He was booked on a flight to New York that left Tel Aviv on Monday. He read it, then glanced over at the clerk. "Is there any way to get to Degania?"

"A bus goes there twice each week. Monday and Thursday."

"So it leaves tomorrow?"

"Yes. Tomorrow is Thursday. It leaves here in the morning. You can catch it on the corner."

"Good."

He turned to leave but she spoke up. "If you take the bus up there tomorrow, you'll have to stay until Monday."

"Right."

"The bus goes up to Degania and no farther. It is only there a short time then makes the return trip. So if you go tomorrow," she repeated, "you would not be able to return until Monday."

"If I go, can I keep my room here until then?"

"That is no problem. You will be booked in your room until you come down here and formally check out."

"Good," he said again. "That's great."

From the front desk, Auerbach crossed the lobby to the elevator and rode up to his room. He sorted through his clothes to find a few things to take and stuffed them into a small satchel he'd salvaged from the plane. All the while he kept thinking, *Suheir is alive. Suheir is alive.* His skin seemed to tingle with excitement. He knew that almost twenty years had passed. Neither of them were young, but still…Suheir was alive and he was determined to see her, even if it meant missing his flight to New York on Monday.

— • —

On Monday morning, as Dayan directed, Shahak left Tel Aviv by car for Galilee. Because of his association with Degania, he decided to start there. He knew the area best and some of the people he'd worked with were still there. That, he reasoned, gave him the best opportunity for gathering useable information. Besides, he had not been back there since the war and he was interested in seeing the place again.

He arrived at the settlement midmorning and stepped from his car. As he pushed the door shut a violent explosion erupted to the west. Far enough away to be harmless but still close enough to hear the detonation, feel the concussion, and sense the ground tremble beneath his feet.

Daniel Erlich, the settlement chairman, came from the cafeteria building to greet him. "Gets your attention, doesn't it?" he said with a laugh.

"Syrian artillery shells?" Shahak asked.

"Yeah," Erlich nodded. "We get a few of them every day from their positions on the Golan Heights." He said it as casually as one might comment on the weather, then the two men shook hands. "How are you?"

"I'm fine," Shahak replied as he glanced around at the compound.

"Does it look different from when you were here?"

"The place looks about the same. But how did you know I was here before?"

"Dayan's office phoned us to watch for you."

"They didn't know I was coming here. I only decided on the drive up."

"Right," Erlich nodded. "But they said you'd probably be by and that we should help you out as much as possible." He gestured with a sweep of his arm, picking up on Shahak's comment. "Most of it's the same. We added a building over by the shop, but other than that, I think the structures are the same."

The remains of a tractor sat to the left. "What happened to that?"

"Artillery shell."

"Wow. We get daily reports about the artillery but they're so regular they've become commonplace. Seeing that makes it a little more real. Was anyone on it when the shell hit?"

"Not that one."

Shahak arched an eyebrow. "There were others?"

"A guy was killed on a nearby farm from the artillery," Erlich noted. "We lost a man who was sitting in a truck out by one of the fields. Most of the rounds fall out there and do nothing but destroy some of the crops. That one hit the truck."

"The Arabs never really liked us before, but it wasn't anything like this," Shahak offered. "Farming in the Galilee is now like combat duty."

"Does Dayan have a plan to do something about it?"

"We're working on it."

"Work a little faster," Erlich said. Without prompting they moved out and wandered across the compound. "They didn't tell us much about your visit," he continued. "Just that we should be ready for you if you came and that we should help if we could."

Shahak took a picture from his pocket and showed it to Erlich. "Know who that is?"

"Yasser Arafat."

"Have you seen him around here?"

"No," Erlich shook his head. "But I don't get much farther than the farm. You looking for him?"

"We've received reports that local Arabs might be organizing more than earlier reports indicated. We were wondering if that was true. I came up to have a look around."

"Well, come on. I'll introduce you to some of the people who've come since you left. I haven't heard anything about any activity in the area, but maybe someone's heard something."

Shahak spent the remainder of the morning talking to workers as they came and went from the compound. Several remembered him from the past but many of them were new. No one seemed to know anything Shahak hadn't already read in field reports from IDF units patrolling the region.

A little after noon he wandered up to the shop where he'd spent most of his time when he lived at the settlement. The building was empty except for one mechanic who was busy repairing the brakes on a truck. "I hear you were asking about Arafat," the mechanic said.

"Yes," Shahak replied. "But no one seems to know anything about him."

"They know. They just don't want to talk."

"Why not?"

"Lot of rumors going around about how the settlements will be treated now that Ben-Gurion's no longer in office."

Shahak had a puzzled frown. "What are you talking about?"

"Some think we may be forced into a more competitive situation. That people in Jerusalem want us to become more like the commercial farms."

"Where did that idea come from?"

"I think they saw that big farm up the road, toward Yavne'el."

"That's a commercial operation, sure. But I haven't heard anyone talking about forcing the cooperatives into that same model. In fact, everything I hear is exactly the opposite. Everyone seems determined to preserve the collective tradition."

"Then why are the commercial farms getting all the government support?"

"I don't think they're getting support to the detriment of the collectives, but commercial farming is good for the economy and they don't want to rule it out for those who want to do it that way."

"I tried to talk to people around here about it but no one's interested in discussing much of anything. They just want to argue."

"Do you think that's why I'm here?" Shahak asked.

"I don't know," the mechanic shrugged. "You said you were here to find out about Arab organizations working in the area."

"You think I'm here for some other reason?"

"I don't really know. Some of them think you're here to find out if forcing us to farm on a commercial basis is feasible."

Shahak chuckled. "I'm not interested in taking over the farming cooperatives."

"Well, if you want to know about Arafat, you should ask the lady who lives up the road."

Shahak was finally glad to have a lead. "What lady?"

"I think their name is Hadawi."

The name caught Shahak by surprise. "They still live here?"

"The girl does. With her brother."

Shahak felt his heart skip a beat. "Are you talking about Suheir Hadawi?"

"Yeah. I think that's her name. Brother's name is Ahmad."

"I thought Suheir was dead."

the mechanic shook his head. "No, the woman I'm thinking of is very much alive. Beautiful woman. Too bad she's Arab."

"We all thought she was dead."

"Go up there and see for yourself." The mechanic gestured with his hand. "If you know them, they might talk to you. She would, probably. The few times I've seen her she's been nice enough."

"What about Ahmad?"

"From what I hear, he's rather deeply involved with Arafat."

"You've seen them together?"

"I haven't seen anything except this shop, the cafeteria, and my room. Most days, I get no farther than those three buildings. But I hear things, and that's what I hear."

"What about Rashid, the father? Is he involved, too?"

"He's dead."

"What happened to him?"

"You remember Thomas Katzenberg?"

"Yes," Shahak nodded. "Is he still here, too?"

"Not now. They transferred him someplace else. He was in charge of the Water Carrier when it first began. Most of the water was sent to the Negev, but the farms around here were supplied from it, too. But Katzenberg refused to furnish water to Rashid Hadawi."

"Why?"

"The Hadawis are Arabs. Katzenberg didn't like them. That was enough reason for him."

"I'm sure Rashid didn't like that."

"No," the mechanic agreed. "He didn't. He confronted Katzenberg and the two got into heated arguments several times. During the last one, Rashid had a heart attack. Ahmad begged Katzenberg to call for help but Katzenberg just walked away. Some of us tried to help but it was too late." He pointed toward the door. "Rashid died right out there in the courtyard."

"Ahmad was with him?"

"Yes. Ahmad used to come around once in a while. Asked me questions about fixing his equipment. But after that, he wasn't the same. I haven't seen him in two or three months."

CHAPTER 17

AFTER TALKING WITH THE MECHANIC, Shahak left the compound and walked up the road to the farm where the Hadawis lived. He knew it well and as he approached from the south he remembered the times he'd been there with his friend Yaakov Auerbach—Auerbach going there to see Suheir, Shahak going with him to keep watch for Suheir's father.

The house sat in the midst of a stand of trees and as Shahak drew near it, he used the trees to shield himself from view. Slowly, he crept closer, picking his way until he was near enough to see the house but far enough away to remain out of sight. He stood there, still suspicious that what the mechanic had said was wrong and hoping to catch a glimpse of Suheir or Ahmad for himself before he approached them directly.

After a moment, Ahmad came from the house and seconds later a car turned from the road. It came to a stop near where Ahmad was standing and the driver's door opened. A man stepped out and as he turned to greet Ahmad, Shahak saw the driver of the car was Yasser Arafat. He and Ahmad greeted each other with a hug and a back slap, then they both got into the car and rode away.

When the car sped away down the dirt road, Shahak left his hiding place among the trees and walked over to the house. As he came into the clear, the door opened and Suheir appeared. "What are you doing here?" she demanded, obviously not recognizing him. "No one is allowed on this property. My brother has warned you people many times to keep away."

Shahak smiled at her. "Hello, Suheir."

She stared at him a moment, as if trying to recall who he was, then her mouth fell open in a look of amazement. "Natan?" she gasped. She took a halting step toward him. "Natan Shahak?"

"It's been a while," he grinned.

She hurried to him and put her arms around his shoulders. "Yes," she agreed, hugging him close. "It has been a long time." Then she looked up at him and her countenance changed. "But this is too dangerous." She glanced around suspiciously. "You shouldn't be here."

"I'm not supposed to be here?" Shahak laughed with an ironic sense of humor. "You're supposed to be dead."

She withdrew and folded her arms across her abdomen. "That could not be avoided."

"What do you mean?"

"Yaakov was about to get us both killed. I knew the only way he would leave me alone was if he thought I was dead."

Shahak frowned. "So you staged the whole thing?"

"No. Of course not. What happened to me was very real and Khalid Suleiman should rot in hell for it. But after it was done, my father decided to take advantage of the situation. He allowed Yaakov to go free, but only after convincing him that I was dead."

"And you were okay with that?"

She looked away. "It had to be done."

"You don't seem convinced it was the right thing."

Her face softened. "Do you hear from Yaakov?"

"I haven't heard from him in a while. I think it's been maybe two years."

"He is well?"

"Yes. He is well."

"And he has a family now?"

"No, he never married."

For an instant a hint of something flickered in her eyes. Interest. Longing. Hope, perhaps? But it quickly disappeared as the look on her face once again turned somber and serious. "Whatever happened between us happened a long time ago. It does not matter how I feel now. You should not be here," she repeated, only this time in a gentler voice. "If Ahmad finds you he will kill you."

"I saw him leave just now. What is he doing with Yasser Arafat?"

"Arafat is a very dangerous man. Come." In spite of her warning that he should leave, she gestured for him to follow her inside. "I will show you what they do." She glanced around once more. "But we must hurry."

Shahak felt uncomfortable entering the house with her but this was the kind of thing he'd come to Degania to discuss and he felt compelled to follow. She led the way through the front room to a room in back. As she pushed open the door he saw rockets, hand grenades, and boxes of ammunition stacked against the far wall. "This is what they do," Suheir said. "They bring weapons here and put them in this room. Ahmad thinks he is one of them, but he does not understand. They are only using him to hide these things and when the soldiers come to take them, they will take Ahmad, too. Only then his friend Arafat will be long gone while Ahmad takes the blame."

"Ahmad is really with them?" Shahak asked.

"Yes," she nodded. "Since our father died he is not the same."

"I heard about your father." Shahak looked over at her. "I am sorry about what happened to him."

"Too bad others were not sorry," she snarled. "Katzenberg should have been shot. Instead, they covered up his mistakes and rewarded him with a promotion. Now he is in the Negev doing the same thing there. But this," she pointed to the weapons, "Ahmad thinks this will make a difference."

"He is angry?"

"We all are angry, but I am afraid it will only get him killed. It almost got me killed when we were in Jerusalem. I have tried to tell him it won't be any different here."

"He was involved with the groups in Jerusalem?"

"He was with Khalid Suleiman."

Shahak was surprised. "The man who tried to kill you?"

"Yes. I was shot by someone Ahmad thought was our friend."

Shahak looked around the room once more and noticed a book lying facedown on a table near the door. He picked it up and saw it was entitled *Report From Iron Mountain*. "Where did you get this?"

"That's not mine," she replied. "Ahmad is reading it. You are familiar with it?"

"It's a hoax."

"Ahmad thinks it is true. He has many other books, too." She led him to the front room and took a backpack from the floor. "These," she unzipped the flap. "These are his, too."

Shahak glanced inside and saw that the pack was filled with books. He recognized many of the titles. Several of them were in French. "Radical left-wing literature," he said. "Where did he get them?"

"Most of them came from Arafat." Suheir dropped the backpack in disgust. "He is no good for us."

— • —

When Shahak returned to the settlement compound he walked over to the cafeteria building hoping to find a cup of tea and a roll. Instead, he found Auerbach seated at a table near the kitchen door. Shahak stopped and stared in disbelief, then Auerbach rose from his chair. "Natan," he had a look of disbelief. "Of all the people I thought I might see up here, I never thought of you."

"The same here," Shahak said as they embraced. "What are you doing? Last I heard you were in New York."

"I was in Jerusalem on business," Auerbach explained, avoiding eye contact. "Thought I'd come up and...have a look around."

Shahak found the moment awkward and he withdrew, shoving his hands in the pockets of his pants. He knew how things ended between Auerbach and Suheir, that Auerbach would want to know that she was alive, but he also knew that would disrupt both their lives and perhaps put them all in danger. Instead of telling him about her, he asked, "How are things? Still with the law firm?"

"Yeah," Auerbach nodded. "That's what got me over here. How about you? Still working for IDF?"

"Not in the IDF anymore. When Dayan was appointed defense minister I became one of his assistants."

"Assistant to the minister of defense. That's a step up in the world."

"Yes," Shahak replied with a nervous laugh. "Definitely a step up."

They took a seat at the table and talked awhile longer, then finally Shahak told Auerbach about his visit with Suheir. "I just came from there. She's alive."

"I know," Auerbach sighed.

"You know?"

"That's why I'm up here. I should have told you from the beginning but I didn't know how to bring it up."

Shahak was curious. "How did you find out she was alive?"

"I located her uncle in Jerusalem. He told me."

"So why were you in Jerusalem?" Shahak asked. "The real answer, not the put-me-off answer."

"I can't talk about it right now." Auerbach looked uncomfortable and he glanced around the room. Then he looked back at Shahak and his countenance brightened. "I want to see Suheir." He said it as if it were the first time he'd had the thought. "I've been sitting here wondering if I should. Worrying about whether I should hold on to the memory and let that be enough. But seeing you, I know. I want to see her."

Shahak shook his head. "I don't think that's a good idea. Things are not as they once were."

"They weren't that good back then," Auerbach commented. "What could make them worse?"

"A lot," Shahak then told Auerbach about Rashid's death.

"The uncle told me he was dead," Auerbach said when Shahak finished. "I didn't really understand what happened, but whatever it was the uncle was mad about it."

"Rashid died while arguing with the Water Carrier director over water for his crops."

"No …" Auerbach whispered in disbelief. "He left that part out."

"After that, Ahmad went a little crazy. He's joined with Yasser Arafat and the FATAH. It's a bad situation."

They sat in silence a moment, then Auerbach said, "I don't care. I still want to see her."

"You shouldn't."

Auerbach stood. "You're probably right, but I've come all this way and I have no idea when I'll ever get back. So I'm going to see her. You want to come with me?"

Reluctantly, Shahak pushed himself up from the table. "I suppose it would be better than you going up there alone."

Auerbach slapped him on the shoulder. "It'll be like old times."

— · —

As they walked toward the house, Shahak told Auerbach some of the rumors they'd heard about Arab activity in the region and reports that some of them were coalescing into viable fronts. "Dayan sent me to find out whether the reports are true."

"You mean reports about Arafat?"

Shahak jerked his head around in surprise. "How do you know about those reports?"

Then Auerbach told him why he was in Jerusalem—the trip to Amman, meeting with Hussein, and the plane crash during the return flight.

"You were on that plane?" Shahak asked.

"Yeah."

"That must have been scary."

"Happened too fast to be scared. But yeah. It was rather unnerving."

"You actually met with King Hussein?"

"Yes. I assume the report about Arafat came from my conversation with him. He told me about it. I told Golda Meir."

Shahak found all this incredible. "You met with her?"

"I met with her yesterday. I wasn't supposed to. I was supposed to return to New York and talk to Abba Eban. He's the one who sent me over here. But with the plane crash, things got a little hectic. She found out I was in Jerusalem and sent for me, so I told her about the meeting."

"Interesting law practice," Shahak suggested wryly.

"Not always. Most days it's just papers on a desk." They walked a little farther in silence, then Auerbach said, "Do you think Arafat is really working here in Galilee?"

"No doubt," Shahak replied. "He's been to the house."

"Whose house?"

"Suheir and Ahmad's."

"You're sure of that?"

"I saw him leave with Ahmad less than two hours ago."

Auerbach shook his head. "Hard to believe Ahmad is one of Arafat's men. I guess he couldn't put it down after all."

"I suppose not."

Auerbach looked over at him. "You know about his involvement with Suleiman?"

"Yes, I knew before and Suheir told me more about it when I was up here earlier."

When they reached the Hadawi house, Shahak insisted they linger among the trees to make sure it was safe. Auerbach obliged him at first. He was uneasy again after seeing the house, wondering if he'd made a mistake. Waiting with Shahak for a moment gave him time to think, but then Suheir came outside and Auerbach saw her. Any hesitancy he'd had before suddenly evaporated. No longer able to restrain himself, he stepped into the open and their eyes meet. She stared at him, a worried look on her face, then her eyes lit up and she rushed toward him and threw her arms around his neck. He slipped his arms around her waist and pressed his lips to hers. They stood like that, arms embraced, locked in a long, slow kiss, until finally she leaned her head away and said, "Why are you here? I can't believe this." She glanced in Shahak's direction. "I don't see you for twenty years and now I see both of you."

"I was in Jerusalem and found your uncle. He told me you were alive. I've been thinking you were dead all these years, but when he told me I had to come see you."

"You found my uncle?"

"Yes."

"You were looking for me?"

"Yes," Auerbach nodded.

"But it has been so long." She gestured to her midriff. "I am no longer a young woman." She looked at him and giggled. "You are no longer a young man."

"Does any of that matter?"

"No," she grinned. "None of it matters." Then she squeezed him close and they kissed once more.

While they embraced, Shahak glanced behind them, checking as he always had for any sign that trouble might be approaching. In the distance, a plume of dust rose from the road and just ahead of it, barely visible in the glaring sunlight, he saw the outline of a car. "Someone's coming," he said. Auerbach still with his arms around Suheir seemed not to notice. "Someone's coming," Shahak repeated, this time louder. He tugged at Auerbach's sleeve. "We gotta go. I can't be seen here by Ahmad or Arafat. That will blow things for me."

Auerbach relaxed his grip on Suheir and let her slowly slip from his arms. "Okay, we'll go." Then he looked down at Suheir and smiled. "But not yet." He leaned forward and kissed her again.

Shahak pulled at Auerbach's shirt. "We have to go," he insisted. "Now."

Suheir pulled away. "He is right. You cannot be here when Ahmad arrives." Reluctantly Auerbach moved his arms from around her and took her hand. Together they walked slowly from the clearing in front of the house toward the stand of trees. Suheir looked up at him. "Will I ever see you again?"

"I hope so, but I don't know how just yet."

Shahak grabbed him by the collar. "I'm sorry," he glanced over at Suheir. "But we have to leave." He pointed in the direction of the car approaching on the dirt road. It was now close enough to see two men sitting in front with a third in back.

Suheir was alert. "Yes," she insisted. "You must go at once."

Auerbach kissed her once more and said, "I'll find a way to contact you."

"We will see. Now hurry."

Shahak pulled Auerbach toward the path that led through the trees and shoved him ahead. "Get moving."

Auerbach stumbled forward, then twisted free of Shahak's grasp. "I'm an adult. I don't need a chaperone."

"If you're an adult, then act like one," Shahak demanded. "Not like some infatuated teenager. You have a career and obligations in New York. You have a job and opportunity. You need to go back to it and never come back here again."

Auerbach glared at him. "Or what?"

"If you stay here, you will die," Shahak argued. "This is not your home."

They emerged from the trees and started across an open field. Auerbach seemed to agree with Shahak and said with resignation, "I'll go. But I don't like it."

"I don't like it, either," Shahak conceded, "but this is how it must be. We have to get you back to Jerusalem."

Auerbach frowned. "What if I don't want to go back just yet? I might want to come back out here tomorrow and see her again, when Ahmad's not there. I meant what I said to her. I'm going to find a way to see her."

Shahak caught hold of Auerbach's arm again and jerked him up short. "Listen," he snapped. "This is not the Degania of our youth. And it is certainly not New York City. You are a valuable intelligence asset. Like it or not, you know things and if you are caught by the wrong people out here, it would be terrible."

"All right," Auerbach conceded. "I'll go with you." Again he pulled free of Shahak's grasp. "But that doesn't mean I'm not coming back."

"We'll take things one step at a time. First, we get you to Jerusalem. Then we worry about what happens next."

CHAPTER 18

THE FOLLOWING DAY, Shahak drove Auerbach to Jerusalem. On the way he asked, "Do you intend to see her again?"

"Suheir?"

"Yes."

"I don't know," Auerbach shrugged. "Why? I thought you said I shouldn't."

"I just think this is going to be a problem."

"Arafat?"

"No, you and Suheir."

"How so?"

"Like I said before, this isn't New York."

"You keep saying that." Auerbach's voice had an edge. "What do you mean?"

"You kissed her."

"Yes," Auerbach smiled. "I did."

"Many in the Arab world don't take expressions of affection quite as glibly as they do in New York."

"Why did you bring it up again anyway?" Auerbach leaned against the door and closed his eyes. "I was thinking about home already."

"Because I know you and I know this isn't over yet."

"Yeah," Auerbach's eyes opened and he grinned at Shahak. "I guess not."

Shahak gave him a friendly punch on the shoulder. "Why did you come up here?"

"Like I said, I went back to the alley where she was shot and then to her uncle's house and I don't know…I just got caught up in it." Auerbach rested his head against the glass and once more closed his eyes. "How long before we get to Jerusalem?"

"We're not going to Jerusalem."

Auerbach's eyes opened. "Why not?"

"We're going to Tel Aviv. You need to see Dayan."

"Moshe Dayan? Why?"

"Because he's the defense minister and if you briefed Golda Meir, you need to brief him."

"Whatever. But I have a seat on a plane leaving Monday."

"Good. I'll make certain you're on it."

— . —

When they reached Tel Aviv, Shahak drove them to the Ministry of Defense building and parked in a lot near the side entrance. He led the way to the building lobby and took the elevator upstairs. Dayan was seated at his desk as they entered the office. He looked up at Shahak with surprise. "That was a quick trip. I thought you would stay up there awhile."

"Long story." Shahak gestured with his right hand, "This is my friend Yaakov Auerbach."

"Auerbach," Dayan frowned as they shook hands. "*The* Auerbach?"

"Yes," Auerbach replied. "I'm afraid so."

Dayan wagged his finger at them. "And you two know each other?"

"We both lived at Degania," Shahak explained. "I found him up there yesterday."

Dayan looked over at Auerbach. "What were you doing in Degania?"

"I wanted to see the old place again."

"He went to see Suheir Hadawi," Shahak added.

"Hadawi?" Dayan had a puzzled look. "She is Arab?"

"Yes. She and her family lived at the north edge of the farm."

"An Arab girl," Dayan nodded.

"I suppose she's not really a girl anymore," Shahak suggested. "We knew her when we lived there."

Dayan glanced over at Auerbach once more. "You should have known better than to go up there. Especially considering the reason you are here in the first place." He looked to Shahak. "Did he tell you why he's here?"

"Yes," Shahak replied.

"What do you think would have happened if Arafat or any of the dozen Arab groups up there had found you?"

"Perhaps it wasn't the smartest thing," Auerbach admitted.

"Perhaps?" Dayan retorted.

"I know," Auerbach said with a nervous grin. "But after all this time, and I was so close. I wanted to see her."

"Well, it's a good thing Natan was there to get you out. If FATAH got hold of you they would figure out who you are, and that would not be good. For you or for us."

"I realize that."

Dayan stared at him a moment, then leaned back in his chair. "Tell me about Hussein."

For the next ten minutes Auerbach described his meeting in the palace, the topics they discussed, Hussein's concern for his own survival, and the suggestion that the Water Carrier would be FATAH's next target. "I suppose you've had time to check out what he said."

"We're working on it."

"Think there's anything to the threat against the water project?"

"Difficult to say," Dayan replied. "But I can tell you this. These people play for keeps."

"What does that mean?"

Dayan leaned forward and rested his elbows on the desktop. "That plane you were on crashed because the engines had been tampered with."

"Tampered with?"

"Yes," Dayan nodded. "We examined the two engines that failed and found a problem with the fuel system. Same problem on both engines. Someone had obviously tampered with them."

Auerbach looked concerned. "So, they were trying to kill me?"

"Apparently so. After we discovered what happened to the failed engines, we looked at the other two engines. They had attempted to do the same thing to them, too, but they failed to explode, though they were running at reduced capacity, which is why you came down the way you did."

"They knew I was there? On the plane?"

"I'm sure they knew you were there, that you were from the United States, and that you work for a firm that represents many of our official interests. Anyone could know that much. I don't think they knew the exact reason for your visit."

"Sounds like the plot against Hussein might have some truth in it."

"It's an intriguing situation," Dayan answered, not really telling him anything.

They talked awhile longer, then Auerbach stepped outside the office so Dayan could meet with Shahak alone. When Auerbach was gone Dayan asked, "Are you sure this guy is okay?"

"Yes," Shahak replied. "I think so. Why?"

"He seems a little…addled or something. Maybe a delayed reaction to that plane crash."

"Maybe so. But he's about the same now as when I knew him before."

"He was like this when he lived at Degania?"

"When it came to Suheir, he was this way and more sometimes. He was madly in love with the girl and refused to listen to anyone."

"But that was…twenty years ago."

"For the mind," Shahak offered. "But not for the heart."

"You need to get him out of here before he causes trouble."

"He's booked on a Monday flight."

"Good," Dayan nodded. "I really wanted you to stay up there awhile and find out what's going on."

"I know, but considering the circumstances, I thought I should bring him down here. I can go back."

"That would be good."

"I know one thing for certain," Shahak continued. "Yasser Arafat is there."

Dayan's brow winkled in a frown. "He's in Degania?"

"They have a cache of weapons at Suheir and Ahmad's house."

"Where you and Auerbach were today?"

"Yes."

"She told you?"

"I saw it."

"You saw it?" Dayan asked in disbelief.

"I asked about Arafat at the settlement compound but no one wanted to talk at first. They seem to think we're trying to force them out of their communal style and into a commercial farming model."

"Where did they get that idea?"

"I'm not sure. But they weren't interested in talking to me. So after a while I wandered up to the shop where I'd worked before and one of the guys in there suggested that I talk with Suheir or Ahmad."

"The Hadawis?"

"Yes. So I went up there to see her. It's not far."

"Auerbach was with you then?"

"No. We went back later. He arrived at the compound while I was up there at the house with Suheir the first time."

"Did she know about Arafat?"

"I saw Arafat. He came by to pick up Ahmad."

"And Arafat saw you?"

"No. The house is in a grove of trees. I was hiding behind them, trying to watch the place for a while to make sure it was okay, rather than just rushing in."

"Good."

"So while I was standing there watching," Shahak continued, "Arafat pulled up in a car. Ahmad got in with him and they left. Then I went over to the house and talked to Suheir."

"She confirmed her brother was working with Arafat?"

"Yes. Then she took me inside the house. Arafat has a cache of weapons in the back room."

"What kind of weapons?"

"Grenades, rifles, ammunition."

"You're sure they're his?"

"She said they were."

"If they have them there," Dayan mused, "they probably have them in other places, too."

"From the look of it, I'd say that's right."

"We need to find those caches."

"I suppose we could send in the IDF," Shahak suggested. "But that would cause more trouble than it would solve. And we'd be finished with gathering intelligence. If the soldiers start raiding houses, no one will talk. Not even the ones who want to."

"What we really need is two operations," Dayan observed. "One to locate the caches and one to clear them out. Use people who are out of uniform. Work it more like a theft than a military raid."

"What we need is our own intelligence network," Shahak added. "I know that would cause problems with Mossad, but we'd have our own information. And it would be suited to our own purposes."

Dayan liked the idea. "It would also give us control over the entire operation. Top to bottom. Intelligence to response."

CHAPTER 19

WHEN GOLDA ARRIVED HOME that evening she found the lights were on and the front door unlocked. She opened the door slowly and called out in a loud voice, "Who's in here?"

A moment later, her sister, Clara, appeared from the kitchen, an apron tied around her waist. "I hope you're hungry," she grinned.

Golda crossed the room and the two women embraced. "Why didn't you call to tell me you were coming? I would have come to the airport to meet you."

"I didn't want to argue with you about whether I should come or not."

"I wouldn't have tried to dissuade you."

"But you would have had reasons why another time would be better," Clara countered. Her face softened and she took Golda's hand. "We need to talk."

"Yes," Golda nodded. "I suppose we do."

"And I didn't want to do it over the phone."

"I'm glad you came," Golda smiled.

"Besides," Clara let go of Golda's hand. "I haven't seen you in three years and I wanted to see how you're doing." She turned back to the stove. "Get cleaned up. Supper is ready."

They sat at a table in the kitchen and talked while they ate, both eager to know what the other had been doing since their last visit. Then after a while, Clara turned to the topic on both their minds. "I know about the doctor's diagnosis."

Golda gave her a knowing look. "Aliza called you."

"Yes."

"I thought she might. She should mind her own business."

"Nonsense! She's a good friend to you."

"She's nosey."

"She's trying to look out for you."

"And that's why you came all the way over here?"

"No, I came so I could fly back with you for your appointment in New York."

Golda's eyes opened wider. "I have an appointment?"

"Not yet. But you're going to make one tomorrow."

"Why are you so sure of that?"

Clara had a kind smile. "Because now that I'm here, you realize it's the right thing to do."

"I ..." Golda looked away. "I can't take time away for that now."

"Golda," Clara said softly, "there will always be one more important thing waiting on your desk. The job will never end. You've done enough. Israel can survive now. Others are here to see it through to whatever it is to become. You did your job." She reached across the table and rested her hand on Golda's. "You've done enough," she whispered.

Tears trickled down Golda's cheeks. "We began with nothing."

"I know."

"Nothing," Golda repeated. "And now we have a country."

"I know," Clara nodded. "You, Ben-Gurion, the men from Haganah, Shimon Peres, you all put it together from nothing. And it worked."

"The people made it work."

"That's right," Clara sensed an opening. "And the people of the next generation will make it work, too. You have to go to New York."

Golda wiped her cheeks. "I suppose so." They looked at each other a moment, then Golda began to cry again. "I'm scared," she whispered.

"That's why I'm here," Clara smiled. "That's why I'm here."

CHAPTER 20

MEANWHILE IN AMMAN, JORDAN, Tareq Ayasrah quietly leaked rumors that he suspected a group of key military officers were plotting to overthrow the king. At the same time, Ayasrah set in motion rumors that his key generals had been ordered to assemble at a palace on the outskirts of town. The location was purposefully vague and the exact time indefinite.

Both rumors quickly came to the attention of Talal, the king's cousin. He shared the news with Fayez bin Wahbi. Both men were giddy with excitement.

"Everything is coming together as planned," Wahbi said. "The gathering of the generals is no doubt a prelude to their execution."

"Nevertheless," Talal cautioned, "I think we must be very careful. Hussein is a crafty man."

"You are thinking it is a deceit?"

"I am thinking we cannot afford to be overconfident."

That evening, Talal's assistant left the residence and contacted an informant within the army. While he was gone Abdullah al-Majali and Abdel Eleyan arrived. The four men reclined together while they awaited news of whether the rumors were true.

Several hours later, Talal's assistant returned with reassuring news. "Every general in the Jordanian army has been ordered to gather at Qasr al-Mushatta."

"You are certain of this?"

"I spoke with Habis."

Talal's eyes were wide. Habis was a well-connected informant whose word had been found trustworthy by Talal's father. "Habis told you?"

"Yes."

Wahbi looked concerned. "Something is wrong?"

"Qasr al-Mushatta is a palace in the country," Talal explained. "It is a place of special significance to our family. Common ancestors many generations removed lived there."

"Qasr al-Mushatta is north of Amman," Eleyan noted. "The first rumors were that they had been ordered to a palace in the city."

"This is the way with rumors," Wahbi responded. "Gossip is always askew of the truth."

"Perhaps it is enough that the generals are meeting," al-Majali suggested.

"And doing so under orders from General Ayasrah," Eleyan added.

Wahbi looked over at Talal. "This is the end for which we hoped. Allah has blessed you. And in blessing you, he has blessed us all. Only a few days more and you will sit on the throne that should have gone to your family years ago."

— • —

Meanwhile, Marouf Rifai, the footman in Hussein's palace, was seated on the bench in the hall outside Hussein's study when the door opened and Hussein appeared. From his brisk gait, Rifai was certain the king was angry. Partway down the hall Hussein was joined by Haider Raimouny, the king's assistant, and they walked together to the rear exit.

As they stepped outside, Rifai rose from his place on the bench and moved down the hall to a window. From it he had a clear view of the courtyard, the garden that surrounded it, and the trees beyond.

Hussein walked with Raimouny from the house to the courtyard and led the way through the garden. When they reached the trees, two men appeared from the left. They were dressed in long black robes that covered them from head to toe. A sash around their waists held their robes tightly against their abdomens. Tucked inside the sashes were curved swords.

"Assassins," Rifai gasped at the sight of them. His heart sank and a sense of sadness swept over him. This was certainly the end for Hussein.

As the assassins stepped forward, Hussein shrank back, hands clasped in front at the waist in a reverential pose. Raimouny turned to face him with arms outstretched and an anguished look on his face. Then Rifai knew it was not the king who would die and watched as Raimouny begged for mercy.

Before Raimouny could finish his plea, the first assassin stepped forward, drew the sword from the sash at his waist, and swung it in a quick, powerful arc. It sliced through the air and landed squarely against Raimouny's neck. Blood spurted into the air. The second assassin followed with his sword from the opposite side. A moment later, Raimouny's head fell to the ground and his body pitched forward in the dirt.

Rifai was shaken by what he had seen, because many in his position had met with death for witnessing such events uninvited. While the king still faced the opposite direction, Rifai backed away from the window and moved quickly up the hall to the bench. He took a seat outside the king's study, folded his arms across his chest as usual, and waited. Before long, he heard the king's footsteps as he came up the hall to the stairway, then ascended to the second floor.

— · —

That night, after dinner was served, Rifai slipped away from the palace through a small service gate in the palace wall. He hurried a few blocks to the east and came to the home of Paul Howell, an American merchant. A wall surrounded the house and grounds but Rifai easily scaled it. Moments later, he knocked on the back door near the kitchen and waited.

An English butler answered the door and Rifai asked to speak with the American. "That is quite impossible," the butler replied in an arrogant tone.

Rifai persisted. "Tell him I am here. My name is Marouf. Marouf

Rifai. Tell him at once. I think his response will surprise you." The butler abruptly closed the door and Rifai listened to the sound of his footsteps as he moved away.

In a few minutes, the door opened and Paul Howell appeared. With the butler watching in horror, Howell stepped outside and closed the door behind him. He gestured for Rifai to follow and they moved a short distance from the house to a small garden with a fountain near the corner of the back wall. "This is very risky," Howell whispered. "Coming here like this. Do you know what would happen if you are caught?"

"It could not be avoided," Rifai explained. "They told me you were my contact. I need to get a message to Tel Aviv."

"I agreed, but only for matters of the direst importance."

"Late this afternoon, the king led his assistant, Haider Raimouny, from the palace, past the garden to the trees in back. There, two men dressed in black cut off his head."

Howell had a look of horror. "Hussein's head?"

"No. Raimouny's. They beheaded Raimouny. The king's assistant. And they did it in the king's presence."

Howell looked puzzled. "But why?"

"I do not know. But I believe from the way in which he was killed that this arose from a matter solely between King Hussein and Raimouny."

"I am not so sure," Howell replied. "You have heard of the plot among the generals?"

Rifai shook his head. "I have heard of it, but I do not believe it."

Howell looked surprised. "Oh? And why is that?"

"All of the generals are loyal to General Ayasrah. And he is loyal to King Hussein. He and King Hussein have met numerous times during the past two weeks. I see no rift between them."

"Perhaps we should pass that on as well."

"You may decide about the generals. I need you to pass the information about Raimouny. It is most unusual. The king never witnesses an execution. He never participates in these matters. They are never done in his presence." Rifai looked over at Howell. "You know what to do?"

"Yes," Howell nodded. "I will take care of it."

— • —

The following day, King Hussein traveled by car to the home of Talal, his cousin. He had arrived unannounced and invited Talal for a ride. Talal had little choice but to agree and joined the king in the rear seat of the king's car. As they rode away, he glanced over at Hussein and asked, "We are going to the palace?"

"I thought we would enjoy the ride for a while," Hussein replied.

"I heard a radio report about the generals," Talal offered. "You must feel terribly betrayed."

"Many have plotted against me, but today I am settling with all of them."

What is he doing? Talal thought. *Is he taking me to witness the execution that will make me king? Surely not, but what can this mean? Is he crazy?* For the first few minutes of their ride he alternated between moments of great joy and deep despair: One minute thinking he was about to die and the next, confident that Hussein was on the verge of collapse. With great effort, he maintained an even, steely look on his face and spoke in an unhurried manner, "I have not heard many details of the plot. Only what was released on the radio. Which generals were involved?"

"Most of the best," Hussein said with disgust. "And I fear the plot runs even deeper."

"You are continuing to investigate?"

"Oh yes," Hussein nodded earnestly. "We are investigating all of them."

A purge, Talal thought to himself. *A purge of army leadership. Nothing would say madman like a purge.* He smiled with confidence. This was turning out better than he'd ever dreamed.

"Soon," Hussein continued, "those who are against me, who wish to bring me down as they did my father, will be no more. All our problems will be eliminated."

They rode on for a while, exchanging bits of conversation between long periods of silence until they came to the gates of Qasr al-Mushatta. The car came to a stop and a servant stepped up to open the doors.

Hussein stepped from the car and waited for Talal to join him, then escorted him up the steps and inside the palace.

From the main entrance, they walked down the hall. Hussein came to a stop in front of large double doors. "Do you remember this room?"

"They used to dance in here, long ago."

"Our grandfather was married in this room."

"I doubt we were in attendance," he quipped.

Hussein smiled. "I doubt our parents were, either." Then he pushed open the doors and gestured for Talal to enter.

Talal bowed respectfully to Hussein and stepped through the doorway to find the room was ringed with soldiers, all of them generals in the Jordanian army. Standing in the center of the room looking ashen was Fayez bin Wahbi. Next to him stood Samer Hattab, Abdullah al-Majali, and Abdel Eleyan.

Hussein urged Talal toward his friends with a nudge. With halting steps Talal made his way in their direction and when he reached the center of the room Hussein glanced around at the generals. "As you are aware," he gestured to Talal and his friends, "these men conspired with my assistant, Haider Raimouny, to depose me from the throne and install Talal as king. And as General Ayasrah has confirmed to your satisfaction, no doubt remains as to their guilt. I leave their final disposition to your discretion." Then he backed away to the hall and closed the doors behind him. Moments later, the crack of gunfire echoed through the halls.

CHAPTER 21

FOUR KILOMETERS OUTSIDE BEIT SHEMESH, west of Jerusalem, Shafi Harel sat at a radio receiver alternating between bands as she listened to broadcasts from Jordan and Syria. Nineteen years old, she'd been assigned to the radio post six weeks earlier.

Late in the afternoon, as Hussein and Talal traveled from Amman to Qasr al-Mushatta, she switched back to a band used by a Jordanian radio station and heard the report about a plot among the generals to remove Hussein. Following standard procedure, she recorded the broadcast and sent it to Mossad headquarters in Tel Aviv.

Broadcast in Arabic, the report was transcribed and translated into Hebrew, then sent to the Mossad Operations Center in the basement of the headquarters building, where it was delivered to intelligence analyst Idan Rechter. He read the transcript, then stepped to the center of the room. "Okay. We've just received this from a listening post near Jerusalem. They've recorded a broadcast from Amman that indicates eleven Jordanian generals have been executed, all of them supposedly with significant ties to officials in either Syria or Egypt. We have copies of the report for each of you and we'll play the tape in a few minutes. As you recall, we've already been through this scenario once, from the front end with the plot our operatives reported earlier. Now it looks like someone followed through with it."

Ehud Katz spoke up, "What happened to the source who gave us that plot?"

"The source in Damascus was captured, tortured, and executed," Rechter answered.

Meir Walder, seated across the room, asked, "Did we share that information with Hussein?"

"I am not aware of what might have been done with the information. We advise; we don't determine and execute policy."

"But if we did share the information with Hussein," Katz argued, "and he executed his general staff, then we could assume he either believed us or confirmed it for himself."

"We could assume most anything we like," Rechter replied.

Walder spoke up again. "We should back up and ask the first question."

"Which is?"

"Is this broadcast valid? Did he really kill eleven generals?"

"Perhaps," Nathan Shlonsky answered.

Walder looked over at him. "Perhaps?"

Before Shlonsky could respond, Katz chimed in, "Eleven generals lying in the street and you still have questions?"

"No," Walder countered. "Nathan's question is more seminal than that. And it's the question we should focus on."

"Which is?"

"Are they lying in the street? That's the question. Has anyone seen any of those eleven generals who were supposedly killed?"

"Do we know the names of these generals?"

Rechter held up a single sheet of paper. "This is a list of the people Research thinks should be among the dead." The discussion continued as Rechter passed around copies of the document.

"If the report is true, doesn't it prove the truth of the plot information?"

"No. If it's true, it proves Hussein *thought* the threat was true."

"If he killed his generals, then we could say he took it seriously."

"Extremely."

"But that could be a reaction based on internal politics as much as anything else."

Rechter spoke up. "So that gets us back to the essential question. Is the information about the killing of the generals valid information? Is it actionable intelligence?"

"Does he have anyone else to lead his army?" Shlonsky asked. "I mean, he might have just solved our problem for us. If he killed off his best leadership, how much of a threat could their army be?"

Someone else spoke up, "Looking at this list, it appears Waleed Obeidat is still alive. And he could—"

The door opened and a staff member appeared with a message for Rechter. He read it quickly, then said, "Okay. Here's some new information. A source in Amman indicates Raimouny, Hussein's assistant, is dead. According to the source, he was killed in the garden at Hussein's palace. Apparently, Hussein did not participate in the execution but was there, watching when it occurred."

"This is serious," Walder noted.

"Yes, it is," Rechter agreed. "Which is why we need to know if the information is valid."

"That lends credibility to the report," Shlonsky added.

"We need to confirm it." Rechter glanced around the room. "Work your sources. We need to get on top of this. Information is only useful when we know it's reliable."

— · —

Within the hour, Shaul Nissany, the Mossad director, received a report from Rechter on the developing situation in Jordan. It was initial and tentative, but in spite of the exceptions Nissany felt compelled to brief Eshkol. It was risky, giving raw intelligence to an elected official, but events in Jordan were critical to the nation's security and he was certain Eshkol would want to know. He left immediately for Jerusalem.

Eshkol was in his office when Nissany arrived. Baruch Shatilov, Eshkol's chief of staff, escorted him into the prime minister's office, but before Nissany could begin, a secretary interrupted to tell them President Johnson was calling. Nissany turned toward the door to leave but Eshkol stopped him. "Stay. This could be interesting."

Nissany and Shatilov stood near the desk as Eshkol waited for

Johnson to come on the line. When the conversation began, Eshkol held the receiver to one side so they could both hear.

"It was good to see you in Washington the other day," Johnson began, his southern drawl noticeably slower and more pronounced.

"We were delighted to meet with you as well," Eshkol replied.

"Those missiles we discussed are on their way. They should be arriving soon."

Eshkol nodded. "That is good news indeed, Mr. President." Eshkol looked over at Nissany and mouthed something to him. When Nissany frowned, Eshkol picked up a pen from the desktop and scribbled on a note pad, *Dean Rusk is with him.*

"I understand there's been a little trouble over there in Jordan."

Eshkol appeared confused and glanced at Nissany with a questioning shrug. "Yes, Mr. President," he answered, treading water in the conversation.

"Our reports indicate he executed eleven of his generals," Johnson continued.

"We are… still…sorting through the information, Mr. President.

"Apparently it was rather brutal."

"This is what we have been trying to tell the world," Eshkol noted. "The Arabs want to portray themselves as peaceful, high-minded, civilized people, but in fact they are barbarians."

"Well, look," Johnson replied, getting to the point of the call. "I don't mind telling you, things are tense everywhere right now. And I need you to hold things together over there for me. We can do a lot together. The American people have a lot of goodwill toward Israel…and that makes things much easier for us with Congress. They're all supportive of you. So if you can give us all a little room on this thing in Jordan, maybe don't ramp things up like it's a threat to you, hopefully we can get through this. Just need a little room to work with. That's all we need."

"Yes, Mr. President," Eshkol answered.

"Let things settle down over there with Hussein and don't push him," Johnson continued, "and if you can do that, I think this will resolve itself without much effect."

The conversation continued a little longer, with Johnson conveying his personal regard for Eshkol's family. When they finished, Eshkol hung up the receiver and turned to Nissany.

"What is he talking about? What incident in Jordan?"

"Reports indicate that Hussein has executed eleven of his generals."

"Why was I not informed of this?"

"I came here to tell you, but Johnson called before I could see you."

"I need to know these things immediately. How long have you known?"

"A tentative report came through about an hour ago. I came to see you as soon as I received it."

"The Americans knew about it," Eshkol fumed, "and they're thousands of miles away. We're right here. Why didn't we know?"

"We have limited sources in Jordan, Mr. Prime Minister. We're working with what we have. Based on the conversation you just had with President Johnson, I'd say he received the information about the same time you would have. That's why Rusk was in the office with him. And if I were to guess, I would say they learned about it the same way we did."

"Which was?"

"From a Jordanian radio broadcast."

"Is it true?"

"We're trying to determine that right now, as it relates to the generals."

"As it relates to the...what does that mean? Is there something else?"

"A source in Amman tells us Hussein's assistant, Haider Raimouny, was executed. This comes from a well-placed, highly reliable operative. Apparently Hussein was present at the time."

"He killed his assistant?"

"No. Our source says he was present but did not participate."

"And is this information the truth?"

"I believe so, Mr. Prime Minister. This information comes with a high degree of confidence. And I doubt the Americans even know it."

CHAPTER 22

CONTRARY TO WHAT HE HAD SAID BEFORE, Auerbach had no intention of remaining in Jerusalem. Suheir was in Degania and he intended to see her again before leaving Israel, if he left at all. He returned to the hotel, replaced the clothes in his satchel with fresh ones, and walked downstairs to the street. There was no bus to Degania that day, as he well knew, so he set out on foot toward the highway to Galilee.

Using the American practice of hitchhiking, he caught a ride from Jerusalem to Ramla, a town two-thirds of the way to Tel Aviv. From there, a freight truck driver took him all the way to Nazareth. A few hours later, he caught a ride with a student on his way to Tiberias. A farmer from Sharona brought him the rest of the way to Degania.

At the settlement compound, Auerbach stashed his satchel in the cafeteria and walked up the road to Suheir's house. As before, he paused in the grove of trees to watch. Ten minutes later with no sign of anyone coming or going from the farm, he moved from the cover of the trees, walked to the door, and knocked. When no one answered, he peered through the windows, cupping his hands around his eyes to block out the glare. Inside, the house was dark and he saw no sign of life.

Reluctantly, Auerbach returned to the settlement compound and entered the cafeteria. Daniel Erlich, the settlement chairman, was seated at a table, reviewing production reports from the previous year. He glanced up with a look of surprise as Auerbach entered. "What are you doing here?" he asked.

"I had a few things to take care of."

Erlich had a quizzical frown. "I thought they were taking you back to America."

"They thought that, too."

"The woman?" he asked with a knowing look.

"She's not just a woman."

"They never are," Erlich grinned.

"I went up to the house. No one—"

Instantly, the look on Erlich's face turned serious. "You shouldn't do that," he interrupted.

"Do what?"

"You shouldn't go up there."

"Why?"

"The Hadawis are not who you think they are."

"Then who are they?"

Erlich glanced around the room as if checking and lowered his voice. "The brother, Ahmad, is with FATAH now. They are very dangerous."

"But what about Suheir? She's not involved with them, is she?"

"She would be all right on her own," Erlich conceded, "but she seems tied to her brother now, since their father died."

"Yeah, well," Auerbach shrugged, "she has nowhere else to go."

"That is true. But it doesn't change things. You should stay away from them."

"I went up there," Auerbach said, ignoring the advice. "No one's home. Any idea where they are?"

Erlich glanced away. "I don't know ..."

"Yes, you do," Auerbach pressed the issue. "I can see it in your eyes."

"I don't think—"

"I'm going to find them," Auerbach said with confidence. "One way or the other."

Erlich glanced around once more and lowered his voice again, this time to a whisper. "They left a few days ago. I'm not sure where they went."

"But you have an idea."

"I have heard that some members of FATAH use a house north of Afula. On the road to Nazareth."

Auerbach had suspected all along that Erlich knew more than he'd revealed during his earlier visit. He thought for a moment about what that meant, then said, "Did you tell this to Shahak when he was up here?"

Erlich turned back to the papers on the table. "No," he said curtly.

"Why not?"

"None of his business."

Auerbach was astounded. "None of his business?" His eyes were open wide. "What are you talking about?"

Erlich looked up at him. "We are suspicious of everyone who comes here from the government. Okay? It's got nothing to do with our opinion of Shahak. He's a good guy. But we don't trust the government."

"Why?"

"Many in Jerusalem would like to eliminate our communal tradition."

"Force you to compete with independent farmers."

"We do not mind the competition," Erlich explained, "but to do as they wish we would have to reorient our lives from the community we've spent decades building to the products we can produce that are commercially viable."

"But you already sell on the open market."

"We produce some things for the open market, but we produce many things for our own consumption. Their model would change that. We are not interested in making that compromise."

"That's the vote of the group?"

"The vote?"

"If it's truly a communal situation, doesn't the community get to decide what they do?"

"The community gets to decide," Erlich agreed. "But this is a commune. Not a democracy." He turned back to the documents before him. "Now, if you don't mind, I need to get busy."

Auerbach stood to leave. "Well," he said politely, "thanks for the information about Suheir. Any way to get to Afula?"

"I'll see what I can do." Erlich spoke without looking up. "But if you intend on staying here, you should get to work."

"Doing what?"

"I'm sure they could use some help in the laundry."

— • —

On Monday, Shahak drove to Jerusalem to pick up Auerbach for the ride to the airport. He parked near the front entrance and entered the hotel lobby. At the lobby desk he asked the clerk to phone the room and waited while she dialed the number. When there was no answer, he showed the clerk his Ministry of Defense ID and pressured her into taking him to the room. The clerk led him upstairs and knocked on the room door, then opened it with a master key.

Inside, they found the bed was made and fresh linens were stacked on the dresser. Shahak pointed to them. "When were those put in here?"

The clerk glanced at her wristwatch. "This room was cleaned yesterday. Those linens were placed here then."

"So, he hasn't been here since then."

"I would say not."

"I knew I should have stayed with him," he mumbled.

"He hasn't checked out," the clerk offered.

"You're sure of that?" Shahak asked as he stepped to the closet.

"He is still listed in the registry. If he'd checked out, his name would not be there."

Shahak opened the closet door and found dirty clothes piled on the floor inside. A sense of dread swept over him. "I don't like this," he said, pointing to the clothes.

"We have a laundry service," the clerk explained, "but guests must tell housekeeping they wish to use it. They don't pick up clothes automatically."

"I'm not talking about that," Shahak growled, gesturing to clothes. "That's the shirt he was wearing when I brought him back from Degania. It looks like he dumped his dirty laundry here. And I'm thinking he got fresh clothes and left." He looked on the shelf overhead. "He had a leather satchel, too." The shelf in the closet was empty and Shahak turned to scan the room. "But I don't see it in here."

"Maybe he wanted to see some sites," the clerk suggested. "Lots of things to see."

Shahak rubbed his forehead. "I'm sure he did. And that's the problem."

"What do you mean?"

"I mean he has gone to Degania." Shahak started toward the door, muttering as he went. "I can't believe he did this."

— • —

From the hotel, Shahak drove quickly back to Tel Aviv and went to Dayan's office in the Ministry of Defense building. "Auerbach is gone," he blurted as he came into the room.

"Good," Dayan smiled. "At least that is over with."

"No," Shahak replied insistently. "He's gone."

"What do you mean?"

"He's not in the hotel."

Dayan frowned. "Not in the hotel? What are you saying?"

"I went to get him just now and he's not there." Shahak gestured with his hands as he spoke. "His clothes are there—some of them, anyway—but he's not there and it looks like he hasn't been in his room at least since yesterday."

Dayan looked concerned. "Any sign of foul play?"

"No. Not that I could see."

"How did you get in the room?"

"The clerk let me in."

"Well," Dayan said as he reached for the phone, "I'm sending over a team to investigate anyway. We have to make sure."

"Good," Shahak said as he turned toward the door. "I'm going to Degania."

Dayan called after him, "I thought about what we discussed earlier. I think we have what we need from there."

"I'm not going for that." Shahak pulled open the door. "I'm going for Auerbach."

"You think he's up there?"

"I know he is."

— • —

Shortly before noon, Auerbach left the laundry room and walked over to the cafeteria for lunch. He came through the back door to the kitchen, filled his plate from pots on the stove, and walked out to a table in the dining hall. Only a few workers were there. Most were still in the field. He took a seat at a table near a window and began to eat.

A few minutes later, someone from the mechanic shop took a seat across from him. They talked about everything and nothing, but somewhere in the conversation Auerbach glanced over the man's shoulder and saw out the window a car that had come to a stop on the driveway. It looked familiar and as he watched, he saw Shahak step from it. At once he knew why he was there.

"Excuse me," Auerbach interrupted the man seated across from him. "I need to check on something."

Auerbach rose from the table, hurried back to the kitchen and made his way to the back door. From the rear of the building, he walked back to the driveway. As he passed down the side of the building, he glanced through a dining hall window and saw Shahak inside, talking to the man he'd been eating lunch with a few minutes earlier. Auerbach hurried to the car.

When he reached the car he found the keys were not in the ignition. He leaned to one side, out of sight beneath the car windows, and felt under the dash for the ignition wires. After a moment, he found them and pulled them free from the switch. Then he touched them together and the engine started. He twisted the wires tightly in place, put the car in gear, and drove toward the gate. As he turned onto the road, he glanced in the rearview mirror and saw Shahak standing on the driveway, his arms flailing in the air in a frantic gesture for him to stop.

CHAPTER 23

FROM THE COMPOUND AT DEGANIA, Auerbach drove west toward Afula. He arrived there an hour later and turned north on the road to Nazareth. After another hour of searching, he located four houses that seemed to fit the description given by Erlich. Two of them were working farms and one was abandoned. The fourth looked promising and Auerbach parked the car down the road, then came back to it from the west. A low hill rose behind the house and he lay atop it, just beneath the crest, watching.

After a while he saw the back door open. Through the doorway he caught a glimpse of a woman about Suheir's height, standing in what appeared to be the kitchen. He moved down the hill, hoping for a better view, and took a position at the corner of a barn that stood to the rear of the house. From there he could see through a window and before long Suheir came into view. His heart skipped a beat at the sight of her. Years before, she'd been the most beautiful girl in the world and now, though time had passed, the sight of her still made him smile. "There's no way I'm leaving without her," he whispered to himself.

Moving quietly, Auerbach left the corner of the barn, crossed the open space between to the house, and crept beneath the window. As he arose for a look, two men grabbed him from behind. The touch of their hands on his arms startled him and he twisted to one side, trying his best to break free.

"Stupid Jew," one of them snarled as they wrestled him under control. "Did you not think we would find you?"

Auerbach struggled with his captors. "Let go of me."

A few meters away, the back door of the house opened and Ahmad appeared. He stalked toward Auerbach with deliberate steps. "Who are you and—" His eyes opened wide and his mouth dropped open in a look of realization. "Yaakov?"

"You know this man?" someone asked.

"Yes," Ahmad sighed. "I know him. And you're right. He's a stupid Jew." He glared at Auerbach. "What are you doing here?"

"I came to see Suheir."

"This guy knows your sister?" another asked.

Suheir appeared at the door. "Yes. I know him." She came toward them from the house, pointing to the man who asked the question. "Let him go, Yezid," she demanded.

Yezid ignored her, grasping Auerbach all the more firmly as they looked to Ahmad for direction. Ahmad glanced back at Suheir. "Stay inside," he said to her. "This does not concern you."

"It most certainly does concern me," she insisted as she came toward them. "What do you intend to do with him?"

"That's a good question," one of the men asked. "What do we do with him?"

Ahmad thought for a moment, then said to the men who were with him. "We don't have time for this now. Tie him up. We'll deal with him later."

"Yasser will not like it," one of them groused.

"Just tie him up," Ahmad repeated in a curt tone. He scanned the area behind the house. "Put him in that shed," he pointed to a building perhaps forty meters away. "Put him in there and we'll take care of him when we return. It's almost time for us to go."

Someone brought a rope and tied Auerbach's hands behind his back, then they led him to the shed. Not more than three meters square, it was made of rough-hewn lumber and had a dirt floor. It was dark inside and with the glare of sunlight over his shoulder he couldn't see past the doorway. He blinked once or twice, hoping his eyes would adjust but before they did someone shoved him inside. He stumbled forward and fell against the back wall. One of the men caught hold of his legs and jerked them forward. Auerbach's feet slipped out from under him and he tumbled to the floor as they tied his ankles with the rope.

"Don't make a sound," Yezid ordered. "Or we'll be back with a gag for your mouth and a bullet for your head." Then they stepped outside, slammed the door shut, and latched it in place.

With his arms pinned behind his back, Auerbach quickly became uncomfortable. Muscles in his shoulders ached and the shed was hot and stuffy. Beads of sweat formed on his brow as he squirmed into a position to rest his back against the wall. Then he drew his knees up against his chest. When that gave his back no relief, he leaned to one side, resting his head against the wall and closed his eyes.

Alone in the dark, with nothing but silence to keep him company, he thought of all that had happened and how he'd come to be in such a predicament—traveling from New York to Jordan, meeting with King Hussein, the plane crash on the way home. Then locating Suheir's uncle and finding her alive after all these years. *This can't be the end of it,* he thought. *Not after all that.* Not after so many years without her and now to find her and wind up like this. Surely this wasn't the end. "It can't be," he mumbled. "It just can't be."

Before long the heat became unbearable and he drifted into a restless, fitful stupor. Not really asleep, not really awake, but somewhere in between. He remained like that for what seemed like hours until the clatter of the latch against the wooden frame brought him wide awake. With eyes open and muscles taut, he scooted his feet beneath his hips, ready to spring into action against the men he was sure had come to kill him.

But the form that appeared before him was not the hulking presence of a man, as he had expected. Instead, it was slender and willowy and moved toward him with halting steps. In the pale evening light that filtered through the doorway he could see it was a woman, and when at last she entered the shed he saw she was Suheir.

Her right hand held a small ewer and in her left hand was a clump of bread. "Oh, Yaakov," she soothed as she knelt beside him. "What have they done to you? Are you all right?"

"I'm thirsty," he croaked in a dry, raspy voice.

She placed the pitcher to his lips and tipped it up. "Drink slowly," she whispered. For the first time that afternoon Auerbach felt cool water against his lips and he gulped every drop that fell there.

After a moment Suheir set aside the urn and broke off a piece of the bread, then placed it in his mouth. He stared up at her as he chewed. "What are they going to do with me?"

"I do not know. But I am trying to find a way to get us both away from here."

"Just think about yourself," he whispered. "Don't worry about me."

Suheir stroked his cheek gently. "I do not think it is possible that I should ever think of anything but you again." She kissed him gently on the lips, then leaned away and raised the urn once more. "Here, drink more. Then I must go."

— • —

A few minutes later, Suheir stepped from the shed and quietly pulled the door closed, then latched it securely in place. As she turned to leave she found Ahmad standing in her way. The sight of him made her gasp with fright. "What are you doing?" she whispered in anger.

"Why are you out here? If I saw you, others could have. This is not good."

"I gave him water and bread. It is what you should have done."

"They will not let him live," Ahmad pronounced in a matter-of-fact tone. "I might be able to keep him alive until we return, but they will not let him live. When Arafat returns they will kill Yaakov to prove their loyalty."

"You must convince them to let him live," she implored.

"I can't convince them. And if by some miracle I did, then his life would be on me. I would be responsible for him. The first time he made a mistake, they would kill both him and me. Then you can imagine what would happen to you."

"They can't kill him," she shook her head violently. "They can't."

Ahmad's voice softened. "Do you really think this can turn out well?"

"I love him."

"But are you thinking about where we are? Who we are? This is what Father tried to tell you."

"I love him," Suheir repeated. "And he loves me." Tears welled up in her eyes. "We have been apart for so long and yet neither of us has married. Why do you think that happened? Is it not a sign?" She began to sob. "We have been apart this long and still he risks his life to come and find me. Why do you think he did that?"

"Because he is crazy... He was always the crazy one. Shahak was the sensible one." He put his arm around her shoulder. "Why couldn't you love Shahak?"

"Because I love Yaakov."

"Look," he led her back toward the house, "we have something to do now. After that, I will speak to the others. But for now, you must keep quiet about this." He looked over at her. "You understand?"

"Yes," she nodded. "I understand."

"If they find out that I might intercede for him, then I will be forced to deny it and all hope will be lost." He gave her a hug. "So keep quiet about it."

— • —

The next evening, Ahmad left two men at the house with Suheir and took the others to join Arafat at the edge of a farm field a little way up the road near Mizra. They arrived to find him sitting in a truck, waiting. "What took you so long?"

"Wanted to make sure this was you before we showed ourselves," Ahmad answered.

"Well, get in. We're running late." Ahmad got in on the passenger side of the cab. The others climbed in back.

From Mizra they drove east, crossed into Jordan south of the Sea of Galilee, then turned north into Syria. Not far from the border they came upon an army truck parked at the side of the road. Arafat brought their truck to a stop behind it. Ahmad glance at him. "You are certain this is the one?"

"Yes," Arafat nodded. "I am certain. Besides, do you see any others?" he asked, gesturing with a sweep of his arm.

Ahmad opened the door and stepped out. "This would be easier if you turned the truck around." He pushed the door closed and stepped out of the way as Arafat put the truck in gear.

While Arafat turned the truck around, Ahmad and the others climbed into the back of the army truck. There they found crates of dynamite and C-4 explosives, along with detonators and wire to set the charges. Ahmad surveyed the cargo and grinned. "This will make a statement."

"A loud one," Yezid added.

As the trucked backed into place, Ahmad jumped to the ground. "One of you stay up there and hand the stuff down. The rest of us will make a line and pass it to the other truck."

In a matter of minutes the men unloaded the army truck and placed the contents in the truck they'd come in. When the cargo was secure and covered with a tarp, the men climbed in back. "Start wiring the charges together," Ahmad instructed. "Just like we practiced."

"We aren't setting them individually?"

"No, we'll blow it all at once. Right from the back of the truck. That way, we can pull alongside the building, leave the truck, and do it all right there."

"We ought to just drive the truck into the building and blow it up that way," someone suggested.

"We would all die in the process," another replied.

"Is that such a bad thing?"

"Get busy on those charges," Ahmad ordered. "We have many more things to do before we die." He climbed into the cab and closed the door. Arafat put the truck in gear and steered it onto the road. As they drove away, Ahmad glanced over at him. "Think this will work?"

Arafat grinned. "This will be the loudest explosion the Zionists have ever heard. And when the dust settles, their beloved water project will be nothing but a mud puddle."

— • —

Not long before sunup, they arrived at a hilltop near Hasolelim. The National Water Carrier stretched out below them. Originating from a pump station at the Sea of Galilee, north of Tiberias, the carrier diverted water from the lake into an open canal that carried it west. At Hasolelim, a second pump station forced the water into a large pipe that lifted it under pressure several hundred meters to a plateau from which it traveled by gravity southward a hundred kilometers to the Negev. Without the Hasolelim pump station, the system would quickly run dry, threatening farms near the Egyptian border with ruin.

Arafat eased the truck off the road at the crest of the hill and brought it to a stop. A pair of binoculars lay on the seat beside him and he used them to scan the station below. "It seems to be just as we were told. Here, have a look," he handed the binoculars to Ahmad. "Not a soldier in sight. But we must hurry. The sun will be up soon."

Ahmad trained the binoculars on the cinderblock building in the distance. "Looks good to me. If anyone is down there, they're inside. Noise from the pumps will mask the truck."

Arafat shifted the truck to neutral. "Good." He opened the door. "You know the plan from here."

"Right," Ahmad nodded. He opened the passenger door and climbed down, then made his way around the front bumper. When he reached the opposite side of the truck he found the others already there. They gathered with Arafat and watched as Ahmad climbed into the cab on the driver's side, slipped behind the steering wheel, and closed the door.

Ahmad glanced out the window at them. "You are certain the charges are wired and ready?"

"Yes." Yezid gestured with a walkie-talkie and smiled. "As soon as I press the button, that thing will blow."

"Make sure you wait until I'm clear," Ahmad instructed.

"Of course," Yezid grinned. "Do not worry."

With little option but to trust them, Ahmad put the truck in gear, steered it onto the road, and started down the hill toward the pump station. Halfway there, he put the transmission in neutral and let the truck roll free, allowing the engine to slow to an idle, making it much quieter. A few moments later, he pressed his foot against the brake pedal and slowed, then made a turn to the right.

The truck rolled to a stop alongside the pump station building and he switched off the engine. Moving carefully, he eased open the door, stepped down from the cab, and ran. Before he was halfway up the hill toward the others, an explosion erupted behind him. He glanced over his shoulder to see the cab of the truck on fire. The roof of the pump station was torn aside, exposing wooden joists. A few cinderblocks were missing and smoke rose in the air, but the building remained intact and he heard the pumps operating at full speed.

At the top of the hill, Arafat was fuming. "What did you do wrong?" he railed against the men.

"Nothing," one of the men replied defensively. "We wired it just like you showed us."

"Did you set the detonators?"

"Yes."

"Then what happened?"

"I don't know."

Ahmad glowered at them and said in an accusing tone, "The cab of the truck blew up just fine."

"What are you saying?"

"I'm saying," Ahmad argued, "if I had waited a moment longer, I would be down there and very much dead, instead of up here."

Yezid snarled at him. "If we wanted to kill you, you would have been dead a long time ago."

"Knock it off," Arafat ordered, then he turned to Ahmad. "This was your idea. What do we do now?" He gestured toward the station. "This makes us look like idiots."

"Go public," Ahmad replied without missing a beat.

"Public?" A frown wrinkled Arafat's brow. "We look like idiots already." He gestured in frustration with both hands. "Publicizing it would make us look stupid."

Ahmad shook his head. "Not if we go public first."

"What do you mean?"

"The Zionists will report it in their newspapers anyway. So, beat them to the story. Claim credit for the explosion. Talk about the liberation of our people. The atrocities committed against us. The need to drive the Jews into the sea." Ahmad grinned. "And claim a victory."

A broad smile stretched slowly over Arafat's face, turning up the corners of his mouth. "This is a good idea." He looked over at the others and nodded. "This is a good idea. I like it." He turned back to Ahmad. "You came up with that yourself?"

"I read about it in one of those books you gave me. How a thing appears is as important as how it really is."

"I like it," Arafat repeated, slapping Ahmad on the back. "I like it."

— · —

Meanwhile, back at the house, Auerbach was once again awakened from sleep by the sound of the latch on the shed door. It was dark outside and once again he looked up to see Suheir standing in the doorway, this time her figure outlined against the pale light that reflected from the house. But unlike before, she held a knife in her hand. "We must hurry," she murmured as she knelt at his feet.

With practiced ease she placed the blade between his ankles and cut through the rope with a flick of her wrist. "The others will be back before long," she said as she reached over his shoulder. Auerbach leaned forward and she cut his wrists free. His arms and legs were stiff from sitting but he pushed himself up from the floor and stood.

"What do we do now?"

Suheir took his hand in hers. "Come," she led him toward the door. "This way."

From the shed they hurried across to the barn behind the house. Suheir unhooked the latch on the door and with Auerbach's help pushed it open to reveal Shahak's car parked inside.

"They put it in here until they could decide what to do with you," she explained. "They were afraid to drive it for fear of being discovered."

"I'm glad of that. But I'm not leaving without you."

"I am not staying," she said as she made her way to the passenger side. "I am going with you."

Together, they pushed the car from the building, then got inside and gently closed the doors. "Are they all gone?"

"No, they are inside now. We must leave quickly before they see us."

Auerbach reached beneath the dash and touched the ignition wires together, then twisted them tightly in place. The engine came to life and he shifted the car into gear. Just then, the front door opened and two men appeared, both of them armed. "Get down," Auerbach shouted, then pressed the gas pedal and the car surged forward.

As they passed the house, gunfire burst from the porch. Bullets made a pinging sound against the side of the car and sparks flew as they penetrated the rear door, but the rounds passed harmlessly through to the other side. Three more rounds struck the trunk, but by then they were making the turn at the end of the drive as they sped away into the night.

CHAPTER 24

WITHIN MINUTES AFTER DETONATION, reports of the explosion at the National Water Carrier reached General Greenberg at IDF headquarters in Tel Aviv. He contacted Dayan who, in turn, called Golda to inform her and coordinate the task of briefing Eshkol. She was unavailable but rather than wait, Dayan rode to Jerusalem to brief Eshkol alone. They met in the living room of the prime minister's residence.

"This is what Hussein warned us about," Eshkol lamented when Dayan finished with the details.

"Yes," Dayan replied.

"We knew about it in advance and still they got away with it," Eshkol continued angrily.

"They haven't gotten away with anything," Dayan corrected. "They did it, but we can always respond."

"Oh?" Eshkol's eyebrows arched in a skeptical look. "Exactly how are we going to respond?"

"We'll figure that out."

"I don't want to figure it out. I want to end it." Eshkol continued to rant. "Why can't we put an end to it?"

"We're doing our best."

"They have outside support and no one in the international community calls them to task for it. But if we try to buy arms to defend ourselves, suddenly every country in the world is against us."

"It's complicated, Mr. Prime Minister," Dayan said, trying to keep things under control while giving Eshkol room to talk. "We've been through this before."

Eshkol gestured in frustration. "Tell me again why we don't simply bomb Damascus and reduce it to dust."

The door opened and Golda arrived. "The reason we don't attack Syrian targets," she answered the question as she entered the room, "is because that is precisely what they want us to do. To engage them in conflict so they can draw all the Arab states into a regional war against us."

"We're already at war," Eshkol retorted. "And they are winning because we aren't fighting back."

"We're behaving responsibly," Golda responded. "That's what's expected of us and that is what we're doing. We're a state, not a roving band of thugs. Arafat and his crowd act the way they do because that's what they are—thugs."

"But our people are dying," Eshkol lamented. "And our facilities are being destroyed!"

"And if we attack Syrian installations," Golda replied calmly, "they will have won."

Eshkol glared back at her. "Won?"

Dayan spoke up. "If we attack Syria, then all of them—Iraq, Syria, Lebanon, Jordan, and Egypt—will attack us in Syria's defense. We can't possibly win a war against all of them at the same time."

A low coffee table sat in front of Eshkol's chair and he pounded it with his fist. "I need better options!" he shouted. "Options that work." Golda glanced over at Dayan but neither spoke as Eshkol continued to rail against the Arabs and Israel's lack of a viable, creative response.

— · —

Later that morning a statement was delivered to the *Jerusalem Post*, announcing the Water Carrier explosion and claiming credit for it in the name of FATAH. It was accompanied by a vow from Arafat to pursue the cause of Arab liberation with more attacks.

At the same time in Damascus, Arafat delivered a live radio address that was broadcast to the region through the Syrian Arab News Agency.

In his remarks, Arafat repeated claims similar to those in the Jerusalem statement, vowed to continue the attacks, and called for Arabs everywhere to join with FATAH in driving the Zionists into the sea. Demonstrations in the streets of Damascus followed.

As reports of the broadcast reached Jerusalem, Eshkol called an emergency meeting of the cabinet to review the attacks and discuss options. Having vented his emotions to Dayan and Golda earlier that day, he appeared calm and collected as they gathered around a conference table in the cabinet room.

"No doubt many of you are already aware," Eshkol began slowly, "early this morning a pump station on the National Water Carrier was attacked. Yasser Arafat and FATAH have claimed credit for it. The attack did little damage but their statements give the appearance that they struck a major blow against us."

From down the table, Amnon Levy, the minister of agriculture spoke up. "We should strike a major blow against them. This attack is not only a threat to agriculture in the Negev, but a threat to our nation. If we lose that water, we'll incur serious economic repercussions. This attack was an act of war."

Others appeared eager to join the discussion, but Eshkol spoke up. "Just a minute," he gestured for silence. Then he glanced over at Dayan. "Perhaps we should hear from our minister of defense first, so we all have the latest information."

Dayan recounted most of what was already known—in spite of Arafat's claims the damage was minimal, most of the explosives in the truck failed to detonate, apparently the detonators were defective.

"But they could have destroyed it," Levy offered.

"Yes," Dayan admitted. "If the detonators had worked properly, the damage would have been extensive."

Amos Avraham, the minister of education, spoke up. "Where did they get the detonators?"

"They were made in the Soviet Union," Dayan explained. Groans rose from around the table. Dayan continued. "I assume they were provided by the Syrians. We've seen no evidence of Russian advisors working in the Galilee."

"Do we have the detonators?" Gideon Baram asked. "The ones that didn't work. Are they in our possession now?"

"Yes," Dayan answered. "Along with the remains of the truck and the unexploded ordnance."

"Then perhaps we should consider releasing this information to the press, with photographs. Submit it to the United Nations. File a formal complaint about Soviet interference in the region and about Syrian interference with our internal affairs."

Someone spoke up from the opposite end of the room. "What good would that do?

"It would give us one more piece of evidence to bolster our argument," Baram explained, gesturing with a raised index finger. "Perhaps one leader in one country—maybe just one—would come to his senses and understand what we are facing."

Akiva Patt, the minister of health, spoke up. "We should bomb Syrian positions on the Golan Heights," he said in an even, emotionless tone. "They've been shelling residents of Galilee for months. That's what we should do. They try to bomb us, we obliterate their artillery." Several members nodded approval.

"Attacks like this," Dayan countered, "even though this one was against a major asset, are merely provocations."

"What does it matter?" Levy shouted. "You call it mere *provocation*. I call it an act of war. What does it matter what we call it? They attacked our nation. We have a right to defend ourselves!"

"And that's precisely what they're hoping you'll say," Golda argued. "They want us to respond and give them a pretext for war. Total, complete war. Involving every member of the Arab League in an all-out attack against us."

"But that's what I'm trying to say," Levy responded. "We're already—"

"Golda," Eshkol waved for quiet. "Why don't you make sure everyone knows the latest information from the foreign ministry."

"As you will recall from our previous meetings," Golda began, "we received reports from two sources—one an operative working in Syria, the other a nongovernmental source, both indicating the recent Arab attacks are part of a coordinated plan by the Syrians using Arafat and FATAH to provoke us into retaliating against Syria. According to these sources, they want us to strike Syrian targets in order to induce Egypt to come to Syria's defense and attack us. The Syrians are angry with the Egyptians because they think the Egyptians have not followed through with their defense commitments. Along with that report came news of a plot to assassinate King Hussein. We forwarded that information to King Hussein through an intermediary. During that exchange we learned that FATAH planned an attack on the Water Carrier. There was no—"

"You knew about this in advance?" Avraham shouted, interrupting her.

"Yes," Dayan responded, coming to Golda's defense. "We knew about it in advance, we discussed what actions we should take, and we redoubled our security up and down the length of the system."

"Then how did they get so close?" Patt asked. "I understand they parked the truck right alongside the building."

"They were close," Dayan conceded with a nod, "but that pump station, although critical, is the least defensible of any in the system and it is also the easiest to replace."

Levy, the agriculture minister, came to Dayan's aid. "Moshe consulted with me on this matter," he explained calmly. "A loss of that site would curtail water flow to the Negev but it would not shut it down entirely. We have a canal that carries water by an alternate route that bypasses that station. We added it last year to give us the ability to increase capacity in the system. Three other stations in the system are far more critical, much more difficult to replace, and were guarded with the strictest security."

"I thought you wanted to retaliate," Patt snapped. "I thought you were ready to blow something up in response."

"I am," Levy said. "These attacks have continually escalated and I think this marks a new turn of events in that escalation. They've shown us now that they aren't merely venting frustration or trying to harass us and make life miserable. They mean to bring us down." He paused for effect before continuing. "But what Moshe is telling you is the truth. We talked about the situation, developed heightened security measures, and took some calculated risks."

"Well," Patt said in a dismissive tone, "I saw the report regarding King Hussein's alleged tip. I must say, even though an attack occurred as he described, I am highly suspicious of any information coming to us from Jordan by way of him or a lawyer from New York."

"But it has happened just as Hussein warned," someone chided.

"Yes," Patt nodded. "But is it not possible that Hussein is merely attempting to deceive us?"

"How so?" Golda asked.

"Very simply," Patt continued. "He passes us information warning us to ignore these raids, that they are an attempted provocation. Then tells us of a coming attack against the Water Carrier, knowing it is a matter of national pride, and knowing it is not fully defensible, and knowing that at least one of the stations along the route will remain vulnerable. FATAH makes a guess at which station that will be, perhaps they even have information from an informant who tells them which one it is. The attack occurs—and even though I believe what we've heard here today, the result of a successful explosion would have been catastrophic—and we see that as validating Hussein's warning and his suggestion that we should refrain from responding. We don't respond because we don't want to be suckered by the provocation, the Water Carrier is shut down, and all the while FATAH is organizing local Arabs and building their forces in northern Galilee while we sit on our hands and turn a blind eye until it's too late."

"You're saying Hussein's *warning* is really a ruse to cover for FATAH and give them more time to build their presence."

"Yes."

Patt's suggestion struck a chord and the room fell silent—awkwardly silent—as cabinet members thought about what he'd said. Dayan shot a glance in Golda's direction. She gave him a worried look that indicated she thought there just might be some truth to that long-winded response. Most members of the Israeli government, both in the cabinet and without, thought well of Hussein. Even those who did not particularly care for him realized he was the most moderate of the regional Arab rulers. All of them wanted to be proven wrong in their suspicions of him, but Patt's argument was effective and cut the legs out from under that sentiment.

After a moment, Eshkol turned to Golda in an attempt to bring the discussion back to the topic at hand. "Have we any further information that corroborates what the American from New York told us?"

Before she could speak, Levy piped up. "What about those reports that Hussein killed his generals? Haven't we learned those reports are false?"

"We are still investigating that," Dayan replied, diving in ahead of Golda. "General Ayasrah, who was supposed to be among the dead, was seen yesterday. That has cast suspicion on the entire episode but we do not yet know the full context." He could have told them about the murder of Hussein's assistant, Haider Raimouny, but he refrained.

Eshkol tried once more. "Golda, is there anything new?"

"Nothing we haven't already discussed," she replied with a tired gesture.

Eshkol looked back to Dayan. "What do you recommend?"

"Mr. Prime Minister, I would like to increase our patrols in the region. We have recently obtained information from a highly reliable source indicating FATAH is holding at least one cache of weapons at a house in Degania. It's our belief that there are many more such caches in the Galilee and that this is a growing problem. One that poses a grave threat to the region and to our troops operating there. We would like to develop the capacity to identify those depositories and conduct raids to confiscate and destroy the weapons."

"Now, that's a good idea," Levy said. Most people at the table nodded in agreement.

"How many more troops can we safely deploy," Eshkol asked, "without weakening our defense of the Negev and exposing the southern region to attack?"

"Without calling up the reserve," Dayan uttered in a contemplative tone, "we could easily deploy another dozen tanks and bring the infantry up to a full battalion."

Eshkol nodded. "Colonel Podell's battalion?"

"Yes. Half his unit is already up there. We would simply bring up the remainder of his troops and his command structure. That would give us about fourteen hundred soldiers on the ground. If we brought him up there, too, we would decrease our response time and increase our flexibility."

"Very well," Eshkol nodded. "Deploy the additional troops and move forward with operations to identify and destroy Arab weapons caches."

— • —

After the meeting ended, Golda left the office feeling more deflated and tired than usual. She had noticed Dayan continually coming to her defense in the meeting, and appreciated his sentiment toward her, but she felt it made her look weak and ineffective—as if she needed a man to protect her, which she most certainly did not. Still, she was too tired to argue with him. Instead, she exited the building, collapsed in the back seat of the car, and stared blankly out the window as her driver took her home.

When she arrived at the apartment, she trudged through the front doorway and dropped onto a chair. Clara came into the room. "You don't look well."

"That's an abrupt greeting," Golda smiled weakly.

"But it's the truth." Clara took a seat across from her. "Tough day at the office?"

"Yes." Golda leaned her head against the chair and closed her eyes. "Meetings. Meetings. Meetings," she sighed. "And it seems like we never get anything accomplished."

"Not like the old days?" Clara prodded.

"In the old days we didn't really need meetings. We just asked Ben-Gurion what to do and he told us. And if he wasn't available we asked Shimon or one of the others and they figured out what they thought

Ben-Gurion would say, and that's what we did. Now everyone wants to protect their piece of the pie."

"You know," Clara chided softly, "you can't continue like this."

"Yeah," Golda whispered. "I know."

"You have to go to New York."

"There's just no way to do that right now. I can't leave."

"You must."

"How?" Golda's eyes opened and she glared at Clara. "How am I going to simply walk out and leave at a time like this?"

"It will always be a time like this. You need to choose someone to take over your job. Someone you trust to continue the work. Perhaps not exactly as you would do it, but in the same spirit with the same goals." Clara paused as if hoping for a word from Golda, then pressed the matter when no response came. "Who is it? Who is that person? Who can pick up your work and continue it?"

Golda looked away. "There is one person," she breathed after a moment.

"Who?"

"Abba Eban."

"Will Eshkol appoint him?"

"I think so."

Clara nodded. "He would be as perfect for the job as anyone you might find."

"Yes," Golda agreed. "He would be. And I trust him."

"Then get him over here."

"I can't do that on my own." Golda closed her eyes once more. "I'm foreign minister, not prime minister."

"You would have to resign first?"

"I would at least have to tell Eshkol that I intend to." Golda opened her eyes. "I could recommend my successor, but there's no assurance he would actually give the job to the person I named."

"You'll have to trust Eshkol to do the right thing."

"Yes, I suppose," Golda said quietly, her mood suddenly distant and contemplative. "Maybe I should trust God to do the right thing instead. I think He's been guiding us all the way anyhow. Maybe He will continue to."

Clara seemed taken aback by the comment and leaned away, resting her hands in her lap with her elbows against the armrest of the chair. "You haven't spoken like that in...ages. Since we were little girls."

"I know. But I've been thinking about how things came together. The desire to return to Palestine. People coming early on. Then gradually more and more." The look in Golda's eyes grew more intense. "People think we reconquered the land, taking it by force, but we did it by purchasing every square inch we occupied. All those settlements that were built before independence, we purchased the land for them from the Arabs." Golda looked Clara in the eye. "What would make an Arab sell his land to a Jew?"

"Money?"

"Maybe, but we didn't pay them more than it was worth. They didn't ask for more than it was worth. Was the conversion of land to money enough to overcome their hatred? If that's true, should we offer to buy them out now?"

"I don't know," Clara shrugged. "What are you saying?"

"I'm saying, I wonder if God didn't have a hand in it after all. I never thought of coming to Palestine as an act of faith in God, but maybe that's what it was. And even if it wasn't that for me, maybe that's how God saw it."

Clara had an amused grin. "Have you been attending shul?"

Golda gestured dismissively. "I haven't been to a synagogue since... I can't remember." She closed her eyes once more to rest. "But maybe I should be thinking about that now, too."

CHAPTER 25

IN THE DAYS THAT FOLLOWED, test flights conducted at Ramat David convinced General Bentov, the Israeli air force commander, that Gur's suggested tactic of increased daily sorties was not only feasible but that it would actually work. Not long after the final analysis of the tests was complete, he issued orders to integrate that practice into all future air force war plans and training exercises.

With that part of the strategy in place, Gur and Major Segev turned their attention to the ground attack. "The problem we face," Segev suggested, "is that most of our neighbors have Soviet tanks—the T-55 tank. We have the Sherman. That puts us at a decided disadvantage in almost every category—armor, firepower, size, speed—everything that matters in combat."

"Yes," Gur conceded, "that's true. And on paper the two are unevenly matched. We just need to focus on the opposite side of the equation."

"Opposite side?"

"Our advantages. The point is to win the battle, not lose it. So we should concentrate on how to win, not how they can defeat us."

"I'm not sure there are any advantages," Segev responded. "The Soviet tank is far more suited to desert warfare than the narrower Sherman and that offsets just about any small advantage the Sherman might otherwise have. Sand is not a friend to the Sherman."

"Well," Gur countered, "we've replaced the 76 caliber cannon with a 105, which helps with the firepower question. The cannon on our modified Sherman is actually bigger than the one on the T-55. Maybe we could modify it to make it more maneuverable."

"We've already shown that widening the tracks helps," Segev replied, "We're in the process of changing them over."

"We're changing them?" Gur asked, unaware the conversion was taking place.

"General Greenberg ordered that last month."

"Good. I tried to get them to do that before any of this planning came up."

"But that only helps," Segev continued. "It doesn't eliminate our problem. Soft desert sand will still make our tanks more cumbersome than theirs."

Gur smiled confidently. "Then we'll have to choose the place of battle."

Segev frowned. "Choose the place of battle?"

"*The Art of War* by Sun Tzu. The army that chooses the place of battle wins."

Segev reached for a map. "In the Sinai, the desert sand limits travel to established roadways and there are only six or eight of those. Which means the battle can only take place here, here, and here," he pointed. "We have maps of Jordan and Syria but I'll have to get them from the map room."

Gur shook his head. "Forget about Syria and Jordan. Syria will never invade and we will fight Jordan in the West Bank."

"You said earlier we couldn't be confident about that. What changed your mind?"

"Time and observation. The Syrians have a strong ally in the Soviets but the Syrians themselves are weak. If they were intent on attacking us, they would have done it a long time ago. When war comes, it will come from the Egyptians and it'll be fought in the south." Gur pointed to the map of Sinai. "We need to find other routes besides these highways."

"They're the quickest way to get men and equipment into the peninsula. The only way, actually."

"But if we know that, they know that. We need to find a different way." Gur leaned back in his chair. "We need to find the hard sand."

Segev frowned. "Hard sand?"

"Hard enough to hold up our tanks."

"You mean compact enough."

"Yes. We need to conduct tests to determine the soil compaction necessary to hold up a Sherman tank."

"They weigh about thirty tonnes," Segev offered. "But that's with the seventy-six-millimeter cannon. They weigh more than that now."

"The ministry of agriculture should be able to help us with some soil experts," Gur continued the discussion. "If we can determine the soil density required to support our tanks—to keep them from sinking into the sand—then we can send teams into the desert. Find the areas and routes with the compaction we need." He had a satisfied smile. "Then we can travel by routes the Egyptians have never considered possible."

Segev looked perplexed. "You want to make a map?"

"Yes."

"Of the Sinai Peninsula."

"Yes," Gur nodded. "A soil compaction map. A density map. Showing the density of the sand."

"You realize the peninsula is Egyptian territory."

"We can put small teams in there. It's a long way from the Sinai to Cairo. The Egyptians will never notice."

"But if they do, they'll see it as a cause for war."

"Relax," Gur slapped Segev on the back. "We'll take it one step at a time. The first step is to figure out what level of compaction we need. Then we'll work on finding it in the desert."

— • —

Meanwhile, in Washington, D.C., Steve Smith, the CIA director, arrived at the White House before sunup for the president's morning intelligence briefing. They met in the Oval Office. A review of the situation in Vietnam took most of their time but as the meeting drew to a close Smith said, "There is one other thing, Mr. President."

"What's that, Steve?"

A leather briefcase rested against the leg of Smith's chair. He reached into it as he replied. "We've seen an increase in the number of Israeli troops operating in the Galilee region. They're confined to the area west of the Sea of Galilee but their numbers have increased." He took several photographs from his briefcase and laid them on the president's desk. "A reconnaissance flight over the area three weeks ago took this," Smith pointed to one of the photos. "That's a regional command center." He tapped the picture. "It's manned but it's not a brigade headquarters."

"How do you know that?"

"By the flags they're flying. And the accommodations. This is a remote location. They would have to bring in housing for anyone manning this station." Smith tapped with his index finger a small white square on the picture. "This is a tent. Sparse, but more than adequate for enlisted men and often used by field officers." He moved to a second photograph. "This was taken yesterday." He pointed to the same location on the picture. "You can see the tent is still in place but next to it a second structure has been added. That is a prefab wooden structure. Comes with heat and air-conditioning."

"An upgrade in living quarters," Johnson noted.

"Exactly," Smith nodded. "Our analysts say it's an upgrade of facilities to accommodate an upgrade in staff."

"More staff?"

"Higher-ranking staff. We think they have a general on site." Smith moved to the next picture. "Which explains this," he pointed once again. "Six Sherman tanks traveling in a column toward Nazareth. That brings the total in Galilee to twelve. Perhaps fourteen by one count."

"They've moved more tanks up there?"

"More tanks and more men, Mr. President. They're up to full battalion strength."

"How many men is that?"

"Depending on their overall readiness, about twelve hundred men. Maybe a few more, probably not less."

Johnson thought for a moment, then reached for the phone. "Just sit right there a minute, Steve. I'm gonna get Dean Rusk over here. He needs to be in on this discussion."

Twenty minutes later Rusk entered the Oval Office. Johnson began before Rusk had closed the door. "Steve here tells me the Israelis have increased troop strength in Galilee. You know anything about that?"

"I saw it in the morning briefing paper," Rusk pushed the door closed and started toward the desk.

A frown wrinkled Johnson's forehead and his eyebrows narrowed. "I asked Eshkol not to do anything that would raise the tension level."

Rusk moved a chair next to Smith and took a seat. "There was an attack on some of their facilities west of Tiberias. I'm sure this—"

"The Water Carrier," Johnson cut him off. "I know about that."

"I'm sure any increase in troop strength is a response to that incident," Rusk said, finishing his sentence.

"Well, I don't like it," Johnson huffed. "I just don't like it. Ask a guy to help you out and this is what he gives you."

"If you feel that way, Mr. President," Rusk suggested, "perhaps you should call Eshkol and discuss this with him directly."

Johnson looked over at Smith. "What do you think, Steve?"

"I think it won't hurt to talk to him. Of course, there's no way to discuss it without letting him know how you know they increased their troops."

Johnson looked puzzled. "You think I should keep that from him?"

"I'm saying, I don't think you can talk about it without revealing that fact. The point of the call is to ask why he increased his troop strength. The next question will be, How do you know? You'll have difficulty finessing your way around an answer to that without telling him about our reconnaissance overflights."

Johnson seemed not to hear the suggestion. "I told him we needed them to hold the line on any broad response. We don't need a full-scale war over there."

Rusk spoke up. "Mr. President, do you want me to arrange the call?"

"Yeah," Johnson sighed. "I guess you better."

"I'll get them on it right away," Rusk rose from his chair and started toward the door.

— • —

Eshkol was in his office when an assistant entered to tell him Johnson was on the line. Eshkol picked up the receiver and Johnson began immediately. "I thought you were going to help us out over there. Hold this thing together for me."

"I'm doing the best I can, Mr. President."

"Sources tell me you might be thinking about a response. I understand they attacked some of your facilities but I really need you to refrain from any serious steps."

"We've increased our troop strength in Galilee," Eshkol snorted with an exasperated tone. He was perturbed at Johnson's arrogance in telling him how to protect his own country. "That is all. The troops are patrolling our own territory. Within our own borders. We've done nothing else."

"I don't think that's such a good idea," Johnson argued. "Syria will know what you're doing. The Russians will tell them. The Russians have as good or better intelligence in the area than we do and we saw the increase. The Russians will see it, too."

"Yes, Mr. President," Eshkol struggled to tamp down the rising anger he felt inside. "The Syrians know many things."

The door to Eshkol's office opened and his chief of staff, Baruch Shatilov, entered. Eshkol pointed to a chair near the desk. Shatilov took a seat as the call continued.

"This will only raise tensions in the region." Johnson's tone became more strident. "Maybe even the entire region, and you know as well as I do, tension over there is high enough already."

"We have been exercising restraint," Eshkol countered, raising his voice in response to Johnson's, "even before you asked, but they have continued to attack us and to kill our people. I do not have the luxury of simply sitting by and watching. My people demand more. The responsibility of my office requires more."

"I know it's tough," Johnson suddenly lowered his voice. "But I'm doing all I can and will continue to do whatever it takes to keep the Syrians from invading, but you gotta help me some."

"Yes, Mr. President."

"We don't need another incident."

"No, Mr. President." Eshkol decided to simply wait out Johnson's call without acquiescing. He would listen as politely as possible, but he would continue to do whatever he felt was in Israel's best interests. "We certainly don't need another incident."

"What do you hear from the Egyptians?" Johnson asked, his voice now calm and even.

"I have heard nothing from them about this."

"The Syrians seem to make a point of using every incident to prod them into action. You haven't seen any troop movements to the south?"

"No, Mr. President. We have not. Have you?"

"No. But I would think activity in the Sinai Peninsula would be an indication of trouble."

"A better indication is the Straits of Tiran," Eshkol suggested, seizing the moment to send what he was sure would be seen and understood as a signal. "A line beyond which the Egyptians could not go without triggering a military response."

"The straits?" Johnson asked. "Why the straits?"

"If they are serious about an attack against us," Eshkol explained, with a knowing glance toward Shatilov, "the first thing they will do is close the straits. That is our lifeline to the Indian Ocean. With it, we have no need of the Suez Canal for shipments in either direction—east or west. If they close the straits, we'll know they are serious."

"Then let's hope they don't do that."

When the call ended, Eshkol returned the receiver to the telephone cradle and looked over at Shatilov. "Can you believe that guy?"

"Think he understood what you were saying?"

"About what?"

"About the straits."

"Was I too strong about that?"

"No," Shatilov shook his head. "Maybe not strong enough."

"I didn't want to be too obvious. I didn't want to box us in on a response."

"But they need to know that if the Egyptians close the straits, we will view it as an act of war and cause for military action."

"Yeah," Eshkol sighed. His eyes darted away. "I suppose they should."

"Are you ready for that?"

"For war?"

"To respond with military force should they close the straits."

"If they close the straits," Eshkol replied with a heavy voice, "we will have no choice."

— · —

Later that afternoon, Golda joined Dayan at Eshkol's office to discuss Eshkol's conversation with Johnson. The meeting began with a review of American consternation regarding Israel's policy in the Galilee and quickly grew into an examination of the likelihood that war would erupt. It was a far-ranging conversation that, at times, became heated as their differing views became evident.

When the meeting finally ended, Golda and Dayan left together. As they walked down the hallway, Dayan glanced over at her. "You seem tired."

"I *am* tired."

"Are you okay?"

"It's just the job," she sighed. "All the tedious points and counterpoints. Sometimes I think Eshkol would be better off being his own foreign minister."

"Is that what you were alluding to the other day?"

"I can't really talk about that right now. Just give me a little more room."

"Take all the time you like." Dayan leaned closer and lowered his voice. "I would hate to see you go, but I understand completely."

"Abba would be a good man for the job, don't you think?" Golda contravened her earlier refusal to discuss the matter and all but admitted she was ready to quit.

"Yes," Dayan agreed. "He would be an excellent choice, but he wouldn't be you."

The words struck deep in her heart and Golda felt a lump in her throat. She swallowed hard. "You do realize, don't you," she changed the subject, "that a policy of constantly raising the stakes will inevitably take us to war."

"Yes," Dayan nodded. "I was thinking about that while we were talking in there," he motioned over his shoulder toward Eshkol's office. "We are becoming a self-fulfilling prophecy. Causing the very thing we seek to avoid."

"Arabs attack our facilities, so we put more troops in Galilee," Golda continued. "A perfectly logical response. But if we put more troops in the Galilee we raise the possibility of actually going to war with our neighbors."

"I've come to see it as a characteristic of...us," Dayan's tone was philosophical. "We have our own identity as Israelis and as Jews. They have theirs as Arabs. But when you put all of us together, you get this other identity. Syrians, Lebanese, Jordanians, Egyptians, Jews—separately we are one thing, but together we form a third person who is constantly at war with themself."

Golda gave him a wry smile. "You were thinking of all that while we were talking to Eshkol?"

"I don't think like that when I talk to him. I think like that when I talk to you."

"Well," she avoided the obvious compliment, "all I know is, if our response to prevent attacks actually incites our neighbors to attack, then the Arabs will have won. FATAH will have accomplished its goal."

"But what else can we do?" Dayan shrugged. "What can Eshkol do? He was elected by the people. They expect him to protect them. And if he can't do that, they won't see him as a viable prime minister. No one will, actually. If he can't adequately address the Arab problem, he'll be gone from office before the end of the year."

"Don't get me started on that topic," Golda rolled her eyes.

CHAPTER 26

ON THE ROAD EAST OF HADERA, Auerbach glanced up to check the rearview mirror and saw a pickup truck closing fast behind them. "This could be trouble."

Suheir looked at him, her eyes wide and alert. "What's wrong?"

Auerbach glanced in the mirror again. "That."

Suheir turned to look through the rear window. By then, the pickup truck was less than five meters away. "That's Ahmad," she cried with alarm. "He's driving the truck."

"How many are with him?"

"I can't tell exactly. It looks like two are in front. One of them is Yezid and I think the man beside him is the one they call Masood. But I can't tell how many more are riding in back." She was frantic. "What will we do?"

"I don't—" Suddenly Auerbach's head snapped backward as the truck rammed their rear bumper. Auerbach struggled to maintain control as Ahmad slid the truck off the bumper and accelerated, ramming the truck's fender against the rear fender of the car. "I can't hold it!" Auerbach shouted.

"Why are they doing this?" Suheir screamed. "We're going to crash!"

The car swerved hard to the right. Auerbach snatched the steering wheel to the left, caught the car once, then back right before it slid down the grade on the shoulder of the road, coming to rest with the wheels buried in the soft dirt of a drainage ditch.

In a matter of seconds, Ahmad stood at the driver's door. "Get out," he demanded and brandished a pistol to reinforce his command. Auerbach pushed open the door and climbed from behind the steering wheel. Ahmad grabbed him by the shoulder and shoved him against the car. "You should have never come back," he snarled.

"I had to. I'm in love with your sister."

"You're an idiot."

"I love her. I have always loved her."

"Shut up!" Ahmad shouted, and slapped Auerbach on the back of the head. "You know nothing of love. Not true love. Not the love that stands up for the truth no matter the cost."

In spite of the threatening tone in Ahmad's voice, Auerbach turned to face him. "I know enough to travel halfway across the world to find Suheir again," he answered calmly.

"You were stupid for doing this." Ahmad leaned closer and lowered his voice. "You have put all our lives in danger." He shoved Auerbach aside and leaned through the car's open door. "Get out," he orderd Suheir.

She slid across the front seat and came from the car on the driver's side. "Why are you doing this?"

"Shut up," Ahmad retorted. "I'll ask the questions."

"You would speak to me this way?" she said in an indignant tone. "Are you not my brother still?"

"Shut up!" Ahmad shouted. "Just shut up."

"We only want to be together," Suheir continued, ignoring his command. "Is that so bad? Can't you see that? Can't you understand?"

"I understand many things."

"Yes, and you know I love him. I have always loved him." She took hold of Auerbach's arm at the elbow. "And he has always loved me. You know these things are true."

Yezid, one of the men with Ahmad, stepped up. "Let's kill them now and get it over with." He was armed with a Kalashnikov rifle and he pointed it at Suheir. "Arafat was expecting us back long before now."

Ahmad's eyes were wide with fright at the sight of the rifle pointed toward Suheir. He reached for it with his right hand to push it away. Just as quickly, Yezid pivoted, turning the rifle toward Ahmad. When Ahmad pulled at it to free it from Yezid's grasp, the rifle fired, discharging a round into Ahmad. He staggered backward, gasping for breath, then collapsed to the ground with blood pouring from his chest.

"No!" Suheir screamed as she lunged toward him and took him in her arms. "No, no, no," she cooed, gently rocking him back and forth. The others who came with Ahmad watched in silence as Auerbach knelt at her side.

Yezid glowered over them. "I hate your brother," he seethed, nudging Ahmad's abdomen with the muzzle of the rifle. "And I hope he dies a miserable death. But I will give *you* a choice. Leave this country with your American boyfriend, and never return, or forsake him and return to your home in Degania. If you stay here with this man," he punctuated his words with a shove against Auerbach's shoulder, "we will find you and we will kill you both." Then he gestured to the others and they started toward the truck. A moment later, with Yezid behind the steering wheel, he drove the truck onto the road and back in the direction from which they'd come.

As the truck neared the crest of the next hill, two IDF jeeps appeared in the distance, traveling from the opposite direction, toward the fleeing truck. In a few minutes they reached the car where Suheir and Auerbach sat with Ahmad. The first jeep continued past them, accelerating as it gave chase in pursuit of Yezid and the others. As it sped by, Auerbach saw three men seated inside.

The second jeep came to a stop at the car. Two soldiers sat on the front seat and one of them stepped out. He approached Auerbach. "What happened to him?" he looked toward Ahmad, whose lifeless body still rested in Suheir's arms.

"Those men in that truck shot him," Auerbach explained.

The soldier knelt next to Suheir and gently pulled back Ahmad's shirt, exposing the gaping wound in his chest, then checked for a pulse. "This man is dead," he stood to face Auerbach. "What is his name?"

"Ahmad Hadawi."

"The men who did this were in that truck?" he asked, gesturing up the highway.

"Yes."

"Any idea who they were?"

"They are FATAH," Suheir said.

The soldier looked down at her, his eyes suddenly alert with interest. "With Yasser Arafat?"

"Yes," she nodded. "We were trying to escape from them and they chased us."

"How do you know they're FATAH?"

"This is my brother," she nodded in Ahmad's direction. "He was one of them."

The soldier looked at Auerbach. "You're an American."

"Yes."

"You're with her?"

"I am Yaakov Auerbach. She is Suheir Hadawi."

The soldier gestured with an open palm. "You have an identity card?"

"I have a passport," Auerbach replied. He dug it from his hip pocket and handed it over.

The soldier opened the passport, glanced at the name, and checked the photograph. "We have a report on you." He handed the passport back to Auerbach. "Important people are looking for you. You'll have to come with us."

"I can't leave Suheir."

"We have orders to return you to IDF headquarters in Tel Aviv. They didn't say anything about her."

"Then I'm not leaving."

"I...don't know," the soldier sighed. "I'm not sure we can—"

Instinctively, Auerbach dropped to the ground at Ahmad's feet. "If she doesn't come, I won't, either."

The soldier still seated in the jeep spoke up. "We can take you by force."

"Please," Auerbach implored the man standing over him. "Just let her come with us."

The soldier thought for a moment, then finally agreed. "All right. But wait here with the girl."

With Auerbach holding Suheir back, the two soldiers lifted Ahmad's body and placed it in the back of the jeep, then pulled the car from the ditch to the road. One of them got in behind the steering wheel while Suheir and Auerbach took a seat in back, then they followed the jeep up the road.

— • —

A few hours later, Auerbach and Suheir arrived at IDF headquarters in Tel Aviv. They were debriefed by two officers, then placed in a lounge room to wait. Half an hour later, Shahak appeared. He glanced at Suheir and pointed to her dress. "You need a change of clothes."

"It's the blood of my brother. What do I do about it?"

"You could start by putting on something else."

"His blood is sacred." Tears formed in her eyes. "He is dead, you know."

"Yes," Shahak nodded. "I know. And I'm sorry."

"He brought it upon himself." She blinked back the tears. "But I miss him." Auerbach slipped his arm around her shoulder and pulled her close.

Shahak glanced at him. "Are you okay?"

"I'm fine."

Shahak shook his head. "What were you thinking when you took the car?"

"Am I in trouble?"

"I don't think so," Shahak shrugged. "They got it back, so they seem happy."

"That day when I took the car, how did you get back here?"

"I caught a ride in a truck. Several trucks, actually."

"Sorry."

"Don't worry about it." Shahak turned again to Suheir. "What do you plan to do now? I don't think you can return to Degania. At least not right now."

"We want to be together," Auerbach offered.

A frown wrinkled Shahak's forehead. "Here?"

"No, in New York."

Suheir spoke up. "I want to go to America with him."

Shahak grinned. "You're both crazy."

"Think you can help us do that?" Auerbach asked with a smile.

Shahak gave a heavy sigh. "I'll make some calls and see what we can do."

— • —

A few days later, Golda asked for a meeting with Eshkol. He agreed to see her late in the afternoon. She arrived to find the office staff was already gone for the day. They sat in comfortable chairs on the far side of the room from the desk.

"So," Eshkol began when they were seated, "what did you need to see me about?"

"My resignation," Golda answered, getting straight to the point.

Eshkol appeared taken aback. "I...know we've had disagreements, but ..."

"You need someone who can take you where you want to go." Golda spoke with confidence and resolve. Her mind was made up. "I'm not that person."

"I'm not sure I know what you mean."

"With me, you will always feel that Ben-Gurion is looking over your shoulder."

Eshkol nodded. "He casts a long shadow over us all."

"And I can't change that." Golda leaned back, resting against the chair, her legs crossed at the ankle.

"I understand what you are saying, but I do not want you to resign. Can't we work this out?"

Golda shook her head. "I was thinking Abba Eban would be a good person to replace me."

"Abba is an excellent choice for almost any position but I—"

Golda continued before he'd finished. "Abba was close enough to events from the past to experience them in their context, but far enough from Ben-Gurion and me to be free of our suppositions. And, he's brilliant."

Eshkol's shoulders slumped as he reconciled himself to the inevitable. "It will take time for him to make the transition. We'll have to find someone to replace him at the United Nations."

"The sooner the better," Golda responded. "We have several people who can step in, at least for the short term. Michael Comay is ready to take over."

"You've spoken to him?"

"No. I mean, in my opinion, he's developed the experience and expertise to handle the job. He's ready for it. Gideon Rafael would be another option."

They talked awhile longer with Eshkol trying again to dissuade her, but finally he realized it was no use opposing her. He never told her the confidence he had in her or how scared he was to see her go. She didn't tell him about her health issues.

Golda's departure from office was explained to the public as a desire for time to rest and reflect after long years of service. A book deal for her memoirs—something that had been in process for months—was announced and several receptions were held to celebrate her contribution to the founding of the nation of Israel. A few weeks later, with Clara at her side, she departed for New York, ostensibly to visit family and friends she hadn't seen in years. Not long after that, Eshkol welcomed Abba Eban to Jerusalem and a seat in the cabinet as foreign minister.

— • —

Abba Eban arrived with little fanfare and went straight to work. One of his first meetings was with Moshe Dayan to review the military situation. They talked about defense of the Negev against Egypt, the threat of attack from Syria and Jordan, and conditions in the Galilee. Dayan provided details of the most recent Arab attacks and the intelligence they'd received that pointed to an Arab-Syrian strategy of provocation in an attempt to create a pretext for war.

"Arafat organizes local Arabs," Dayan explained. "The Syrians finance him and support him with logistics, but the attacks are not committed by marauding gangs coming over from Syria. These attacks are committed by people who live in the Galilee. Recruited and trained by Arafat."

"I'm not sure it makes any difference to the people who live up there where they come from. Either across the border or within, they're the ones forced to endure the hostilities," Eban replied. "But our greatest threat isn't that they will provoke us into attacking Syria. If we did that, we would have bigger problems than the Egyptians."

"You mean the Russians?"

"Yes," Eban nodded. "If we attack the Syrians, they will attack us. That's what Nikolai Suslov told me before I left New York."

"Eshkol knows this, so there's not much chance of that happening."

"All the same," Eban cautioned, "we would do well to remind him often."

"Outside of that," Dayan continued, "what do you see as our greatest threat?"

"That Syria will succeed in pressuring Egypt to attack us. Egypt is our greatest threat. The traction they get with their own people from the lies they tell about us indicates to me that they could attack us at any time with no domestic repercussions. In fact, the momentum is starting to shift in the opposite direction. They've talked about attacking us so long their people are now agitating for it."

"I don't know how they get away with it, either," Dayan said, shaking his head. "Arafat attacked one pump station in an attempt that failed miserably, but they said, 'We attacked. We will not be held down by the imperialists. We will drive them into the sea.' And the people rejoiced, having no idea that the explosion had no effect."

"It's madness, I agree," Eban replied. "And that's the part that frightens me most. The shift from the lie as the lie, to the lie as the truth."

CHAPTER 27

THE NEXT DAY, YEZID ARRIVED at the farmhouse in Afula with his clothes torn and tattered. Clumps of dried blood were caked on his shoulder from a flesh wound and his face was streaked with grim. Arafat met him on the porch at the front door. "What happened?"

"We found them—the girl and the American—on the road east of Hadera," Yezid reported wearily. "But the Zionists surprised us."

"Where is Ahmad?"

"Dead."

"Dead?" Arafat seemed genuinely troubled by the news. "What happened to him?"

"We stopped them and took them from the car. Ahmad, to his credit, was prepared to shoot them but—"

"He was willing to kill his own sister?"

Yezid nodded proudly. "They begged for their lives, but he said we had no choice. That they knew how to find us."

The troubled look on Arafat's face turned to skepticism. "Why did you bother to take them from the car? Why not shoot them right there, while they were still inside?"

"The American was already out. Ahmad used the truck to force them from the road into a drainage ditch. The American jumped out as soon as the car came to a stop. Before we could deal with him, the girl came out, too."

"Then Zionists attacked?"

"We had them behind the car, ready to shoot them. I offered to do it, but Ahmad said the girl was his sister and he'd do it. Before he could shoot, Zionist soldiers topped the hill and were coming toward us. Masood shot at them."

"And then they shot back."

"Yes. They shot at us and killed Ahmad. The rest of us made it to the truck but the Zionists continued to fire at us. Then they chased us as we drove away."

"Where is everyone else?"

"Two were shot. Masood is dead. The others were captured."

"And you alone escaped?"

"Yes."

"Where is the truck?"

"Destroyed. The Zionists forced it from the road."

Yezid, of course, knew better than to tell Arafat the whole story and continued to describe events in a light most favorable to himself, omitting the part about how Ahmad really died, how he drove the truck from the highway and crashed it into a dry wadi, then left the others to fend for themselves as he fled. Instead, he told about how they fought from behind the truck until the ammunition was gone, then set the truck on fire to cover their escape, all of which was untrue.

Apparently satisfied with the story, Arafat led Yezid inside where he repeated the story to the rest of the men. They welcomed him as a hero, but after listening to his version of events several of them became concerned that he might have been followed. Arafat agreed. To protect themselves, that night they packed everything inside the house, wiped the place clean of any indication they'd been there, and moved to a remote area not far from Beit Hillel in the extreme northeastern corner of Israel. There they discussed strategy for the future.

"Ahmad and Masood are dead," Arafat began. "I know many of you followed him faithfully." His eyes darted from man to man, searching for the slightest sign of a reaction. "Others of you are not sorry to see him go." He paused a moment as if expecting a response, "Regardless of how you feel about him, we must continue the fight."

"Should we not attempt to free those who were captured?" someone asked.

"It is of no use," another replied. "If they were wounded as Yezid has informed us, they are better off there than here. We cannot care for them."

"Besides," Yezid offered, "they are likely dead by now."

"Our sources have indicated they were taken to a secure facility in the Negev," Arafat explained. Yezid was surprised to learn that Arafat had extensive contacts among the Zionists and worried that he might actually know the truth of what happened with Ahmad and Suheir. Still, he dared not say anything and did his best to hide his concern. Arafat continued, "Recovering them would be highly problematic, but we should not forget our obligation to them and, if the possibility to free them arises, we should be ready to take full advantage of it."

Izzat Farsoun, who had been with Arafat from the beginning, spoke up. "What do we do next?"

"I must confess," Arafat answered, "that is a most frustrating question, and one I ask myself continually. We have done all this and still there is nothing. Surely we have not pleased Allah, but I do not know where we have failed."

"We must target more places," Farsoun suggested. "Redouble our efforts. The water carrier, local farms, businesses."

Others in the group nodded in agreement. "Hit them all."

"Hit them everywhere we find them."

Comments continued around the room. "Get our people to attack wherever they are. See a Jew, shoot him. Just like the Nazis in Germany. With the help of people on the street, they almost killed them all."

"If the Americans hadn't stopped them."

"We should make the Zionists pay a price too heavy to bear."

"Hitler made them pay and they got out. That's why they are here. We should send them on somewhere else, too."

Farsoun returned to his earlier suggestion. "We need to hit many places, but we should choose locations closer to the Syrian border. That way, there would be a greater possibility they will drift across the border. Then the Syrians could attack them for their intrusion."

"The Syrians are supposed to be our allies," someone said. "They should come across the border and help us like true friends, instead of staying up in the hills with their artillery, where it's safe. We take all the risk. We are the true liberators of Palestine. None of the others will act without prompting from us."

"But if they come across the border," Yezid argued, "then they will be invading Israel. *They* will be starting the war. If *they* start it, there is no assurance any of the others will come to their side."

"There is no assurance if they do not start it, either," Farsoun argued.

Yezid shook his head. "I do not think you understand these things."

"It is only a matter of time," someone else suggested. "We will get them if we simply continue to attack."

"No," Farsoun argued, his voice becoming more strident. "The Jews have tolerated us so far because not many people have been killed."

Arafat had a puzzled frown. "What are you saying?"

"Our attacks here have been too small," Farsoun explained. "That is the problem. If we make more people die, they will be forced to do something. And then we'll have war. A war in which they will be seen as the aggressor. Then we will achieve the liberation of our people. Then Allah will be proud."

— • —

A few nights later, Arafat and his men attacked Ramat Yosef, a small village east of Alumot near the Syrian border. Using munitions and explosives obtained from the Syrian army, they blew up a dozen houses and set others on fire. When the people ran from the burning structures, Arafat and his men shot them down, brazenly standing in the street, firing at will while the houses went up in flames. Dozens were slaughtered.

Within minutes of the attack, an IDF infantry squad responded and engaged Arafat and his men. In the face of a withering onslaught, several of Arafat's men turned to run but Arafat badgered and cajoled them into fighting a little longer. Then two of his men were killed and he gave the order to run.

As they fled, two IDF tanks arrived, accompanied by three trucks carrying infantry troops. The trucks and one of the tanks pursued Arafat and his men as they dashed eastward to the border, but the IDF units stopped short of crossing the border and their guns fell silent. Arafat was frustrated. "What happened?" he asked as he pounded the steering wheel with his fist. "What happened? Why didn't they follow us?"

"They know," Yezid replied calmly.

Arafat looked over at him. "They know what?"

"They know where the border is located, and they know what will happen if they cross it. They also know what we are trying to do."

"How do they know what we are doing?"

"I don't know," Yezid shrugged. "But they know." He gave Arafat a faint smile. "We need a different strategy."

"Now you sound like Ahmad," Arafat grumbled.

"He was right about this. I hated him. And I still hate him. But he was right. If we want to provoke the Zionists, we should be attacking positions near Jerusalem."

— • —

While the attack on Ramat Yosef was still in progress, Dayan received a report from General Greenberg, the IDF commander, providing him with details of the conflict. Dayan reviewed it, then traveled to Jerusalem to brief Eshkol. After listening to Dayan's report, Eshkol said simply, "Make sure you brief Abba Eban."

"This might be too terrible not to respond," Dayan suggested. "You will call a cabinet meeting?"

"Yes, but not right now. I want to think about what we should do, and I want you to have time to talk with Eban first. And," he sighed, "I suspect President Johnson will be calling soon."

"No doubt they've heard by now."

"Yes," Eshkol said slowly. "No doubt they have."

Before Dayan could leave, the office door opened and Eshkol's assistant entered, informing him that President Johnson was calling. Eshkol glanced over at Dayan. "I told you he would call."

"I'll let you handle it," Dayan chuckled as he turned toward the door. "I find it difficult not to laugh when he speaks."

As Dayan left the room, Eshkol took a seat at his desk and lifted the telephone receiver from its cradle. "Yes, Mr. President," he began.

"These calls are getting to be a regular thing, Mr. Prime Minister," Johnson responded. "A little too regular."

"Yes, Mr. President." Eshkol leaned back in his chair and used a lower drawer of his desk for a footrest. As he'd resolved last time, he decided to listen and say as little as possible.

"My people tell me one of your villages was attacked," Johnson continued.

"Yes, Mr. President."

"I'm sorry to hear about that," Johnson soothed in his best southern drawl. "They also tell me your troops responded to the attacks and chased them as far as the border but no farther."

"Yes, Mr. President. That is correct. We're doing our best to keep things together over here," Eshkol remembered the phrase Johnson used in their previous conversation.

"I'm glad to hear that. I know you have to make a show of force from time to time, but I just want you to remember it's not just the Syrians on the other side of that border. We have to be concerned about the Russians. They're heavily involved in this thing."

"Yes, Mr. President, I'm aware of that."

The conversation continued another ten minutes with Johnson doing most of the talking. When it ended, Eshkol convened the cabinet for an emergency session. They gathered around the conference table in the cabinet room with Eshkol seated near the center, his back to the door. He spent the first five minutes bringing everyone up to date on the call with Johnson. "They're worried about the Soviets," he admitted finally. "Not sure that I blame them, but that can't set our policy."

"Johnson is well-advised to be concerned about Russia," Eban offered. "We should be, too."

Eshkol acknowledged him with a nod then turned to Dayan. "I'm sure everyone already knows about the most recent attack, but perhaps you should recount the details all the same. Arab terrorists led by Arafat attacked Ramat Yosef and—"

"I've had enough of this," Akiva Patt shouted from the far end of the table. "At first they hit a site here and there. Mostly harassment. And we looked the other way. Then they struck the pump station on the water carrier. And we looked the other way again. Now they've slaughtered an entire village. We can't look the other way!"

"Our troops responded," Dayan replied calmly. "They attacked. We struck back and chased them as far as the Syrian border."

"We have the right to pursue them, especially given the fact that the Syrians won't stop them."

"If we do that," Dayan began, "then I am sure we would see—"

"We would see the Soviet army deployed in Syria," Eban interrupted, speaking up without prompting. "Forget about the Egyptian army coming up from the Sinai. We would be facing the Russians. In Galilee."

"They come after us, we go after them, and we're the bad guys?"

"Lebanon, Iraq, Jordan, and Egypt are waiting to attack. I'm surprised it's taken them this long. We can't keep—"

Eshkol cut him off and turned to Dayan. "What troops do we have in the region?"

"We're up to battalion strength with the infantry now. Thirty-six tanks."

"Where are they deployed?"

"They are spread across the region. Not really concentrated in one location, which is how they were able to respond to this attack."

"I still think they are attacking us from inside Syria."

"As I reported before," Dayan continued, "we received information that led us to believe that they have caches of weapons and explosives throughout the region and that they use those when making these attacks. We also believe from local interviews and internally developed information that they have safe houses where they actually stay in the region. After each attack, when we give pursuit, they dash across the border but it is in the hope that we will follow them. Hoping we confront them there."

"On the Syrian side of the border."

"And if we did that," Eban added, "I am certain we would face an ambush by Syrian regular troops."

"What they want is an attack on Syrian soil so they can induce their neighbors to attack us. An attack against us for invading Syria, which they would sell to the international community."

"Syria has been agitating for another war since the end of the War of Independence."

"If we pursue these attackers and engage them in Syria, we will give them that war."

— · —

After the meeting, Eban took Dayan aside. "This level of frustration among cabinet members is not good," Eban observed.

"No, it isn't," Dayan agreed.

"This will drive us toward war as much as tension among the Arabs drives our neighbors."

"I realize that," Dayan nodded. "And I've thought of the next thing, too."

"Which is?"

"If their agenda is driving them toward poor decisions, how good are ours?"

Eban stopped and frowned at him. "You think we're making a mistake?"

Dayan shrugged. "I think we understand that our neighbors intend to attack and that the question is not *if* they attack but *when*. But we might want to ask ourselves if this is the right time for fighting and we might want to consider whether we are prepared for the kind of fighting a war like this would entail."

"You have planners asking these questions?"

"Yes."

"Will anyone listen to them?"

"I am. And General Greenberg is."

"That's encouraging. Who's running it?"

"A young major is in charge of the group, but Mordechai Gur is working with them."

"Mordechai?"

"Yeah."

"How'd you get him to give up his command for planning?"

"This isn't just another planning group exercise. We plan to use what they develop."

"Then it better be good."

Dayan nodded in agreement. "That's why we brought in Mordechai."

CHAPTER 28

AFTER TALKING WITH EBAN, Dayan became concerned about the way events were propelling them toward war. The escalating cycle of troop movements into Galilee, along with the increasing frequency of attacks by Arafat and other Arab groups, and the growing frustration at the cabinet level, seemed like a toxic mix. Momentum was shifting away from peace toward war throughout the region. The cabinet was right. Their policy of ignoring the attacks wasn't having any effect on reducing the number or severity, but responding to each and every attack seemed to only bring more attacks.

With that concern in mind, Dayan focused on the defense ministry's planning efforts with renewed interest. Like many other cabinet officials, he was convinced war was coming, sooner rather than later. This one, however, would be unlike the others they'd fought. The world had changed since the Arab riots of the 1930s and the War of Independence in 1948. Life was more complex, more sophisticated, more technically oriented. For this war, they would have to be prepared in ways few of the older leaders could have possibly foreseen.

In the days that followed the attack on Ramat Yosef, Dayan called a meeting of the Planning Group to which he invited General Greenberg, IDF Commander, and General Bentov, the air force commander. They gathered with Major Segev, Mordechai Gur, and other members of the group to review the group's work.

Segev briefed the gathering and gave them an overview of the group's developing strategy. Dayan was impressed, as were Greenberg and Bentov. "What else do you need to complete your work?" Dayan asked.

Everyone glanced in Gur's direction. Segev nodded for him to respond and Gur rose from his chair to face them. "As we have discussed," he began, "our single greatest threat would come from Egypt. With that in mind, our overall strategy attempts to shape any battle with Egypt into one that appeals to our strengths and forces them to use only their weaknesses. These plans we have developed, if properly executed, would do that." He gestured to a collection of maps and papers that lay on the table. "These plans will dictate the location of the battle and its magnitude. But to execute it properly, we need one missing component and that is the timing of an attack. These plans hinge on Israel attacking first, with IAF making the initial strike. For that to work, the timing would be crucial."

Dayan had a wry smile, "I'm afraid I can't tell you the time of an attack. At this point, any discussion of that would be purely theoretical. Just a scenario. We have no way of knowing if an attack will even transpire, much less a date and time."

"I don't mean a calendar date," Gur explained. "We haven't yet determined which time of day is to our greatest advantage and their greatest weakness. We haven't worked on that part yet and that's the one piece that is missing."

Dayan gestured to a map that lay in front of him. "How would time of day affect these plans?"

"We would open an attack against Egypt with two waves of air raids against their bases." Dayan nodded in agreement. Gur continued. "In order for that to be successful, we need to know which times of day their air force lapses into its lowest state of readiness."

"No one can remain on high alert all the time," General Bentov interjected.

"That's our point," Gur said. "Readiness undulates throughout the day. There is always a point in the daily routine when a force is least prepared to fight. We need to figure out when that point occurs in the Egyptian air force's daily routine."

"I'm not prepared to send spies into Egypt for that kind of information," Dayan replied with a shake of his head. "Not now. Not with things the way they are. If war is to come, we don't want to be the direct cause of it."

Dayan looked curious. "What do you suggest we do?"

"We're talking about the Egyptian air force, right?" The question was rhetorical but Gur looked around the room as if expecting an answer. When no one replied, he continued. "If they fly their planes, they have to talk to someone. We could monitor their radio traffic and figure out what they're doing."

"I don't think they'll be giving out any secrets over the radio," someone scoffed.

"I'm not talking about that. Not directly. Look," he leaned forward in his chair. "They take off. They fly around. They land. They do something next. There's chatter back and forth all day about that stuff." Heads around the room nodded in agreement. "So, we listen to their conversations and extrapolate what we need to know. Log their routine. Listen to their chatter. I think we'd get all the information we need for free. Without sending people down there to collect it."

An aide shouted, "That's a good idea."

"I agree," Dayan nodded. "It's a very good idea. What do you need to do it?"

Someone said, "We'd need the cooperation of Mossad."

General Greenberg spoke up, "Why would you need their help?"

Bentov seemed uncomfortable at the mention of that topic but Gur let it pass. "We would need to monitor Egyptian radio transmissions, and that's part of Mossad's responsibility."

"But it doesn't have to be only their responsibility," Greenberg countered. "Not exclusively." He looked across the table to General Bentov. "You have several bases near the Egyptian border, don't you?"

Bentov cleared his throat. "Yes, we have bases down there."

"Don't those bases have the capability of monitoring radio traffic?"

"We listen to everyone. Jordan. Syria. Egypt. At least we do when our aircraft are aloft."

Gur was surprised. "You already listen to them?"

"Not constantly," Bentov countered. "Just to monitor whether they've seen our planes, how they react, that sort of thing."

"We do the same with their ground forces," Greenberg added. "When we're out on patrols or conducting exercises, we listen to them."

Gur liked what he heard about the ability to monitor Egyptian radio traffic, but he was a little put off by Bentov's reluctance to come forward with the information earlier. "So we're already doing some of this," he was doing his best to speak in his most ingratiating tone. "We just need you to focus on the part we need. Record the transmissions between their planes and their air traffic controllers. Get it on tape." He looked over at Bentov. "You can do that, can't you?"

"As I said," Bentov nodded, "we do that already, on a limited basis."

"On tape?"

"Yes."

"What happens to the tapes?"

"Mossad has agents working with us," Bentov elaborated. "They're on site and they listen to the tapes, screen them, send some of them to Tel Aviv. But they don't take very many. Most of the tapes are simply stored at the base."

Now Gur understood what the matter was with Bentov. The air force had a standing relationship with Mossad. Shaul Nissany, the Mossad director, could be brutal in dealing with those who opposed his policies, one of which was a confirmed belief that Mossad should control every form of intelligence. That's why Bentov was reluctant to share anything about the program. Apparently, Dayan understood it, too.

"Okay," Dayan began drawing the meeting to a close. "Let's leave that existing air force operation intact. We don't want to spend a lot of time sorting through tapes. Let's start our own listening program, run by our own people. That way, we can gather whatever information we need." He looked over at Segev. "You have analysts who can analyze that kind of information?"

"Yes," Segev nodded. "We can do that."

Dayan turned to Greenberg and Bentov. "Let's keep this separate from whatever you're doing with Mossad. They don't need to know about this right now. When the time comes, I'll be the one to tell them but for now let's keep this to ourselves. We need to see whether it will work before anyone else knows about it."

"Very well," Greenberg replied.

When Bentov didn't respond immediately, Dayan caught his attention. "You're good with that?"

"Yes, sir," Bentov nodded stiffly. "That will work."

Dayan turned to Gur. "If we get you the information you want about the Egyptian air force's daily routine, can you figure out the time of day when they are least ready?"

"Yes, sir," Gur replied. "I can."

"Good." Dayan glanced around the room. "Let's get this right. Lives depend on it. Perhaps even our own."

— · —

After Dayan and the commanders left the meeting, Gur and Segev met with several Planning group members.

"I've been thinking about those initial air strikes and I believe we have a problem."

"What's that?"

"We need to know whether the attacks are successful. The second wave depends on the first wave making the runways inoperable. If our first wave isn't successful, and we send the second wave into Egyptian air space, they could be waiting for us. That would be devastating."

"I hadn't thought all the way through that."

"Neither had I, and I was surprised General Bentov didn't bring it up."

"He seemed to have something else on his mind."

"Yes. Well, I suppose we could include a reconnaissance plane with the sorties."

"Maybe one day. But right now, IAF only has a few of those aircraft and they fly slowly by comparison to the jets. Sending them to each location would be a time-consuming process."

One of the others spoke up. "Just use the gun camera footage."

Gur had a blank look. "What do you mean?"

"All of our jets are now equipped with gun cameras. When they come in, we can take out the camera footage from the run, and replace the tapes with new ones. Add it as another step in the reloading and refueling process. Have the tapes analyzed on a rolling basis as the attacks continue. That will give us up-to-date information on each of the runs."

Gur looked over at Segev. "This man has a great idea," he joked. "I think you ought to buy him lunch."

"Maybe I will."

"I'll join you."

CHAPTER 29

AS PLANNED, ARAFAT AND THE MEN he'd gathered in Galilee shifted their focus to Jerusalem. For the next several weeks they ferried explosives and weapons from Syria, through Jordan, to the West Bank town of al-Khader, about twenty kilometers south of Jerusalem. When they had collected enough for two truck bombs, they went to work recruiting young men from the village to join them. Meeting in back rooms and alleys, they sketched their plans for an attack more aggressive than anything they'd ever attempted before, always with enough detail to intrigue, never with enough information to implicate anyone. Their message met with acceptance and enthusiasm among many who were frustrated, angry, and ready to act.

"This time," Arafat promised, "we will not attack unmanned pump stations in the Galilee or helpless farmers in the field. This time we shall strike at the heart of the Zionists, put fear in their souls, and drive them from our land."

Arafat did most of the recruiting. Yezid handled the training, teaching men from the village how to wire explosives, set a charge for maximum effectiveness, and shoot a fully automatic Kalashnikov rifle.

A few weeks later, early on a Saturday morning, the men were divided into two groups. Arafat led a gang of twenty, mostly young and inexperienced Arabs, to attack Beit Aharon Synagogue in a neighborhood on the southwestern edge of Jerusalem. Yezid took a group of fifteen men, most of them older and experienced who'd been with them in the Galilee, to the Chesed El Synagogue in the Old City.

Dressed in traditional garb, most of the men with Yezid posed as typical Jews making their way to synagogue for Saturday services, but beneath their clothes each of them carried half a dozen sticks of dynamite and a firearm. Yezid carried a detonator. Two of the men arrived in a delivery truck packed with explosives, which they parked near the front entrance.

Working quickly but quietly, they planted charges along the foundation of the synagogue building, near the rear wall. When they were set and ready, three of the men took up positions a safe distance from the building but within sight of the front entrance. Most of the men, however, simply walked away, blending into pedestrian foot traffic that filled the street.

When he was certain those who were leaving had time to get safely away, Yezid took the detonator from beneath his jacket and connected it to the wires from individual charges. He twisted the wires tightly in place, gave them a tug to make sure they had a good connection, and pressed the button on top. Immediately, the charges along the foundation exploded.

The force of the blast separated the rear wall of the building from its footing and pushed it out at the bottom, exposing the ends of the floor joists. Windows along both sides shattered, but the roof remained in place.

At the explosion, those who were inside the building ran to the front to escape. They poured through the doorway in a panic, pushing and shoving in a dash for the safety of the street. From his position in back, Yezid heard them shouting and screaming. He chuckled to himself as he took a small two-way radio from his pocket. "Now we finish the job," he whispered as he pressed the radio's talk switch. Instantly, the delivery truck parked at the curb out front exploded. Dust and smoke filled the air as the roof of the building collapsed to the ground. Most of the people who'd been inside were crushed beneath its weight. Those who managed to escape the blast were gunned down by Yezid and his companions.

— • —

That night, Arafat and Yezid combined their teams to hit the village of Even Sapir on the western outskirts of Jerusalem, setting houses on fire and killing residents as they fled. When men arrived to extinguish the flames, Arafat and the others shot them, too, with Arafat himself leading the way. As a result, fire quickly spread from house to house, engulfing block after block in flames as the killing continued through the night. By morning, a majority of the men, women, and children from the settlement were dead and the town was in ruins.

At sunrise, Arafat and his men arrived back in al-Khader where they were greeted with a loud and boisterous celebration. Villagers and calloused members of FATAH danced and sang together as if they'd won a great victory. But as midmorning approached, Arafat quietly passed word to those he'd brought from Galilee. "Gather at the trucks."

One by one, the men drifted from the party and made their way to the house where they'd been staying on the east side of the village. Many of them were drunk. Several were reluctant to stop the celebration. "What are we doing here?" someone complained. "The women are over there," he said, gesturing over his shoulder.

Others laughed but Arafat gestured for quiet. "We must leave," he ordered firmly. "We must leave now."

"Leave? Why?"

"The Zionists will have no choice but to respond," Arafat explained. "And when they do, they will come here. We should be far away by then."

"You think they will come here?"

"I think we don't want to wait around to find out."

"But how would they find us? How would they know?"

Yezid spoke up. "Someone always knows."

"Let them come," another said in a boastful tone. "We'll destroy them just like we destroyed their synagogues and their village."

Yezid gestured toward a truck parked nearby. "Let's go before they figure out where we are."

"Just like that?" another questioned. "We would leave, just like that?"

"You want to stay here," Arafat's eyes bore in on him, "you can die here. There's no middle ground. Get in the truck."

— • —

Within hours of the attacks on the Jerusalem synagogues, Shaul Nissany arrived at Eshkol's residence to brief him. Dayan, preoccupied with the defense ministry's effort to treat the injured and recover the bodies of the dead, let Nissany meet with Eshkol alone.

By evening, as details of both attacks became more apparent, most suspected Arafat was the instigator but specific evidence was still not available. Some focused on elements of the Jordanian army as the culprit, others were convinced both attacks were the work of Arafat and his FATAH cohorts. While the debate continued, Mossad analysts sifted through the growing mound of information gleaned from electronic and human sources. IDF operatives combed through the rubble on the ground, searching for telltale signs that would identify the explosive devices used in the attacks.

Early the following morning, that debate came to an end when Nissany returned to Eshkol's residence to inform him of the attack on Even Saper. Eyewitnesses reported seeing Arafat in the village, directing the killing of innocent women and children. Nissany, bent on seeing retribution dealt out in kind, spared no detail as he described the brutal executions for Eshkol.

While they were talking, Dayan arrived to find them already well along in forming a potential response. Eshkol, seated on a sofa, was visibly shaken. Nissany, seated in a chair to his left, seemed cool, calm, and under control. Eshkol glanced up as Dayan entered the room. "You heard about Even Sapir?"

"Yes," Dayan replied grimly. "We've dispatched units there now."

"Any reports from them on what they've found?"

"Not yet," Dayan answered. "Shall we call a cabinet meeting? Make sure the others are aware?"

"No," Eshkol shook his head. He gestured toward Nissany as he spoke. "I want the two of you to give me recommendations about how to solve this problem. We've been talking about it, but I want you two to discuss the matter and get me a plan...today."

Dayan looked puzzled. "The problem of the attacks?"

"No," Eshkol snapped. "The Arab problem. The Arafat problem. I want you to tell me how to stop them."

Dayan glanced over at Nissany. "You know for certain this was Arafat at the village? The last information we had from you indicated that was a rumor."

"We'd had a rumor that he was at Beit Aharon Synagogue during the attack there," Nissany said, correcting him, "but no one could say for certain. This time, we have more than a dozen people who positively identified him at Even Sapir. He personally killed women and children. This is a fact. Not a rumor."

"That would have been good information to include in your memo to us," Dayan snipped. "Where is Arafat now?"

"It looks like he has been working from al-Khader."

"Looks like?" Muscles along Dayan's jaw tensed. "Is that fact or rumor?"

"It's our best estimate," Nissany pronounced coldly, his calm demeanor beginning to crack.

Eshkol spoke up. "We don't have time for the two of you to waste arguing." He was obviously aggravated and his voice grew louder as he spoke. "Get your best information together and come up with a plan."

Dayan turned to him. "Al-Khader is in the West Bank," he explained. "In territory controlled by Jordan."

"I don't care who controls it," Eshkol shouted. "Level the town if you have to!"

"Mr. Prime Minister," Dayan replied calmly, "that village is in an area controlled by Jordan. If we go in there—"

"I don't care if it's in Hussein's backyard," Eshkol shouted. "If destroying that village will help end this, then level it to the ground! And from now on, when they strike one of our locations, I want one of theirs destroyed in response!" Eshkol leaned forward, pounding a fist against his open palm. "I want to solve this Arab problem, and I want a plan from the two of you to show me how it can be done. No more excuses."

"We can provide you with plans," Dayan's look turned cold as stone. "But you will not want to use them."

"Why not?"

"Because doing what you suggest would require total and absolute war."

"We're in absolute war already," Eshkol fumed. "This is what I mean! I ask for plans, you give me excuses. No more excuses!"

"Eliminating the Arab problem would require us to eliminate the Arabs," Dayan explained in a careful, even tone. "We'd be turning IDF loose to slaughter men, women, and children. They would become like the SS units in Poland and the Russian front. Every nation in the world would turn against us."

"They're already against us," Eshkol snarled.

"Our own people would turn against us," Dayan continued, ignoring the comment.

Eshkol's shoulders slumped and he collapsed back onto the sofa.

"But we have to do *something*," Nissany chimed. "We can't let this one go."

Dayan knew where Nissany stood but chose not to engage him in debate. Instead, he kept his attention focused on Eshkol, who appeared to be backing down from his hard-line position. "Call for a cabinet meeting, Mr. Prime Minister. Let's begin there."

"What good will that do?" Eshkol groused.

"We can inform everyone," Dayan suggested. "Let them have their input about a solution. Bring them along with us."

"But that's just it," Eshkol snapped in frustration. "Where are we going? What does that mean?" He shook his head. "I have no idea what we're doing."

Dayan gave him a knowing look. "I think you know where we're going."

Eshkol stared at him. "Where?"

"To war, Mr. Prime Minister," Dayan said resolutely. "We're going to war."

Eshkol had an incredulous look and his voice grew loud again. "But you just said we shouldn't do that. And I agreed. What are you talking about?"

"Not a war against the Arabs," Dayan explained. "Not a slaughter of innocents. But a war against Egypt. Perhaps against all our neighbors. That is where this conflict is headed and that, I hope, is where it will end."

"We should attack Egypt? Arabs attacked one of our villages, so we should attack Egypt?"

"That's not what I'm saying," Dayan elaborated. "I'm saying the real war is still ahead of us. Out there in the future. These attacks from the Arabs on our synagogues and villages are terrible, but they will not destroy us unless we overreact. Egypt is the enemy that can destroy us. And they are coming, Mr. Prime Minister. Maybe not today. Maybe not tomorrow. But they are coming and we must be ready when they do. And when that day comes, support of the cabinet will be crucial for our effort." Dayan gestured to the telephone that sat on a table near the sofa, "Call your office. Tell them we need a meeting."

"And talk some more?"

"Yes," Dayan nodded. "Talk some more. For now. Because soon we won't have time to talk. We won't have time to convince them of what we must do. We must bring them along every step of the way. This is one of those steps."

— • —

Late that afternoon, for yet another time, Eshkol convened the cabinet to discuss options for dealing with an Arab attack. Nissany was present and briefed members on the latest information. By then there was little doubt, Arafat participated in planning the attacks, recruited local Arabs to assist him, and used the village of al-Khader as his staging ground. Witnesses not only placed him at Even Sapir, they also linked him personally to the death of hundreds. Cabinet members sat in stunned silence as Nissany finished.

General Greenberg was also in attendance and, at Eshkol's invitation, offered plans for a reprisal raid against al-Khader. The mission would be quick, effective, and proportional. Two hundred homes had been damaged or destroyed at Even Sapir, Israel Defense Forces would secure a perimeter around al-Khader and inflict similar damage there. Not by killing civilians but by bulldozing their homes to the ground.

A heated debate ensued over whether to implement the plan. "This is too much," some suggested.

"It is only what they did to us," others countered.

"It's precise," Akiva Patt, the minister of health, noted. "Measured, controlled, and precise. Exactly as it should be."

"We couldn't attack Syria because of the Russian retaliation threat," someone noted. "But we can attack villages within the Jordanian territory without that fear. And we have good reason to do that in this case."

"Villages throughout the region must know," another added, "they cannot allow these groups to operate in their territory."

Gideon Baram spoke up. "Where is the Jordanian army?"

"Our latest reports show most of their units in the south," Greenberg replied. "Near the border."

"Do they have units near the village?" Baram pressed.

"They're about two or three hours away from al-Khader."

Baram found the answers evasive. "We don't know for certain that they don't have units near the village, do we."

"Not for certain," Greenberg sighed. "But that shouldn't be a problem."

"It *shouldn't* be a problem?" Baram asked rhetorically. "What you mean is you *hope* it's not a problem."

"What are you saying?" Patt asked.

"I'm saying that attacking a village is one thing. Encountering the Jordanian army would be quite another."

"We can take them," Greenberg assured.

"I'm certain we can," Eshkol interjected. "And that is the trouble.

And I'm sure it's the point Gideon is making. If the Arabs are looking for a pretext for war, and we enter their territory and engage one of their armies, we'd be handing them more than a pretext. We'd be giving them cause."

"We have a relationship with Hussein," Eban suggested. "One we've been cultivating since...the beginning. Great effort has been expended trying to win him over to our side. An attack into territory under his control would undo that, regardless of whether we encounter his army."

Greenberg bristled at the suggestion that his plan would not work. He glanced over at Eshkol and, without prompting, said, "Mr. Prime Minister, as military responses go, this is a low-risk response."

"Well," Eshkol sighed. "I suppose we have to do something. We can't just sit by and let these attacks go on unimpeded."

"Why?" Eban asked. "Why do we have to issue a military response?"

"Because it was a military attack," Nissany countered.

"It wasn't a military attack," Eban argued. "Saying this armed gang of Arab thugs was military suggests they're part of an army, which suggests the Arabs constitute a separate nation. They don't. We've argued this point for the past twenty years. The Arabs are simply a people. An ethnic group living within the same region as us. They are not a country."

"Be that as it may," Eshkol replied with an indulgent smile, "Akiva and others we've heard here today are correct. We have to respond."

"Then respond by imposing sanctions...close the border with Jordan, ban their commercial flights through our air space—"

"Commercial flights?" Nissany scoffed.

"Yes," Eban argued. "Cease all commercial flights going to or from Jordan through our air space. They'd have to fly all the way around to get to Amman."

"Hundreds of people die," Greenberg chided, "and you propose we stop a few airline jets from passing overhead?"

"I'm suggesting, Mr. Prime Minister," Eban added forcefully, "that we find a diplomatic way to express our indignation."

"Did *they* find a diplomatic way to express *their* sense of indignation?"

Patt shouted from the opposite end of the table. "No! They blew up two synagogues and slaughtered a village!"

"And that is my point," Eban replied, refusing to cower to the verbal barrage. "That is the way criminals act. We are not criminals. We are a nation and if we want to be respected as a nation, we must continue to act like one."

Eshkol looked over at him. "You are opposed to a military response?"

"I think this is a trap," Eban replied. "I know General Greenberg and Moshe think it's a safe play and Shaul thinks it's a good idea, but I think this is a trap."

"Well," Eshkol said calmly, "I think we're about to find out." He looked down the table at Greenberg. "Do you have a timetable for this response?"

"Yes, sir. We can be ready to go within three hours of your order."

"Very well, you have that order. The plan is authorized."

— · —

Late the next afternoon, Israel Defense Forces under the command of Colonel David Laslov surrounded the village of al-Khader. When all access to the town had been cut off, six bulldozers approached from the north and began leveling houses. Residents and onlookers screamed and shouted in protest but the dozers kept moving back and forth, smashing through houses and pushing the debris into a pile.

As they moved through the first block and on to the next, an armed gunman appeared in the street. A shot rang out, striking one of the dozers, followed by five more in quick succession. As the dozer operator ducked out of sight, three more gunmen appeared and a hail of bullets peppered the dozer. Still, it kept moving methodically through first one structure, then another until four men emerged from the last house remaining on the block. They carried glass bottles rigged as Molotov cocktails, which they lit as they ran toward the bulldozer. Seconds later, one of the bottles sailed through the air, smashed against the front of the dozer, and burst into flames. The driver abandoned the equipment and ran. Shots rang out and dust flew as bullets struck the ground behind him. Then a bullet struck the driver in the back and he fell forward, landing face first in the dirt. While he lay there, writhing in agony, one of the men from the house walked calmly over to him and shot him in the head.

Laslov, who'd been watching from atop a tank at the perimeter, keyed the microphone on his radio. "Get the dozers out of there," he ordered. "We'll use the tanks."

Moments later, the turret of a tank to Laslov's right spun around, aiming the barrel of the cannon in the opposite direction, away from the town. Then the tank started forward, crawling slowly in the direction of the nearest house.

Three boys, not more than fifteen years old, ran toward the tank with a bottle in each hand. A burst of fire from the tank's forward machine guns ripped their young bodies in half. Bloody spray filled the air around them as the force of the rounds ripped their arms and legs from their torsos. The bottles they'd been holding fell with them and burst into flames.

All the while, the tank never stopped or even slowed, but kept going until it reached the nearest house. Then the tracks dug into the stucco finish of the wall, climbed partway up the side, and fell forward as the weight of the tank pushed it down. With the wall gone, the roof collapsed atop the tank, but still it never stopped and plowed through the building as easily as if it weren't even there. The tank continued on to the next house and the one after that, working the entire block, moving forward and back as it crushed the structures to dust.

While Laslov watched, the speaker on the radio crackled and an excited voice said, "Colonel, we've spotted a unit of Jordanian regulars headed our way."

"How many?"

"Company size. Looks like about two hundred men, sir. Traveling in trucks."

"Any armor?"

"Yes, sir. Three tanks. Russian. Not the T-55. These appear to be 41s."

"How long do we have?"

"I'd say, at the rate they're traveling, they'll arrive at your position in about twenty minutes."

"Do they know we're here?"

"Difficult to tell, sir. They're traveling at a high rate of speed, but I don't think—" An explosion interrupted the conversation. "Sir, they know *we're* here. I gotta go."

"Meet us at the point."

"Yes, sir."

Laslov pressed a button on his microphone and called Captain Feldman, who was in charge of the perimeter on the south side of the village. "Rabin's got Jordanian regulars in his sights. We're about to have company. Break this off and let's get out of here."

Ten minutes later, Laslov and the units under his command evacuated and headed north, hoping to get beyond the West Bank line before the Jordanian unit caught them. That, however, proved impossible. With no other choice but to defend his troops, Laslov and his men turned to face the Jordanians and for three hours fought a pitched battle. When it was over, the Jordanian tanks were on fire, along with fifteen trucks and two jeeps. Worst of all, 198 Jordanian soldiers were dead.

CHAPTER 30

AS INITIAL REPORTS OF THE RAID on al-Khader reached IDF headquarters, Dayan was concerned that the situation had gotten out of hand. Armed civilians, he thought, posed the worst scenario possible. His evaluation of that "worst case" scenario changed with news of the approaching Jordanian army unit. When the firefight ended with most of the Jordanians dead and a dozen in custody, Dayan knew their worst nightmare had come true.

True to form, Dayan briefed Eshkol, prepared to take the brunt of the blame. Eshkol, however, sat in stunned silence. When he finally did speak, it was only to ask about IDF casualties and whether the men had been properly cared for.

"I suppose the world will condemn us," Dayan muttered.

"I suppose they will," Eshkol replied. "And they will probably spread that blame around to everyone. But before they do I want you to know, this was all my fault. I should have listened to Abba Eban. And to you."

"You did listen, and then you made a decision. That's all anyone can do. Listen and decide. The rest is up to everyone else."

"This will turn out exactly as you said," Eshkol lamented, "with the world lining up against us."

"No one will ever know what I or anyone else said."

"Someone will tell them."

"They will never hear it from me. And you shouldn't tell them, either."

"Why not?"

"You are the head of state. You should have some distance between yourself and operations. Some diplomatic room."

"I'm not going to lie," Eshkol retorted with disdain. "I made a mistake. I'm not covering it up with a lie."

"That's the—"

Just then, the door opened and Abba Eban entered. "The first responses are arriving now."

"How bad is it?" Eshkol asked.

"As we expected, the rhetoric is rather caustic. Everyone so far has condemned us."

"The Americans?"

"Johnson issued a statement castigating us, but I've talked to Rusk. He assured me that while the public conversation would be rough, they would not back down on their support for us. They will honor the deals you signed with them earlier."

"Good."

"See," Dayan said with a gesture of his hand. "We can get through this."

Eban gave Eshkol a questioning look. "You were thinking this would end your government?"

"No," Eshkol replied. "Just the end of many friendships."

"I don't think we'll lose any friends." A wry smile spread across Eban's face. "We didn't have that many anyway."

"I think we'll get through it with the international community," Dayan continued. "The big question is whether our neighbors will react."

"There's news on that front, too," Eban offered.

"What is it?"

"Apparently, Nasser is ordering Egyptian troops into the Sinai."

Eshkol looked over at Dayan. "You knew about this?"

"I didn't know they had sent them, but I knew they were considering it and I assumed he would do something like that."

"Should we be concerned?"

"Not yet," Dayan replied. "It's an obvious move. Let's see how many troops he actually sends. We still have time."

— · —

In the aftermath of the attack, Arafat and FATAH blamed Jordan and berated Hussein for not defending al-Khader. "We who are part of FATAH, the most powerful Arab organization in Palestine," he announced in repeated radio broadcasts, "are the only ones doing anything to combat the Zionists and to protect our people. Jordan leaves them defenseless. Egypt struts around with its chest out proudly, but when trouble comes they cower behind words and fancy language, choosing the turn of the phrase to the turn of the sword."

Syrian officials picked up the accusation, blaming Jordan and Egypt. In a public address shortly after the attack, President al-Atassi, noting Hussein's execution of leading generals—a statement al-Atassi knew was false—argued that Hussein had abdicated his moral responsibility as a ruler and should be overthrown by the people. Later, in an interview with members of the Foreign Press, he said that al-Khader's fate lay at the feet of the Egyptians and that Nasser had fallen under the influence of his colonial imperialist allies. Accusations against Israel, always laced with calls for the dissolution of a Jewish state, seemed mild by comparison.

In the midst of that, President Johnson placed a phone call to Eshkol and blasted the prime minister for blundering into such a volatile and polarizing situation. "You make me look like an idiot. Here I am telling the Russians you can hold this together, and there you are blowing up a village of women and children."

"Mr. President," Eshkol said, trying not to upset Johnson even more, "I am sure you are aware that—"

Johnson seemed not to hear him. "Hussein is barely hanging on over there and now your attack has put him in a bad spot. He can't stand down—you've entered his territory. Violated his sovereign authority. And he can't keep quiet—he's got streets full of protesters demanding his head. And now you have me right in the middle of it."

The tone of Johnson's comments put Eshkol on edge. "Mr. President, this could not be avoided any longer." Anger rose inside as he spoke. "In less than twelve hours, they destroyed two synagogues in Jerusalem and slaughtered men, women, and children in one of the outlying villages. I am their prime minister. I could not avoid the situation." His voice grew more forceful and he pounded his fist against the desktop as he spoke. "If these radicals continue to attack, we will continue to pursue them until they are gone."

"Do you realize how close to war we are over there?"

"Perhaps you should talk to the leaders of Syria, Lebanon, Jordan, and Egypt. They have been sponsoring these attacks." Eshkol was on a roll now and he had no intention of backing down. "Everyone asks us to have patience but no one confronts them over their continued atrocities. The United Nations, which was supposed to protect us from this kind of problem, refuses to even consider our protests. Yet every time we try to defend ourselves, a job the UN should be doing itself, the UN condemns us. You would not allow such attacks to go unpunished in America and we will not allow it here. We will do all we can to keep our citizens safe!"

Baruch Shatilov, Eshkol's chief of staff, stepped into the office as the call ended. Eshkol dropped the telephone receiver in the cradle and shook his head. "He wants us to give them advance notice in the future."

Shatilov's eyes opened wide. "He said that?"

"Not explicitly," Eshkol replied. "But I know that is what he wants."

"We can't do that," Shatilov cuontered, crossing the room toward the desk. "We could never do that."

"I know," Eshkol nodded.

"If we tell them in advance," Shatilov continued, "they will use that knowledge to derail us to suit their purposes. They will exercise a veto over our own decisions."

"I know. I know," Eshkol sighed impatiently. "But we can't survive without them."

— • —

Like most IDF officers, Gur was at first surprised by the death and destruction inflicted by the IDF against the Jordanian army units. But as he focused again on his work with the Planning Group he realized the IDF unit's performance against Jordanian troops might provide useful information for the group's attempts to evaluate IDF's battlefield effectiveness. Combat conditions were impossible to simulate, which meant raw data from actual conflict was the only way to understand a unit's fighting capability. As distasteful as it might seem, Gur wanted detailed information about the battle with the Jordanians and he took that request to Segev. "I've been thinking about this incident with Colonel Laslov."

"It was more than an *incident*."

"It was a battle," Gur replied tersely. "It happened. They did what they were supposed to do. What they were ordered to do. Everyone should get over it."

"I think everyone is trying to forget it."

That comment angered Gur but he pushed his emotions aside and continued. "Colonel Laslov's unit was using the rebuilt Shermans, right?"

"Yes."

"And they have the new 105 Cannon."

"Yes," Segev acknowledged with an exasperated tone. "What's your point?"

"Those rebuilt Sherman tanks have gun cameras, as do the machine guns on the half-tracks. Cameras record every shot."

"Right."

"Images from those cameras could tell us how effective the tanks were in battle."

Segev arched an eyebrow. "You want to see the gun camera footage from those tanks?"

"Yes."

"I'm not sure we can get them."

"Why not?"

"I don't think they want that information disseminated. Most people are running as far from that incident as possible."

"Will you ask?"

"Yes," Segev agreed reluctantly. "I'll ask, but I'm telling them you're the one who wants it. I'd rather not touch this and I'm certain no one else does, either."

"Just ask," Gur said. "I don't think we'll get in trouble for asking."

Later that day, Segev met with General Greenberg and told him of Gur's idea. "Tell him to forget it," Greenberg replied. "No one wants to discuss that incident, much less resurrect images of it."

"I told Gur you'd say something like that."

"This is the kind of thing that ends careers. No one wants to get near it. Gur should know that. And he should stay clear of it, too. I suspect he wants to return to the field one day. He wouldn't want to have something like this anywhere near his record." Greenberg looked Segev in the eye. "Neither would you, for that matter."

"Don't you think that's odd?"

"What?"

"Laslov and his men were simply following orders, executing an operation approved at the top, and doing so quite well. Yet he is the one who is receiving the brunt of criticism."

"What are you saying?"

"I'm saying if there was a problem with what happened, it was with the strategy of attacking the village in the first place, not in Laslov's performance on the field."

"You should be careful what you say about that. You might be talking to someone who approved that strategy."

"But why should Laslov's career be over simply because he followed orders?"

"Laslov will finish out his career with distinction."

"As a colonel."

"Generals have public exposure. If he were elevated to a general, he would be questioned about this matter every time he appeared in public. He wouldn't be able to do his job. Now, was there a point to this meeting?"

"We need the gun camera images from the tanks."

"As I said, you and Gur should stay away from that if you want to go any further than where he is right now."

"I don't think he's thinking of his career, sir."

"I suppose you *are*?"

"Look, we're just trying to come up with the best plan to defend our country."

"And Gur has convinced you that information from the gun cameras can help?"

"Yes, sir. It would help us determine how effective our battlefield tactics are and how well our tanks perform against the Jordanian tanks. They use an older Russian version than most, but seeing them perform on the battlefield would be helpful."

Finally Greenberg agreed. "I'll give you what you want, but I don't think you're going to like it ten years from now."

"If we're still around ten years from now, we might find out. Right now we need to have a look."

A few days later, gun camera tapes from Colonel Laslov's tanks arrived at Gur's office. He and Segev viewed them together, playing them over and over, analyzing every move, shot, and reaction. The Russian tanks obviously had more firepower than the Shermans, but the Russian tanks' bigger, heavier configuration made them difficult to maneuver in soft, sandy conditions and they were all but useless in tight spaces. Gur pointed to the screen. "They had the advantage of speed, which is how they caught up to Colonel Laslov and his unit. But the location of the battle negated their better firepower and made speed a nonfactor. If we could somehow develop strategy and tactics that trap these tanks in similar limiting locations, we could eliminate their advantage every time."

"Those mapping teams are becoming more important every minute that passes."

"Yes," Gur agreed. "We need them now more than ever. Any report yet on what they've found?"

"Their first week's data is just now being collated."

CHAPTER 31

SIX WEEKS LATER, THE RAMAT RACHEL, a dry-cargo vessel of moderate size, departed from the port of Eilat and sailed down the Gulf of Aqaba to the Straits of Tiran on its way to India, fully loaded with grain. As it neared the mouth of the Gulf, an Egyptian naval destroyer came alongside. A sailor at the bow of the destroyer with a megaphone began to speak. "Captain of the *Ramat Rachel*. This is the Egyptian naval ship *Al Gatar*. You have entered Egyptian territory without authorization. Bring your engines to full stop and prepare to be boarded!"

When the *Ramat Rachel*'s captain failed to stop, the Egyptian sailor repeated the warning in Hebrew, English, and Arabic. Still the ship did not stop and the crew of the destroyer manned a small cannon at the ship's bow. Moments later, they fired a warning shot over the *Ramat Rachel*'s bow. At the same time, cannon at fortifications near Sharm el-Sheikh opened with three salvos, dropping shells in the water on the starboard side of the *Ramat Rachel*.

The captain of the *Ramat Rachel* turned to his second mate. "Come about," he ordered and the ship began a slow, steady turn to the left, toward the destroyer.

"Sir!" the second mate shouted. "They'll ram us!"

"No they won't," the captain replied dryly. "They don't intend to start a war over a load of grain."

As the *Ramat Rachel* continued in a lazy arc, the Egyptian destroyer gave way, allowing the cargo ship to continue unimpeded. Slowly, the ship came around to a heading that took it back in the direction from which it came as it sailed up the Gulf toward Eilat. For a while, the destroyer followed at a safe distance, but as the *Ramat Rachel* neared the head of the Gulf, it turned away and passed out of sight.

— • —

Within the hour, news of the *Ramat Rachel*'s encounter with the Egyptian destroyer reached General Greenberg at IDF headquarters in Tel Aviv. He reviewed the captain's report of the incident, then met with Dayan to discuss the situation.

"You realize what this means, don't you?"

"If this really happened," Dayan replied, "and the straits are closed, they've crossed Eshkol's proverbial line in the sand."

"You disagree with the notion that free shipping through the straits is vital to our economic survival?"

"I'm not certain we ship enough through there to fight over it, but that's not my decision."

"No," Greenberg replied. "And neither is it mine, but I suppose we should inform the prime minister of what has happened. If we don't, Nissany and some of his Mossad analysts will beat us to it."

"Let them," Dayan said tersely.

Greenberg seemed taken aback. "Let them?"

"If we tell Eshkol about this now, he'll want to respond. Can you imagine what that response might be?"

"Call up the reserves. Deploy units along our southern border. That's what I intend to recommend."

"Yes. I agree. And when we do that, the Egyptians will send more troops into the Sinai, along with armor to defend them." Dayan's earlier conversation with Golda and later with Eban was now foremost in his thoughts. "And the cycle will continue. They add more, we add more, until we've both reached a force that can no longer be easily sustained. And then we on both sides will inform our leaders that they must decide, war or withdrawal. No head of state, elected or otherwise, wants to be the first to back down. Not in a situation as volatile as this. So we will go to war."

"That may be true, but that is not for us to decide. It is simply the nature of the situation we have at hand. This is what we have inherited and we have no choice but to follow through. We can't simply sit back and watch while they assemble an overwhelming force against which we could not possibly hope to defend ourselves."

"Well," Dayan sighed, "we can't brief him with this kind of information, either."

"Why not?"

"There isn't enough for anyone to make an informed decision, much less a head of state on the verge of sending his country and the entire region into war. We need more details."

"What do you propose we do?"

"Send a surveillance flight."

"Over the Sinai?"

"Yes. It's the only way to know for certain what they are doing."

"If the Egyptians see it—if the Russians see it and tell them about it—we'll be at war before morning."

"Technically, we're already at war. Let's make certain we can talk about it in an accurate manner."

Rather than brief Eshkol immediately, Dayan ordered an aerial reconnaissance flight over the affected area. The aircraft flew to Eilat, then proceeded down the Gulf to the Straits of Tiran, up to the Suez Canal, and back over the Sinai Peninsula, taking thousands of photographs in the process. When it returned, IDF analysts spent the night processing the film and reviewing the images. What those pictures revealed was even more unsettling than the report of the ship's encounter.

"Egypt has moved thousands of troops into the Sinai Peninsula," Greenberg said as he dropped the analysts' report onto Dayan's desk. "And many more are on the way."

"The Straits of Tiran are closed?"

"Yes," Greenberg replied. "Our trade route to the Indian Ocean is blocked."

Dayan spent the next two hours with Greenberg, preparing for yet another meeting with Eshkol to deliver bad news. As they left the office for the ride up to Jerusalem, the phone rang with a call from Abba Eban. Greenberg continued out to the hall. Dayan lingered in the office to take the call.

"I've heard rumors...," Eban began.

"Right."

"You'd better brief Eshkol quickly, before he finds out about it from someone else."

"I'm on my way there now."

"Shall I join you?"

"Yes. By all means. Greenberg is with me. You might as well meet us there."

"I'll be waiting."

Just then, Natan Shahak, Dayan's assistant, entered the office. "There's a report on television you need to see," he said in a whisper.

Dayan covered the receiver with his hand. "I'm on a call."

Shahak ignored him, crossed the room to a bookcase opposite Dayan's desk, and switched on a television monitor. Seconds later, an image of Egyptian president Nasser appeared on the screen. He was standing at a podium delivering a message from the hall of what looked to be a government building. "And so," Nasser said, "I have today ordered troops into the Sinai Peninsula to protect and defend our sovereign claim to the territory. We expect to send additional units as needed to reinforce our ban on all Israeli vessels traversing the Straits of Tiran. And, in conjunction with that effort, we are today calling up all additional reservists to ensure adequate manpower is available to meet our ongoing security concerns."

Dayan moved the telephone receiver back to his lips. "Turn on your television, Abba."

"I have it on now," Eban replied. "You better get moving. Eshkol will see this for sure and he'll want to know why we didn't tell him first."

— • —

When Dayan and Greenberg arrived in Jerusalem they found Abba Eban waiting outside the door to Eshkol's office. "Are you ready for this?" Eban asked.

"We may be at war before morning," Dayan replied.

"I hope not," Eban added. "But it seems inevitable."

"Relax, gentlemen," Greenberg said with a nonchalant attitude. "We're not quite there yet."

Dayan led the way as they stepped into Eshkol's office. Eshkol was seated at his desk, scribbling a note. "I saw Nasser's broadcast," he advised in a flat monotone without looking up. "I'll skip the part about why I had to learn about this from a television broadcast instead of from my own advisers." He glanced up. "I assume that's why you're here."

"Yes, Mr. Prime Minister," Dayan replied.

"Well, give me the briefing so we can get on with what we have to do."

"Yesterday, the *Ramat Rachel*, a cargo vessel loaded with grain, sailed from Eilat bound for India. As the ship entered the Straits of Tiran it was met by an Egyptian destroyer and ordered to halt for boarding. The captain of the *Ramat Rachel* refused to stop and, instead, turned the ship around and sailed back to Eilat."

"They allowed it to do that?"

"Yes, Mr. Prime Minister. And I think that is important to remember as we go through this. They could have fired on it and—"

"I understand they did fire on it," Eshkol interrupted. "The destroyer and a shore battery."

"Those were warning shots," Eban offered, "not meant to strike anything, but rather to reinforce the command to halt."

"And you think that is significant?"

"I think allowing the ship to return to port was significant," Eban continued, picking up with the point he thought Dayan was making.

"How so?"

"According to standard naval procedure followed by navies throughout the world, after the ship refused to stop they should have fired on the rudder to disable it. They did not."

"And you think that's important?"

"Yes," Dayan rejoined the dialogue. "I think it indicates the Egyptians knew you had said that closing the straits was a cause for war and was their attempt not to cross that line."

"I did say that, and despite your opinion, they *did* cross the line."

"I think, to the Egyptians," Eban continued, "refraining from firing on the ship and allowing it to return to port was an indication that they thought they were right at the line, but not over it. That they'd taken steps just short of causing an armed conflict."

"You think they wanted to provoke us so that we would go first, but hold back just enough to argue they didn't cause it?"

"I think they wanted to go right up to the line to satisfy their Arab neighbors, while hoping we would understand the gesture and refrain from making a military response."

Eshkol looked over at Greenberg. "What do you think?"

"Moshe and Abba make an interesting point," Greenberg replied. "But we took the liberty of sending a reconnaissance flight over the area." He produced a packet of photographs. "Pictures from that flight show troop movements into the region, as Nasser announced, with more on the way."

"But," Dayan interjected, "all of them are deployed along the Gulf of Suez and around to the coast of the Gulf of Aqaba, areas well to our south. None of them are deployed near our border."

"How many mechanized units have they deployed?" Eshkol asked.

"None," Dayan replied.

"Their mechanized units will follow," Greenberg added.

Eshkol turned back to Dayan. "You agree with that? They'll put armor in the Peninsula?"

"Yes," Dayan nodded reluctantly. "What they've deployed includes support units for a mechanized division. That would indicate an intention to deploy tanks and other armored vehicles."

"How soon do you think they will deploy those mechanized units?"

Greenberg sighed. "I expect they will begin deploying elements of their Third Mechanized Division within the next few days."

Eshkol leaned back in his chair. "You do realize we'll have to do this briefing again with the full cabinet."

"Yes, Mr. Prime Minister," Dayan replied. "I understand."

— • —

Two hours later, Eshkol convened the cabinet in another emergency session. Dayan, with General Greenberg's assistance, provided members with the latest information, including the suggestion that Egyptian actions may have been an attempt by Nasser to placate his Arab allies, while falling just short of starting a war. When they were finished, Eban spoke up. "This is the threat I warned about. The threat that our neighbors would goad each other into attacking us."

"I don't think that matters much now," Gideon Baram said with a dismissive tone. "How we got here is irrelevant. The question before us now is what we shall do."

Akiva Patt asked, "So, is Egypt really preparing for war?"

"That isn't altogether as clear as it might seem," Dayan replied and offered more detail about the steps they could expect in the coming days should this actually be a move toward war—establishment of staging areas for supplies, introduction of armored units and their support elements, and a continued sustained buildup of ground troops. "The first troops are positioned at strategic points along the Suez Canal, down the coast of the Red Sea, with additional forces at Sharm el-Sheikh. Those are key sites for Egyptian interests and they are far enough away to avoid provoking a direct response from us. At the same time, they would provide a base from which they could operate in a push north toward the border if that becomes necessary. All of which makes the situation difficult to assess."

"How long before they could begin moving northward?"

"Once those first positions are secure and operational," Greenberg answered. "Which should take several weeks to obtain."

"We've told them before," Eshkol added. "We've told everyone repeatedly. If they close the straits we will consider it a cause for war. Now they've closed the straits. We have no choice but to respond."

"We always have a choice," Eban offered.

"Not in the real world," Eshkol barked coldly. "In New York, at the UN building, perhaps. But not out here, where lives are on the line." He glanced down the table to General Greenberg. "Short of launching an attack, or provoking one from them—if that remains avoidable—what can we do as an effective response to Egypt's actions?"

"Call up the reserves," Greenberg replied. "Move three armored brigades to the Egyptian border. Two to the border with Gaza."

"Call up the reserves to active duty?"

"Yes, Mr. Prime Minister," Dayan interjected himself into the discussion. "Each of these steps will send a message that we have an interest in the region and we intend to protect it, without demanding a counter move from the Egyptians. If we must act, these are the most direct and least provocative moves we can make."

"These steps are also necessary preparation for anything else we might do and would be required regardless of what comes next," Greenberg explained.

"What's our state of readiness for a deployment like this?"

Dayan nodded to Greenberg, who answered, "The first units of the army can be in place within the week. The air force is ready to fly now."

Eshkol looked back to Dayan. "We have final plans in place for an attack on Egypt?"

"Yes, sir. They are final enough."

A frown wrinkled Eshkol's forehead. "And by that you mean …"

"Planning is a never-ending process. The longer planners and logisticians have, the deeper they go into the process. But the plan is ready. We can implement it now."

"I need you to brief me on those plans."

"Certainly," Dayan replied.

"Very well." Eshkol glanced around the room. "I'm ordering a callup of IDF reserves and the deployment of three armored brigades to the southern border and two to the border with Gaza. Defense Minister Dayan and General Greenberg can work out the details of which units go to those locations."

CHAPTER 32

THREE WEEKS LATER, A routine—and now daily—IDF reconnaissance flight took off from an Israeli base near Nevatim, south of Hebron, and flew over the Sinai Peninsula. Within the hour, an additional flight left from a base southwest of Beersheba and passed over Egyptian bases at Mansura and Biyala. Both aircraft returned later that day and technicians worked around the clock to process the film.

Pictures from the first flight showed additional troops, along with an accompaniment of tanks and armored vehicles, moving southward from Suez on the Sinai side of the canal. Photos from the flight over Egyptian bases showed fighters and bombers in the process of being loaded with munitions.

General Bentov brought the results to Dayan at his residence. It was almost midnight when he arrived.

"Sir, I hate to disturb you, but we have photographs from the daily reconnaissance flights and I thought you should see the results as quickly as possible."

"Certainly," Dayan said. "Show me what you have."

They stood at the dining room table as Bentov took photographs from a leather satchel and spread them on the tabletop for Dayan to see. "What am I looking at?"

"These first photographs show troop movements," Bentov pointed to apicture on the table. "This is a column moving along the road from Suez down the Gulf toward Sharm el-Sheikh."

"How many men?"

"Best guess is fifteen hundred to two thousand in this group."

"This group? There are others?"

"Yes." Bentov moved to a second photograph. "This is a column moving toward Suez from Cairo."

"Tanks."

"Yes. This is part of the armored brigade General Greenberg told you about earlier."

"Part but not all?"

"Right. This appears to be an initial unit of about one hundred."

"So," Dayan mused, "they're continuing to build up their troops and reinforce their presence."

"Yes, but that's not all." Bentov took additional photographs from the satchel and laid them on the table. "These are fighters," he said, pointing to those pictures. "And these are bombers," he added, moving to yet more photos.

"What are they doing with these?"

"Arming them." Bentov pointed to a photograph. "These fighters are being loaded with rounds of ammunition for the guns. That white patch you can see just there is a hatch that's open on the side of the fuselage. It's an access hatch to the magazine." He moved to another picture. "These are fighters also. Those rectangle objects beside them are dollies for missiles that are being loaded beneath the wings." He gestured to a group of photographs that lay to the left. "These are carts for bombs that go inside the bombers. As you can see, some of the carts are empty and some are full."

"How long until they are fully loaded?"

"To load them all, fighters and bombers, two days at most. But they wouldn't need to load them all to pose a threat."

"Are the planes fueled?"

"Difficult to determine from these photographs alone. Arming is normally the first step. Fueling is normally the final step in the process. They top them off before leaving."

"Have they begun the fueling process?"

"We don't see any signs of it." Bentov took another photograph from the satchel. "These aircraft are parked by groups. We think these have been fully armed. The fueling area is over here," he explained, pointing. "As you can see, the planes are parked quite a distance from the fueling area."

"They can't fuel them there with a truck?"

"Yes. But normally they do not do that." Bentov pointed to the right side of the picture. "Planes move from the area where these are parked, over to the fueling station." He traced the route with his finger. "And then out to the runway. It's an orderly process. Something they learned from the British. But it usually begins as part of the sortie. Fuel and go."

"This looks like a large number of aircraft."

"Yes, sir. Very large."

"Enough for a preemptive attack on our positions?"

"More than. They wouldn't need half this many to take out most of our defenses."

"How long before they can fly?"

"If they were launching a preemptive strike, they'd want to take out as many targets as possible on the first attempt. To get that many planes airborne in a single sortie they would need twenty-four hours. But they could mount a formidable force within minutes."

"How old are these photographs?"

"They were taken about twelve hours ago."

"So we could be looking at an attack within the next twelve hours."

"In a worst-case situation," Bentov replied. "Yes."

"Any hint the Americans know about this?"

"Nothing from the usual channels."

"If they knew, do you think they would tell us anything in advance of an Egyptian attack?"

"Difficult to say," Bentov answered. "The Americans are so caught up in their internal politics right now—Vietnam War and all that. I don't know whether they'd tell us or not. But I don't think we should count on their assistance."

Dayan sighed. "Has the prime minister seen these?"

"No, sir. Not at all."

"What about General Greenberg?"

"No, sir. Came straight to you with it."

"Well, then, come with me and we'll brief Eshkol together."

"Shouldn't we include General Greenberg?"

"I'll tell him to meet us at Eshkol's residence."

— · —

Dayan and Bentov arrived outside Eshkol's home just ahead of Greenberg. They waited while Greenberg's car turned in off the street, then briefed him on the Sinai situation while standing in the driveway. Afterward, all three went inside to see Eshkol. It didn't take long for Bentov to run through the details.

"So," Eshkol said as Bentov finished. "The buildup continues, the straits are closed, and there is nothing left for them to do but fuel their planes and attack us."

"Yes," Dayan agreed with a nod.

"What do you gentlemen suggest we do?"

"As difficult as it is to say this," Dayan began, "I think we have no choice but to attack now."

"Difficult? Why is that difficult? It's obvious."

"Obvious, yes," Dayan conceded. "But difficult because I know what the men on the ground will face. I've been in battle before. It's not easy, even under the best of circumstances."

"Are we prepared to launch an attack?"

"We can be ready to initiate our plans within two days."

"Two days," Eshkol grumbled as he looked over at Greenberg. "You agree with that?"

"Yes, Mr. Prime Minister." "The first wave of the attack will come from the air force. That will give us an extra two days to move ground units into position. So we should be in good shape."

Eshkol had a puzzled frown. "An extra two days?"

"An attack on Egyptian air force targets would likely take two days to complete," Dayan explained. "The first day would concentrate on disabling their runways. The second wave would destroy their airplanes. With the armored units already positioned along the southern border, we should have plenty of time to move the infantry into place. We can continue adding troops as they become available but we should be up to sufficient strength by the time the air force completes its initial mission."

"You still intend to siphon off some of those aircraft and use them to support the tanks in the desert?"

"Yes, sir," Greenberg interjected. "That's the plan."

Eshkol gave Dayan a weary look. "We can't wait any longer. We'll attack on Monday."

Dayan nodded. "Should we inform the Americans?"

"Not now," Eshkol replied. "If we tell them now, they will only try to persuade us to wait. I do not want a debate with Johnson about what we should do. We are a sovereign nation. We have the right to defend ourselves, and we have a right to take preemptive action when necessary. We go on Monday."

CHAPTER 33

ON THE MORNING OF MONDAY, JUNE 5, Major Segev walked from the hallway into Gur's office. Standing just inside the doorway, he gestured toward the hall and said, "Come down to the map room, please."

"I'm in the middle of something," Gur countered without looking up. "Can it wait?"

"No," Segev replied impatiently. "It cannot wait. Do I need to give you an order?"

Gur gave him a puzzled look. "We have a meeting today?"

Segev came closer and lowered his voice. "The prime minister has ordered a preemptive attack on Egypt. It's starting now. I thought we should monitor things for a while."

Gur rose from his chair, his eyes wide with amazement. "We're doing this now?"

"Yes."

"But I've heard nothing—"

"Apparently, that's the way they wanted it," Segev cut him off in midsentence. "I didn't find out about it until just a few minutes ago. Hurry up."

Gur took his jacket from a coatrack in the corner and slipped it on as he made his way toward the door. "Are they following our plan?"

"Word for word," Segev led the way down the hall.

In earlier days, the map room was just that—a room where maps were stored. Detailed maps of the region were available from cubbyholes that once lined the walls, but the room's main feature was a large permanent map the size of a conference table that dominated the center of the room. On it, both in peacetime and in war, assistants identified the position of every IDF unit by placing small wooden tokens at each unit's location—tank-shaped ones for tank units, soldiers for infantry, and planes for the air force. That system, a remnant of World War II, had long since been replaced by a screen on the wall to the left of the door that provided up-to-date information of each unit's position, along with the last known position of units from the armies of neighboring countries. Across the room to the left, a modern communications center was in constant contact with IDF units wherever they were located, feeding a constant stream of information to the room and providing a vital command and control link between the defense ministry, IDF general staff, and troops in the field.

When Gur entered the room that morning he found it already packed with officers far beyond his rank and experience. He wedged himself into a corner and watched as information on the screen was continually updated, showing mechanized and infantry units poised near the southern borders, ready to enter the Sinai and Gaza. All the while, radio traffic played through speakers arranged in the corners of the room.

Segev pointed in the direction of the nearest speaker and leaned closer to Gur. "The airplanes are taking off now," he noted in a quiet but excited tone.

Gur checked his watch. "It's 7:45."

"This may take some time to develop."

"Right," Gur said with a nod. "It'll take an hour for them to reach the first targets and at least that long to get back. That's two hours before we can see the gun camera films."

For most of the morning, Segev and Gur watched the screen as sortie after sortie of the first wave tracked across the map toward the coastline, continued out over the ocean, then turned back toward the mainland. Traveling just above the water, the planes reached the Egyptian shore without being detected and arrived on target without incident. By midmorning it was clear, things were going far better than Gur or anyone else imagined.

− • −

Shortly before noon, planes from the initial attacks began returning to their bases. Gur, still standing near the corner of the map room, looked over at Segev. "Any chance we could see some of the gun camera footage now?"

"It's early," Segev replied. "And the tapes are still at the bases."

"Think they have a way of showing them to us over a telephone line? Don't we have a video link to our bases?"

"We have the link," Segev shrugged. "But it's mostly so they can meet without having to leave the base. I'm not sure they can transmit the tapes like that."

"See if you can find out."

Natan Shahak, Dayan's assistant, stood nearby and Segev made his way in that direction. Shahak listened to Segev's request, then nodded in response and started toward the door. Segev caught Gur's attention and gestured for him to follow.

With Shahak leading the way, Segev and Gur walked down the hall to a door guarded by an armed soldier and secured with a coded lock. Shahak entered a code on a keypad near the knob and opened the door. Gur followed them inside to find all four walls lined with television screens. Most of the screens were blank but three along the back wall showed grainy black-and-white images from an airplane looking down on a runway.

A console sat to the left with an operator seated behind it. Shahak caught the operator's attention and pointed to one of the screens. "Roll this footage, please."

Moments later, images on the screen began to move as an IAF fighter bomber flew over an empty field. Below the aircraft, a runway came into view. It was smooth at the approach end, but farther up, large gaping holes appeared. The operator at the console explained, "These images are from the second attack wave at Bir Gifgafa Airfield. Just east of the Suez

Canal. The shot you see is from a plane in the lead of that wave. Those holes are bomb craters from an earlier run." The operator stopped the film with an image of a truck sitting nose first in a hole. "That will give you an idea of how deep the bomb craters are."

"Those runways will be unusable for days," Gur sported a satisfied smile.

"If not longer," Segev added.

The gun camera footage continued as the plane passed over the airfield and four heavy bombers appeared below, parked on the runway apron. White tufts of smoke appeared as bullets from the IAF fighter bomber hit the pavement, then black smoke boiled up, enveloping the plane and obscuring the ground from view. "That smoke is from the bombers," the operator explained. "Black smoke is good. It means we hit the target. Whiter smoke would indicate a miss."

Gur and Segev grinned with satisfaction. Their plan was working perfectly. Israel controlled the skies.

— · —

In Washington, D.C., Robert McNamara, the US secretary of defense, informed President Johnson of Israel's attack against Egypt. "Our sources indicate this is an Israeli rout so far."

Johnson seemed both surprised and relieved. "They're winning?"

"Yes," McNamara assured. "They control the skies. We're ready to brief you in the situation room."

"Good." Johnson came around his desk. "Let's have a look."

Johnson and McNamara walked downstairs to the White House situation room, where they were met by Dean Rusk, Steve Smith from CIA, and General Earle Wheeler, chairman of the Joint Chiefs of Staff. "What happened?" Johnson asked as he took a seat at the head of a long conference table.

"The Israelis executed a brilliant strategy," Wheeler boasted from his position at the opposite end of the room. "They attacked first and hit every Egyptian base of any significance, disabling the runways. Then they launched a second wave and went after the planes that were trapped on the ground. More than half the Egyptian air force has been destroyed. Virtually all of their bases are inoperable and will be for days to come."

Johnson seemed amazed. "I thought the Egyptians outnumbered them three to one in aircraft."

"They did," McNamara replied. "But the Israelis have done more with less, while the Egyptians have done almost nothing."

"The standard assumption is that the most you can get out of an air crew is three sorties per twenty-four hours," Wheeler offered. "The Israelis are getting an average of five and sometimes six sorties per day from their pilots and aircraft. That means some of their wings are doing seven and eight missions per day."

Smith spoke up. "This gives them a seven-hundred-plane air force out of three hundred fifty aircraft."

Johnson gave an approving nod. "Any move by the Russians to respond?"

"No, sir," Wheeler replied.

"Any change in Russian troop positions or deployments?"

"None."

"What about their readiness?"

"No change in status, sir."

"Interesting." Johnson looked across the table to Rusk. "I think I should meet with the Soviet ambassador and make sure everyone is understanding this situation the same way."

"That would be a good idea. I'll call over to the embassy and set up a meeting."

— • —

Later that morning, in the Oval Office, Johnson met with Alexander Zarubin, the Soviet ambassador. Johnson began with his best southern drawl. "I'm sure you've heard of the latest developments in the Middle East."

Zarubin acquiesced grimly. "I understand the fighting is going badly for the Israelis."

Johnson had a wry smile. "Is that what you're getting from Soviet sources, or something you're hearing from your contacts in Egypt?"

Zarubin had a timid smile. "One hears things," he shrugged. "From many sources."

Johnson opened a desk drawer and took out a photograph. "This picture is a few hours old." He handed it across the desk to Zarubin. "I think you know what I'm talking about."

The photograph showed an Egyptian air base, its runways pocked with bomb craters. Zarubin glanced at it and sighed. "Mr. President, my country has no interest in involving itself in a conflict with the Israelis, if that is what you are worried about." He tossed the picture casually onto the desktop. "So long as the United States does not enter the fray, we are content to let the countries of the region decide their own fate."

"That has to include arms, logistics, and intelligence," Johnson replied.

"We have no intention of sending any more armaments into the region. But I am certain you would appreciate our sharing genuine intelligence with our allies."

"What do you mean?"

"Truth, Mr. President, is your most powerful weapon," Zarubin answered.

"The truth," Johnson scoffed, "has been sorely lacking in the Middle East. We need you to talk some sense to them."

"Nasser is an idiot and the Syrians are worse," Zarubin continued. "But we cannot order any of them to do or not do anything. That is not our relationship with them. In fact, we have very little influence over them and it is a major sore spot within our government."

"But you armed them."

"True," Zarubin nodded. "We supplied arms, which they were glad to get, and we showed them how to use them, but they do not reciprocate with allegiance."

Johnson had a knowing smile. "You might not be able to control the Syrians, or the Egyptians, but you can control your advisers."

Zarubin had a puzzled expression. "What are you suggesting?"

"Recall them," Johnson said flatly. "Recall your advisers."

"I do not think my country would do that." Zarubin shook his head slowly. "Why should we abandon an ally?"

"For the sake of peace."

Zarubin looked Johnson in the eye. "But for what strategic reason?"

A satisfied grin spread over Johnson's face. He loved this moment in a conversation with the Soviets, when both sides understood without saying so. Zarubin wasn't refusing to cooperate, he was asking for something in return and Johnson knew just what to give him. "Tell Brezhnev I'll announce an arms embargo on the region," Johnson said eagerly, "if he'll withdraw Soviet advisers from Syria."

"You think he will accept such a proposal?"

"I think he will be forever grateful to you for bringing it to him," Johnson beamed.

"I will pass along your message, but I am not certain it will be well received."

Johnson rose from his chair and came from behind the desk. Zarubin stood also and Johnson came alongside him, draping an arm over Zarubin's shoulder as they walked toward the door. "If I know anything at all, Alexander, I know you have a way with words. You can convince anyone of anything when you want to. When you tell Brezhnev about our offer, with some of that warm, soothing charm of yours, I think things will work out just fine."

CHAPTER 34

AFTER TWO DAYS OF RELENTLESS BOMBING, and with no threat of attack from Egypt by air, Israeli ground forces crossed into the Sinai from the Negev and sped toward Suez. Within hours, they drove deep into the desert and were well on their way to cutting the peninsula in half. Covering their flank along the coast, units reached the outskirts of El Arish, well past the Egyptian border, by nightfall.

With those fronts well in hand, IDF troops arrived by sea at Sharm el-Sheikh, quickly subdued the Egyptian troops there, and pushed west. Before sunset of the fourth day, they reached Abu Zenima, halfway up the Gulf to the Suez Canal.

Surprised by the speed of Israel's invasion and caught off-guard by its success, the Egyptian army was thrown into disarray. With no air support and no hope of stopping the advancing IDF, the Egyptians retreated in a headlong dash toward the Suez Canal and the safety of the Egyptian homeland on the opposite side. Unwilling to let them escape, IDF units pursued the Egyptians with diligence and caught most of the force at Mitla Pass east of Suez. Trapped at a location that minimized Egyptian strengths, the pass became a killing zone where thousands of Egyptian troops were struck and countless pieces of equipment destroyed.

Meanwhile, in Amman, Jordan, King Hussein was both perplexed and confused by conflicting reports from the field. In an effort to sort through available information, he summoned General Ayasrah to the palace for a review of the war's progress. Seated in Hussein's study, they reviewed reports, trying to decide which course of action to take. Information, even from previously reliable sources, was murky at best with some reports indicating the Israelis had attacked and met with great success, while others suggested the attack came from American planes flying from an aircraft carrier off the Egyptian coast.

"The planes that struck the Egyptian bases came from over the sea," Ayasrah noted. "That much seems clear and they very well could have been American."

"Perhaps that is the direction from which they came, but an American attack on Egypt would make no sense," Hussein countered. "The Americans have no reason to get involved. How widespread is the damage?"

"No one seems to know for certain. There are reports of smoke from several air force bases, but Egyptian sources say the smoke came from aircraft they shot down."

Hussein and Ayasrah continued discussing the situation, going back and forth between them as they debated what they should do. Then an aide entered the study. "President Nasser is on television," he announced with a bow.

Ayasrah's eyes were wide with surprise. "On television?"

"Yes, sir."

Hussein stood. "Is he surrendering?"

The aide bowed again. "Come and see, Your Majesty."

Hussein and Ayasrah came from the study to the outer office and watched as Nasser gave his address. Far from surrendering, he was defiant to the point of absurdity. "The Zionists attacked us with airplanes," Nasser ranted, "but we shot down one hundred fifty-eight of their planes. Their air force is decimated. Their tanks crossed into Sinai but we destroyed them. Our valiant and courageous army is now pushing toward Tel Aviv and Jerusalem, with the Zionists fleeing before them. In two days we will be in Haifa!"

Hussein looked over at Ayasrah. "That changes things."

"Yes," Ayasrah nodded. "If we do not get involved, we could lose the West Bank and eastern Jerusalem."

"But are we too late?" Hussein worried. "Will our involvement now stop them from attacking us, too?"

"That does not matter," Ayasrah slowly shook his head. "We cannot survive long with Egypt in control of Palestine. The Negev, Jerusalem, Galilee, in their hands it would be too much. We must occupy the West Bank, strengthen our grip on eastern Jerusalem, and prepare to take the entire city. If we do that, Egyptian intentions will be irrelevant."

"Rather than shrink back or defend, we must pursue and go deeper."

"Exactly, Your Majesty," Ayasrah smiled approvingly and bowed his head. "From Jerusalem we can move west toward the coast and cut Palestine in half. Then we can argue with the Egyptians about which portion we should keep permanently."

"I prefer the northern half," Hussein said with a chuckle. "It is far better territory. The Negev is nothing but desert."

Ayasrah laughed, "Let it be so." Then he bowed once. "We shall mobilize our troops at once, Your Majesty."

— • —

Back in Jerusalem, Abba Eban stood in his office watching the Nasser speech as it was broadcast live. Arms folded defiantly across his chest, Eban's jaw was slack and his mouth gaped open in a look of wonder at what he was hearing. "He's out of his mind," Eban whispered. "Totally out of his mind."

When the speech ended, he reached for the phone on his desk and called Dayan. "You saw Nasser's speech?"

"The man is insane," Dayan replied.

"This is not good."

"In so many ways," Dayan quipped.

"If we heard it," Eban continued, "then Hussein heard it. Most of the world heard it, including al-Atassi and Arafat and anyone in FATAH with a radio. All of them—everyone who hates us—will feel compelled to attack us now."

"They aren't that crazy. And they have nothing to attack with. The Egyptian army is all but defeated."

"But no one knows that," Eban shouted. "We have to issue a public statement."

"No." Dayan's reply was swift and forceful. "I don't want to do that."

"Our people need to know the truth."

"But we can't issue a statement just to our people," Dayan argued. "The entire world will hear us and if we offer the world the truth, the Soviets will seize upon our pending victory as an opportunity to prompt the UN for a cease-fire. Everyone will join them in supporting it. I don't want a cease-fire. I want a victory!"

"Then you should be prepared to defend against a major attack from Syria and Jordan," Eban warned.

Dayan brushed his concern aside. "The Syrians don't want to fight. They want Egypt to fight for them."

"Yes," Eban countered, "and now that they think the Egyptians are winning, they will cross the Jordan River to join them rather than be left behind. They can't sit this out now. Hussein can't, either. He has to allay the fear and anger of his own people and he has to protect himself against Egyptian domination of the region."

"Our latest intelligence shows no major troop movements by the Syrians. Nothing has changed on the northern border."

"I'm telling you," Eban insisted, "this is not good. You should make plans to evacuate us from Jerusalem."

"We can't do that any easier than we can issue a statement. It'll look like defeat."

"Moshe!" Eban shouted. "You can't make this situation disappear simply by ignoring it. You're doing exactly what Nasser is doing."

"But we are winning," Dayan chided. "You don't concede defeat when you are winning."

— · —

As the attack on Egypt began, Jerusalem was a divided city, separated by a line extending north and south along the western boundary of the Old City, leaving Israel in control of the largest portion of the city. Jordan, however, controlled the rest of the Old City and most of the important religious sites—the Temple Mount, the Mount of Olives, and others. A system of walls and defenses marked the boundaries of the two zones, defended on the Israeli side by a force of several hundred guards spread among towers and gates along the wall. As the invasion of the Sinai moved forward, guards in Jerusalem were supplemented by a small infantry force under the command of General Uzi Narkiss.

Narkiss had enjoyed a long and illustrious career since joining a unit of Haganah as a teenager. He had served admirably in the defense of Jerusalem during the 1948 War of Independence and continued afterwards as a career officer. He was educated, trained, and seasoned in combat. His troops, however, were mostly young and inexperienced, those with combat training having been assigned to the fighting in the Sinai.

Though untrained and untested, Narkiss's troops held several important positions in southern Jerusalem, most notably the hill and surrounding compound of Government House where UN peace-keepers had been stationed since 1948. The remainder of his force was spread along the western boundary of the city to guard against the possibility of being attacked from the rear, and as a defense against access to Tel Aviv. Adequate to maintain order in times of peace, they were wholly inadequate to defend Israel's portion of the city from a full-scale onslaught by a well-armed, well-trained army like the one at King Hussein's disposal.

In an attempt to minimize the risk posed by his thin and ill-prepared force, Narkiss placed scouts across the Jordan River to the east of Jerusalem, deep within Jordanian territory. One of those scouts, Yona Gronich, was perched atop a hill overlooking an encampment of Jordanian troops ten kilometers beyond the river. He'd been there almost a month, living off the land, hiding in the rocks, keeping watch over the Jordanian troops below.

Not long after Nasser's address, those troops assembled in formation dressed in full battle gear. Trucks arrived and soldiers loaded into them. Gronich took a pair of binoculars from his backpack and focused on the trucks. Soldiers were crowded in back with rifles at their side, the muzzle pointed up toward the sky. "They're armed," Gronich whispered. "That's how you carry an armed weapon."

Not long after the trucks were loaded, a column of tanks appeared over the hill to the south. They streamed through the camp and moved in front of the trucks, then the entire caravan started forward, traveling west toward the Jordan River.

Gronich scooted out of sight and removed the pack from his back. Inside was a small two-way radio. He extended the antennae, held the radio in his left hand, and squeezed a button on the side with his thumb and sent a message to Narkiss's headquarters tent. Jordanian troops were moving west, toward the city, apparently intent on engaging anyone who opposed them.

Fifteen minutes later, a messenger brought a note to Narkiss with the news. He read it, then gave it to a young lieutenant standing nearby. "Jordanian troops are headed west, toward the river."

The lieutenant read the note, then handed it back. "Does this movement mean they intend to attack across the armistice line?"

"I'm not waiting to find out," Narkiss turned to the messenger. "Radio Jerusalem and tell them what's happening. The Jordanian army is headed this way. Tell General Greenberg we need reinforcements immed—" He stopped in midsentence and turned away. "Never mind. I'll send the message myself."

Narkiss walked quickly to the headquarters tent, where a radio operator was seated just inside the flap. "I need to get a message to General Greenberg," Narkiss growled. "Can you do that?"

"Yes, sir." The operator was startled at Narkiss's sudden appearance.

"Good. Here's what I want to say ..." Narkiss paused a moment, as if thinking, then started. "Enemy advancing on ..." He paused once more, then tried again. "Enemy approaching ..." Finally in frustration he gestured to the operator. "Just get them on the air and give me the microphone."

Moments later, Narkiss spoke with Greenberg. "Look, General, the Jordanian army is on the move. Yesterday they were camped ten kilometers beyond the river. Now they're moving in this direction. I need those reinforcements you promised me two weeks ago."

"We don't have reinforcements to send you right now," Greenberg replied. "We're sending everything south to the Negev."

"Then give me some air support."

"You want us to hit them from the air while they're still in their own country?"

"I want you to keep them from getting to me," Narkiss argued. "They've got crack troops, I've got kids younger than my grandchildren out here walking around in uniforms, with guns, playing army. Half of them don't even know which end of a rifle to load."

"We can't bomb them while they're in Jordan," Greenberg countered. "They haven't done anything yet. And we can't bomb them in Jerusalem; we'd destroy the place and kill our own people."

"Are we still recruiting?"

"Recruiting?" Greenberg had a puzzled tone. "We don't recruit."

"You know what I mean," Narkiss retorted. "Are we still taking new conscripts?"

"Yes."

"Good," Narkiss barked. "Send me a busload. I'll train them up here. They won't be any worse than what I've already got. I need bodies. People I can put on the line."

"You're impossible," Greenberg scolded.

"Well, what about—"

Just then, an artillery shell whistled overhead, interrupting Narkiss's train of thought as he instinctively ducked. The round exploded a hundred meters beyond the tent in a blast that shook the ground beneath his feet.

"General," Narkiss shouted, "the shelling has begun. Send me those troops." Then he tossed the microphone to the operator, charged from the tent, and started toward the front line at a trot.

CHAPTER 35

IN TEL AVIV, REPORTS OF JORDANIAN troop movements reached the map room communications center from multiple sources. First indications showed them preparing to cross the river at two locations south of Jerusalem. Two more columns of men and tanks were proceeding west from Amman. Dayan was in the room when the reports arrived. "Does General Narkiss know about these movements?"

Natan Shahak, who stood nearby, spoke up. "Yes, sir. He called just now asking General Greenberg for more troops, air cover, tanks."

An operator at the communications center called out, "Sir, we have reports of artillery shelling Jerusalem."

Just then, the door to the map room opened and General Greenberg entered. "The Jordanians are shelling Jerusalem!" he exclaimed.

"We're just getting the report now," Dayan replied.

"They started while I was talking to Narkiss."

"Are you sending him the troops he requested?"

"We don't have them to send," Greenberg lamented.

"We'd better find them," Dayan said grimly, handing Greenberg the latest report. "He's about to be hit with ten thousand Jordanian infantrymen, and more are on the way."

Greenberg had a puzzled expression as he scanned the report. "Is this an attack or is Hussein merely reinforcing his claim to the West Bank?"

The operator at the communications desk called out again, "Government House is under attack."

Dayan looked over at Greenberg. "Narkiss is doing his best but he won't be able to hold out for long. He needs more men."

Then the phone started ringing with calls from the prime minister's office, Abba Eban, and a dozen other officials, all of whom were in offices located in Jerusalem, calling to say they were under constant shelling from artillery. "We took a direct hit," Eban shouted in an excited voice. "I can see the sky from the hallway. There's a big hole in the roof."

Dayan called out, "Do we have any troops we can deploy to help them?"

Shahak, reviewing a troop roster, spoke up. "The Fifty-Fifth Paratroopers are still at their base in the Galilee. They were supposed to deploy to the Sinai but the campaign there is going so well they were put on hold."

Greenberg stepped to his side. "Let me see that." He took the roster from Shahak's hands. His eyes moved quickly down the page, then he looked over at Dayan. "He's right. They're up there."

"Tell them to prepare for mobilization," Dayan ordered, then he looked over at Shahak. "Call IAF. Find out what aircraft they can divert to attack Jordanian artillery positions east of Jerusalem. Tell them to send what they have right away." He started toward the door. "Get me a car and driver. And call Narkiss. Tell him I'm on my way. I want to see what's going on."

"I'll go with you," Shahak called after him.

By then, Dayan was in the hallway. He stopped at the doorway and turned back to face Shahak. "Stay here. Call IAF. The plan depends on siphoning aircraft from the initial attack and using them for ground support. Find out what they can send to Jerusalem. Get moving." Then he turned away from the door and was gone.

— • —

Dayan arrived at Jerusalem amid a constant barrage of shelling from Jordanian artillery. He found Narkiss on a ridge near Government House, directing his men as they fought to stave off the advancing Jordanian army. "This isn't good," Narkiss mumbled with a worried look. "Our men are fighting much better than their training suggested, but they can't keep this up."

"We're sending the Fifty-Fifth Paratroopers to help you," Dayan replied. "Maybe you should withdraw. Fight your way back. Prolong this awhile longer but save as many men as you can until the others get here."

"Can't do that," Narkiss shook his head.

"Why not?"

"If we lose this ridge, we lose the entire city."

Dayan looked perplexed. "What do you mean?"

"I've been trying to tell you—you and everyone else I see. Government Hill in the south, Ammunition Hill to the north, Mount Scopus in the east. Temple Mount in between. Those are the key sites for controlling the city. Any army that controls those locations controls the entire place."

"And you are worried that if they take this one hill, they will take them all?"

"They already have Temple Mount. Mount Scopus was neutral before the fighting started but it's inside Jordanian territory. They can take it anytime they want and maybe already have. That's two hills already. With this one, they have three and that leaves us with only Ammunition Hill, which is the least important of them all."

"Show me," Dayan ordered. "Take me up to Scopus and show me."

"Come on," Narkiss waved his hand. "If we can get up there, I'll show you what I'm talking about."

From Government Hill they rode through the city, dodging craters and debris from the shelling, and an hour later reached the top of Mount Scopus. From a vista at the northern end of the crest, Dayan and Narkiss looked out over the city as artillery shells whistled overhead and exploded in the valley below.

"That's Government Hill," Narkiss pointed to the south. "You know Temple Mount here in front of us," he said, nodding in that direction. Then he turned to the right and pointed once more. "Ammunition Hill is over there."

Dayan scanned the terrain and nodded. "I see what you mean. If they take Government Hill and Mount Scopus, they can control the entire city."

"I've been trying to explain this to you."

"And you were right," Dayan nodded.

"We must take the entire city. If we defend just our portion, we will lose the entire thing. To save it, we must take it all."

"I agree."

"The Fifty-Fifth Paratroopers are on their way?"

"Yes," Dayan nodded. "They should be here shortly."

"Good. Colonel Gur knows how to fight."

"Colonel Gur?"

"He's still in command of them, isn't he?"

"No. He was assigned to planning months ago."

"Planning? What's he doing there?"

"He's the one who came up with the plan for this war. One that's working far better than expected, I might add."

"Well, it's not going to work here."

"This part wasn't his idea. This was my decision." Dayan smiled at Narkiss. "Gur said we should take the whole thing from the beginning. But we had to commit everything to the Sinai in order to defeat the Egyptians."

"Well, you better commit something to Jerusalem or you'll lose the whole place."

"We can't lose the city," Dayan groaned. "That would be terrible. Win the war and lose the city? Most of our people would trade the entire country if that's what it took to defend this city."

"I don't mean the city," Narkiss corrected. "I mean the country. If they take Jerusalem, they can drive straight across to Tel Aviv. There's nothing between here and there to stop them. They'll control our two most important cities, and the country will be divided in half."

"We won't let that happen."

"Get me Gur," Narkiss commanded tersely. "He's wasting his time in planning now."

— • —

Back in Tel Aviv, Gur walked down the hall to the map room to check on the progress of the war. The screen on the wall showed a map of the region with Jordanian units plotted on the west side of the Jordan River. As he studied the situation, the door opened and Major Segev entered. "This isn't good," Gur pointed to the map. "Jordan has increased its troop strength in the West Bank. New units have crossed the river." He shook his finger for emphasis. "Some of them are even in the eastern part of Jerusalem."

Segev nodded. "The Jordanians are advancing on Jerusalem. They're shelling the city, too."

Gur looked stricken. "I tried to warn you. I tried to warn everyone. They intend to occupy the entire city." Gur turned back to the map. "They will move additional troops here, here, and here," he indicated each location on the map. "When those are in place, they'll attack across the line, gain control of the highways to Tel Aviv, and drive straight across to the sea. We will win the Sinai but lose everything else."

"I know," Segev agreed with a knowing smile.

"You know this?"

"That's why you're going to Jerusalem."

"What for?"

"To take command of the Fifty-Fifth Paratroopers."

A grin spread across Gur's face. "I'm going to the field?"

Segev handed him written orders. "Your unit will meet you there. You are instructed to link up with General Narkiss and put that plan of yours into action."

"That plan won't work. We can't defend the city."

"That was my plan. Not yours. And that's not the plan they want. They want the one you wanted."

"To take the city?"

"All of it."

Gur leaned forward and kissed Segev on the cheek. "Always Jerusalem!" he shouted as he darted toward the door.

— · —

In Amman, King Hussein was just in from a meeting with his interior minister when he heard airplanes flying overhead. Thinking they were Egyptian aircraft, he rushed from the palace to see.

Moments later, three bombers came into sight. Hussein shielded his eyes from the sun's glare with his hand and stared up at them. While he stood there, gazing into the sky, a car turned onto the driveway and screeched to a halt near the front steps. A rear door flew open and General Ayasrah climbed from the car. "Your Majesty!" he shouted. "What are you doing?"

Hussein glanced in his direction and pointed to the sky. "The Egyptians have arrived to finish off the Zionists."

Ayasrah hurried toward him, his face white with fear. "Those aren't Egyptian aircraft!" he shouted, taking Hussein by the arm. "Get inside, Your Majesty. Those are Israeli planes!"

"Israeli?" Hussein looked confused. "What are they doing here?"

"We will talk inside," Ayasrah said as he guided Hussein toward the front steps.

Before they reached the entrance to the palace, a bomb struck the grounds, shattering windows and destroying the trees that stood in back, beyond the palace garden. A second bomb fell farther away but close enough to shatter the remaining windows on the first floor.

Ayasrah hustled Hussein inside the palace and they hurried down the hall to the study. Hussein paused as they entered the room, staring at the shattered glass that covered the floor. "This has made a mess. We'll have to get someone in here to clean this up."

"Not now," Ayasrah replied. "There isn't time for that now." His voice sounded nervous and he had a worried frown as he hurried around the desk and grabbed the telephone. "Hah," he said with a note of surprise. "It still works." With a flick of his finger he dialed a number, waited while the phone on the other end rang, then shouted into the receiver when they finally answered.

While Ayasrah talked, Hussein moved near an open window and

gazed out at the tangled trunks and splintered logs that once had been trees growing near the house. He thought of the day he had walked out there with Haider Raimouny and of the end that came to him with the swing of the executioner's blade.

In the distance, bombs continued to fall across the city. An explosion caught Hussein's attention, diverting him from the stand of trees beyond the garden and he turned to the left to watch as smoke and dust rose in the air from the bomb. It was so close, and yet it seemed distant, remote, a matter of little interest to him. The Egyptians would provide air support. Nasser had promised it. The Zionists were all but finished anyway.

Here and there across the city, columns of smoke rose toward the clouds. Beneath them, flames were visible and in spite of the lives that undoubtedly were lost as a result, Hussein thought to himself, *This is but a minor inconvenience, for soon the Zionists shall be no more.* "The Egyptians will destroy them," he mumbled.

A moment later, Ayasrah slammed down the phone and came from behind the desk. "Your Majesty, we must vacate the palace at once."

Hussein looked perplexed. "Vacate the palace? But why?"

"The Israelis are attacking."

"Can we not shoot them down?"

"They have destroyed all of our aircraft. And now they are attacking us with artillery located on the opposite side of Jerusalem."

Hussein still did not seem to grasp the gravity of the moment. "But what about the Egyptians? Will they not send their aircraft to defend us?"

"They have no aircraft, either," Ayasrah groaned with sadness. "The Zionists destroyed them."

"But Nasser said—"

"Nasser was lying," Ayasrah cut him off. "He was lying."

Anger flashed over Hussein. "I forbid you to talk of President Nasser in such vulgar terms!" he snapped.

"It's the truth, Your Majesty. I mean no offense. He did not tell the truth. I just spoke to our command center. They have confirmed it. The

Zionists bombed the Egyptian bases on Monday, disabling all their runways. Then they returned to destroy the aircraft that were trapped on the ground. The few that managed to take off were quickly shot down."

Darkness came over Hussein's face. "The Americans," he scowled. "The Americans helped them. They could not have done this if the Americans had not helped them."

"Perhaps that is so, and there will be plenty of time to discuss it later. After we get you to safety." Once again, Ayasrah took Hussein by the arm and guided him toward the door.

When they reached the hall, Hussein glanced over at him. "Why would he do such a thing? Why would he say they had defeated the Zionists if it wasn't true?"

"For the same reason we would. If he tells the truth, his own people will turn against him. If he lies, he buys himself a little more time and induces others of us to join him in his madness." Ayasrah pointed up the hall toward the main doors. "Come. We must go."

Before they'd gone two more steps, a bomb exploded in front of the palace. Smoke and dust billowed down the hall, obscuring everything from view. Ayasrah grabbed Hussein by the shoulder and shoved him to the floor. "Get down!" he shouted. "We can crawl under the smoke."

Dust covered them from head to toe as it settled to the floor, but the toxic smoke from the explosive passed overhead as they crawled on hands and knees toward the front doors.

By the time they reached the main entrance the dust was gone and the smoke had thinned enough to permit them to stand. The palace doors, blown loose by the force of the explosion, dangled from their hinges. Hussein rose to his feet and brushed off his robe while Ayasrah straightened his jacket. After a moment, both men turned to start down the steps but came to a sudden halt when they looked out at the driveway where Ayasrah's car sat upside down, its frame twisted and mangled from the blast.

CHAPTER 36

IT WAS LATE IN THE AFTERNOON when Gur joined his paratrooper unit on the western edge of Jerusalem. Five minutes later, Narkiss arrived. After a round of handshakes among the officers, Narkiss took a map from the pocket of his jacket and unfolded it across the hood of a jeep. As he spread it flat, he glanced over at Gur. "Do you have a good map?"

"One just like this," Gur replied.

"Good. When this thing is over, we need to make new ones. This version is usable but not very good and most of the others are junk. Maybe now that you've straightened out planning," Narkiss quipped with a twinkle in his eye, "you can fix the mapping department."

"After we get this over with," Gur tilted his head to indicate the seriousness of the moment.

"Right," Narkiss agreed, then he turned his attention back to the map. "My men are down here, near Government House in the south," he indicated. "Your men need to take up positions here and here to the north." He tapped the locations with his index finger. "Take Ammunition Hill first. That way you can protect your northern flank. Then turn southward toward Mount Scopus. We must occupy Mount Scopus before the Jordanians reach it. If you do that, we can take the city."

"Are you holding Government Hill?"

Narkiss exhaled. "We held out for a while but Jordanian troops outnumbered us by...a lot. They eventually pushed their way up to the top. Our men escaped down the steep side but they've gathered near the base and will concentrate their effort there. Even if they can't recapture the hill, they can hold some Jordanian troops there and give you time to take Mount Scopus."

"Do you have enough men to do that? I can send a company—"

"No," Narkiss interrupted. "The Tenth Brigade is on its way and I've instructed them to deploy part of their force to the south to help us." He folded the map and returned it to the pocket of his jacket, then looked over at Gur. "We've been promised air cover. I understand they've begun hitting positions across the river. If they keep it up, maybe we can end most of the artillery. But whether we get air force help or not, we still have to fight our way through the city."

"We're ready."

Narkiss looked him in the eye. "Mount Scopus is the key. Take it. Secure it. And move toward the Old City as quickly as possible."

Gur's eyes opened wide. "We're moving across the armistice line?"

Narkiss slapped him on the shoulder. "Take all you can get. You and I both know we can't defend the city without seizing control of it. The Jordanians attacked us. As far as I'm concerned, that put all their claims on the line."

After meeting with Narkiss, Gur moved his forces north toward Ammunition Hill. Located on the outskirts of the city, it was named for a former police training station used by the British when they controlled Palestine. Perched at the top of a steep incline, it was heavily fortified with bunkers and trenches that offered a well-protected location from which to launch subsequent operations. Scouts working ahead of the main force indicated the hill was unoccupied. Gur meant to take it quickly.

As they neared the base of the hill, a portion of Gur's force broke off from the main unit and started up the hill. The remainder took up positions near the base. When word came down that the site was unoccupied, the bulk of Gur's force then turned toward Mount Scopus.

All was quiet as they made their approach, but as they drew near the base of the mount, machine guns opened fire from positions near the top, bearing down on them with lethal accuracy. Four of Gur's men were hit immediately. Everyone else ducked behind boulders, trees, and any outcropping or post that seemed to offer cover. For the next three hours they fought hard, moving forward from one rock to the next, one tree to the next. Ducking and shooting, then diving and rolling, in an effort to move forward while staying alive. Yet for all their effort, as midnight approached, they still were no more than ten meters up from the bottom.

Captain Harnoy, a veteran under Gur's command, was tucked behind a boulder with Gur at his side, both of them pinned down by a fresh and concerted round of machine gun fire.

Gur peeked out for a look, then quickly shrank back. "I can't see a thing. What about from your side?"

Harnoy braced himself against the boulder, then leaned out for a quick view only to jerk back out of sight as bullets whizzed past his head. "There's a machine gun about halfway up the hill. That's the one that has us pinned down here."

"We need to take it out," Gur noted. "Then we can move around to the left and flank most of their positions. Come at them from the left instead of straight at them."

"Right," Harnoy nodded. "I'll get some men up there." He turned and called out in a loud voice, "Resnick!"

A man, hiding behind a burned-out truck several meters away, turned in their direction. Harnoy gestured for him to come and the man started in their direction. A burst of gunfire from the machine gun sent him diving for the ground but he quickly scrambled to his feet and ran, with bullets hitting the dirt just behind him every step of the way. Obscured at first in darkness and shadow, as he came closer Gur recognized him as the lieutenant from the airplane the night he had made his last jump, just before joining the planning group.

Resnick reached the boulder and squeezed himself between Harnoy and Gur. "That was close," he gasped.

Gur gave him an amused look. "Your first time in combat?"

"Yes, sir," Resnick nodded.

"Nothing like live-fire drills, is it?"

Resnick replied, "Nothing like it."

Harnoy looked over at him. "Get me two men and bring them over here. I have an assignment for you."

"Any special men, Captain?"

"Brave ones, Resnick. We need brave ones. But right now anyone will do. Just pick two and bring them over here."

Resnick asked nervously, "You want me to go back out there, get two men, and come back with them?"

"Yeah," Harnoy nodded. "That's what I want you to do."

"They're shooting at us, sir."

"Just get the men and bring them back," Harnoy ordered with an exasperated tone. "Get moving."

Resnick took a deep breath, then pushed himself away from the boulder and ran, disappearing into the shadows near the truck where he'd been hiding. While he was gone Harnoy looked over at Gur. "Do you remember being that young?"

"I don't remember being that inexperienced," Gur replied. "But young? Yes," he nodded. "I remember being young once."

In a few minutes Resnick returned with a couple of men who looked to be no more than twenty years old. One of them, a redhead, was someone Gur had never seen before, but he recognized the other one immediately. He was the kid on the plane that night with Resnick and the others. *Strauss*. A good kid with a good heart. Gur remembered him because he didn't want to jump and they had to push him out the door. That made them late, but they went down together and hiked across the field in the dark to catch up with the others.

With the men at Harnoy's side, Resnick turned to leave but Harnoy grabbed him. "You're going with them." Resnick's face turned pale but he kept quiet and waited while Harnoy outlined the assignment. "There's a machine gun up there," he pointed toward the hill. "Your job is to work your way up the hill to the left, come around to the machine gun from the side, and take it out."

Strauss nodded confidently. "Got any extra grenades?"

Harnoy unhooked three from his belt. "Take these," he handed them to him.

Strauss tucked the grenades inside his shirt and picked up his rifle. "Let's go," he said to the others.

"Wait," Resnick snapped. "I haven't given the order yet."

Harnoy's eyes bore in on him. "What is it, Resnick?" he asked with a hint of irritation.

"There could be others up there," Resnick said nervously. "You know, Jordanians."

"Right," Harnoy nodded. "So be careful."

"But what do we do if we stumble on to them?" Resnick was obviously frightened. "What do we do if they just pop out of nowhere?"

"We'll take them, too," Strauss replied.

"Nobody asked you," Resnick snarled.

"Look," Strauss continued, ignoring the insult. "I had four grenades already. The Captain gave me three more." He gestured to the guy next to him. "Ziffer's got four, don't you, Ziff?"

Ziffer nodded and patted his belt as he spoke, "I got four."

Strauss looked back at Resnick. "Don't you have four, too?"

"Yeah," Resnick said. "What of it?"

"That's fifteen grenades between us," Strauss noted. "We could take the whole hill with fifteen grenades. Now, come on. We gotta get—" The look on Ziffer's face brought him up short. "You scared, Ziff?"

Ziffer answered with a hint of embarrassment. "Yeah, I'm scared."

"Me too," Strauss replied. "Being afraid is natural. We ought to be afraid. Those machine guns could cut us in half."

"Thanks for reminding me."

Resnick lurched as if he was about to be sick. "I don't want to die," he whimpered.

"Nobody wants to die," Strauss said with an ironic smile. He turned to start up the hill, then paused and glanced back once more. "Look, it doesn't matter that we're afraid. We can still do our job. We can knock out that machine gun even if we are afraid. This rifle I'm carrying doesn't know I'm afraid. The grenades I'm lugging don't know it, either. They'll work just fine and so will yours. Now, come on. I'll take the lead."

Gur had heard that speech before, at least a version of it. He'd given it to Strauss that night when they were trying to convince him to make the jump. Hearing him repeat it now was like catching a glimpse of yourself in someone else. Gur felt a lump in his throat as Strauss led the way from the safety of the boulder.

A hail of gunfire greeted Strauss and the others but they made it to a rock ten meters away, then continued on, disappearing in the shadows only to emerge in the moonlight a moment later. Gur peeked out from behind the boulder to check on them.

Halfway up to the machine gun, Strauss led Ziffer and Resnick, where they paused behind a boulder for a moment to catch their breath before continuing higher, working their way between rocks and boulders. When they were above the machine gun's position, Strauss reached inside his shirt and took out a grenade. "Wait here," he whispered. "And watch my back. Don't let anybody slip up behind me." Ziffer nodded in response and Strauss gestured to his rifle. "You got that thing on automatic?"

"Yeah," Ziffer glanced down to check. "Moved the selector switch when we started out."

"Good," Strauss grinned. "Look sharp."

Holding it at his side, Strauss stepped away from the others and inched toward the gun emplacement, coming toward it from the side and slightly above.

Down below, Gur peered from behind the boulder and caught a glimpse of Strauss's arm as he tossed the grenade. For a moment there was nothing but the continual sound of machine gun fire, then a loud explosion shook the ground. The machine gun, tossed in the air by the force of the blast, sailed overhead and crashed to the ground a few meters away from where Gur and Harnoy were crouched.

"Let's go," Gur yelled, then ran from behind the boulder and started up the hill.

Harnoy followed and shouted as he went, "Go! Go! Go! Let's take this hill!"

With the echo from the blast still reverberating through the valley, men of the Fifty-Fifth Paratroopers came from hiding and charged up the hill, following Gur and Harnoy as they led the way.

Up above, Strauss turned from the machine gun emplacement in time to see a Jordanian soldier appear to the left. Strauss raised his rifle to fire and shouted, "Ziffer, look out!"

Ziffer wheeled around to face the soldier and opened fire. With the rifle on automatic and his finger wrapped tightly around the trigger, a stream of lead poured from the muzzle. Bullets struck the soldier in the abdomen, causing his body to jerk and convulse in response. Mortally wounded, he dropped the rifle he'd been holding, fell to the ground and clutched at his stomach with both hands. A moment later, as Ziffer eased his finger from the trigger and the shooting stopped, the man suddenly froze in place—hands at his waist, eyes opened wide with a look of fear— then pitched forward and tumbled headfirst down the hill, landing with a thud at Ziffer's feet. Blood rushed from a gaping wound in his chest and quickly formed a puddle near the toe of Ziffer's boot. Ziffer stared at him a moment, then turned away and vomited.

With a few quick strides, Strauss was at Ziffer's side and slapped him on the back. "That's what I'm talking about. I knew you could do it. You saved our lives, then you puked. Good job."

Meanwhile, Resnick, who should have been leading the detail, cowered in the shadow of a large boulder. Strauss glanced over at him and saw his face was white and his hands trembled. "It's okay, Lieutenant," Strauss said quietly. "You're okay. We're all okay. We're gonna make it."

"No," Resnick shook his head from side to side. "I'm not okay. I can't take this."

Just then, Gur appeared with Harnoy behind him as the men from below moved past them toward the top. Gur slapped Strauss on the back. "Been jumping out of any airplanes lately?"

"Yes, sir," Strauss nodded. "Haven't missed a jump since you showed me how to do it."

"Good," Gur smiled proudly. "Good job tonight." Then he gestured toward the top. "Now get moving."

Strauss nudged Ziffer. "Come on, Ziff. We gotta keep moving."

"Yeah," Ziffer sighed as he wiped his mouth on his shirt sleeve. "I'm with you," he mumbled as he picked up his rifle and followed Strauss.

As they moved out to join the others, Gur glanced back at Resnick. "Come on," he waved his hand. "It's safer at the top. You can catch your breath there."

CHAPTER 37

WITH AMMUNITION HILL and Mount Scopus under IDF control, Gur turned his attention to the Old City, the most ancient part of Jerusalem, which lay at the base of Temple Mount. Clearly visible in the night, it seemed only a short walk away, but between Scopus and the temple was the American Colony. Its narrow streets, with buildings jammed together side-by-side, meant most of the fighting would be done on the ground. Tanks and armored vehicles, even if they had them, would be unusable there.

Gur radioed his position to Narkiss, then turned to Harnoy. "We'd better get moving." Harnoy rallied the men and they followed Gur down the hill toward the colony, expecting to fight for every building and block. Instead, they encountered little resistance and easily took control of the district.

As the sun came up in the east, Gur found himself standing at Lions Gate, the entrance to the Old City through the northern side of the ancient Jerusalem wall. Even more crowded than the American Colony, taking control of this part of the city posed the greatest challenge of all. Narrow streets—some barely wide enough for two people to pass on foot—buildings on top of buildings, foundations with subbasements connected to passages long forgotten made subduing the area a seemingly impossible task. But controlling the entire city was essential to protecting any of it from Jordanian domination. Not only that, since the armistice of 1948 that ended Israel's War of Independence, Temple

Mount had been off-limits to Jews. Now they had the opportunity to change that, but it would not be easy.

Gur looked over at Harnoy. "This is going to be rough."

"Yes, sir."

"Not like that neighborhood we just came through," Gur said, gesturing over his shoulder.

"Right," Harnoy said with a nod. "How do you want to do it?"

Gur looked him in the eye. "Have the men fix bayonets."

Harnoy turned to the men behind him and called in a loud voice, "Fix bayonets!" The clatter of metal against metal followed as each man attached his bayonet—a heavy steel knife about thirty centimeters in length—to the muzzle end of his rifle.

"I don't want a slaughter," Gur cautioned.

"I understand," Harnoy replied.

"And we can't save the city by destroying it, so no unnecessary grenades or mortars."

"Very well."

"But we aren't risking lives for buildings, either."

"I understand," Harnoy concurred. "You stalling, or preparing?"

"I'm not sure," Gur sighed. "Lot of people could die doing this."

"They'll die right here if we wait much longer."

"Yeah, let's go." And with that, Gur started forward, leading his troops into the oldest portion of the city.

Just beyond the old wall they were met with withering gunfire from snipers perched atop a building on the first block. Men from the Fifty-Fifth Paratroopers crouched along the walls, in doorways, and in the nooks and crannies of every available structure.

Gur, hunkered down in a doorway with Harnoy, glanced out at the ancient stones that paved the streets. "Can you imagine the feet that have walked on those stones?"

Harnoy had a puzzled frown. "We're about to die and you're talking about the stones in the street."

"We're not going to die," Gur replied with a smile.

"Stick your head out past the edge of the entryway and you'll have a different opinion."

"I'm not sticking my head out there, but I'm also not going to panic." Gur looked over at Harnoy. "Take a deep breath." Reluctantly, Harnoy did as he was told. "Now," Gur continued, "think of the men who walked these streets. These streets have been here at least a thousand years."

"Sir, we have to get these—"

"I know what we have to do," Gur interrupted. "But think about it. We've been a country less than twenty years. These streets have been here a thousand years."

"This time," Harnoy said in a matter-of-fact tone.

Gur frowned. "What do you mean?"

"We've been a country less than twenty years, this time," Harnoy explained.

"Hah," Gur laughed. "You're right."

"Now can we stop with the history lesson and get on with it?"

"Send the men up the next street behind us," Gur instructed. "Tell them to keep close to the buildings on this side. The gunfire is coming from that tower at the end of the block. If they stay in the lee of the buildings, all the rounds will pass over them and they can come around from the other side."

"How will I get out of here to tell them?"

"I'll cover you."

"You weren't kidding about not sticking your head out, were you?"

"Not until you're ready to go," Gur smiled. "Get ready." Harnoy adjusted the straps of his pack and checked to make sure his rifle was fully loaded, then nodded at Gur. "On my count," Gur said. Then he paused a moment longer. "Just don't forget where I am."

"When we take out that sniper, you can make it to the corner on your own."

"Right. Here we go." Gur counted to three, raised his rifle to his shoulder, and stepped out from the doorway, firing at the tower as he did. Peppered by gunfire, the sniper ducked behind the parapet of the roof. By the time Gur's magazine was empty, Harnoy was out of sight.

Twenty minutes later, the machine gun on the tower fell silent. A moment later, Gur heard Harnoy shouting. He exited the doorway and walked up the street to join the others.

At the corner, Gur found several of his men were wounded and two more were dead but the others had fought their way up the street and inside the building, then made their way floor by floor to the top and took out the sniper. Gur stood outside and watched as the bodies of six Jordanian soldiers were brought down. He looked over at Harnoy. "This is going to be a block-by-block battle."

"Yes, Colonel, I'm afraid you're right."

— • —

At IDF headquarters in Tel Aviv, Dayan was in the map room with Natan Shahak, reviewing reports of hand-to-hand combat in the Old City. "Gur and his men are going from house to house."

"Yes, it's difficult, but they appear to be making progress."

"This printed report is a couple of hours old. Do we have anything new?"

"Just what you've heard from the radio. Clear one building, move to the next."

"What about General Narkiss?"

"They retook Government House and turned back the Jordanians from the southern flank of the city. As of his last message to us, they were driving them out of the West Bank and sending them back across the river."

"Air cover has decimated the Jordanian air force," Dayan noted, pointing to the latest aerial photographs. "They should have listened to us when we asked them to stay out of this."

"Most of their artillery is gone, too," Shahak added. "Only a few pieces are still functioning."

"Concentrate on the artillery," Dayan cautioned. "We don't want to bomb Jerusalem itself and destroying Amman would do us no good. But we don't want them shelling us, either." He gave Shahak a knowing look. "We also don't want them to have those artillery pieces for use after this is over. The more we destroy of their army now, the less they can use against us later."

For the remainder of the day, Dayan monitored events in Jerusalem from the map room where he remained, listening to radio traffic from the field and checking for updates on the screen. To that he added the latest bits of news picked up by Shahak from Mossad and American contacts.

The Americans were officially uninvolved. Johnson made that clear in public statements made after the attack commenced on Monday. In private, however, he turned around a carrier group, passing the Straits of Gibraltar on its way home as the attack began, and repositioned it at the eastern end of the Mediterranean. With military muscle in place, he followed up on his conciliatory conversation with Soviet ambassador Zarubin, passing word through him to Moscow and Cairo that his earlier offer of a regional arms embargo in exchange for Soviet neutrality in Palestine would be honored but that outside interference in the current hostilities would not be tolerated.

That stance strained US–Soviet relations, so much so that McNamara would later suggest the two sides came close to war over the matter, but in June of 1967, the public didn't know much about it. Eshkol knew, as did Abba Eban and Dayan. That was one reason Dayan spent time in the map room keeping an eye on IDF's progress in clearing Sinai of Egyptian troops and the West Bank of Jordanians. "We have to get what we want now," he kept telling Shahak. "After this, we won't be able to get any more. This is our final opportunity."

As the day wore on, fighting in Jerusalem dwindled to only an occasional exchange of gunfire except in the Old City, where Gur and his men continued the laborious and dangerous task of moving from building to building, block by block, methodically clearing structures one at a time. As action in the field slowed, Dayan became restless, alternately pacing back and forth in the map room, then phoning bases and outposts for updated news. Later, he turned to radioing units up and down the Levant to check on their status so he could hear the raw information of battlefield commanders. Frustrated at being confined in Tel Aviv, he longed to be on the ground, able to observe the action for himself.

Finally, late in the afternoon, speakers in the corner of the map room crackled with Gur's excited voice. "Temple Mount is in our hands!" he shouted. "I repeat. Temple Mount is in our hands!"

A grin spread over Dayan's face. "That's it," he clapped his hands together. "That's it!"

"We have the city?" Shahak asked.

"Yes, Narkiss is holding the hill at Government House. Gur took Ammunition Hill and Mount Scopus last night. Now he has Temple Mount. That's all four hills, plus the Old City. It's ours."

Tears streamed down Shahak's face. "I can't believe it. After all we've been through."

Dayan put an arm around his neck. "And you saw it all from the front row. Galilee in '48. The Negev, too. And now this."

"I was just following you."

"No. You were in the fight. In the future, when they tell schoolchildren about our history and speak of the men of old, you will be one of those men."

"I just tagged along with you."

"And some tagalong, huh?"

"Yeah," Shahak grinned. "Some tagalong."

— • —

In Jerusalem, Gur was still holding the radio receiver as he stared across the way to the western wall of the ancient temple. Already men were gathered there praying while others, overcome with emotion, stood weeping. A group of six or seven were singing and to the right others were dancing. It was an odd mixture of sights and sounds—joy, sorrow, and reverence set against a backdrop of misery, death, and destruction. In the distance, artillery shells were still exploding and every once in a while there was a burst of small-arms fire from the Muslim Quarter. Yet there it was, the western wall of Temple Mount, one of the retaining walls that allowed Herod's expansion of the courtyards and galleries that once stood farther up the hill.

The temple was gone, along with its porticos and courts, but the wall remained and for centuries Jews had come there to pray at what had become one of the holiest sites in all of Judaism. That is, until 1948 when the Old City fell under Jordanian control. *Today,* Gur thought with a smile, *that all changed.*

As Gur stood there, thinking of what they'd accomplished, a single, mellow note blared in a long and continuous sound. He turned to see Shlomo Goren, a rabbi, making his way toward the wall. He held a shofar—a ram's horn used in ancient times as a musical instrument to mark the highest ceremonial occasions. As Rabbi Goren continued to blow the shofar, men gathered from every direction, clustering around him. Their grimy cheeks were streaked with the traces of tears that no one tried to hide. They stood with their hands raised toward heaven, many of them crying out aloud to God.

And then Rabbi Goren began to pray. "Blessed are you, Lord God, King of the Universe, who has granted us life, who sustained us, and enabled us to reach this occasion." The men recited the prayer after him.

"Blessed are you," Goren continued, "who comforts Zion and builds Jerusalem."

Goren's voice seemed to fill the space before the wall with peace, and a sense of tranquility settled over Gur. As Goren continued to pray, those words, *"comfort Zion and build Jerusalem,"* kept playing over and over in his head. And as they did, Gur found himself lost in memories of the past. Once again he was a young boy seated next to Rabbi Breslov as they read from the prophets.

"I am the Lord," he remembered reading, "who has made all things, who alone stretched out the heavens..." He whispered them now as he remembered the verses. "...who spread out the earth by myself, who foils the signs of false prophets and makes fools of diviners, who overthrows the learning of the wise and turns it into nonsense, who carries out the words of his servants and fulfills the predictions of his messengers, who says of Jerusalem, 'It shall be inhabited,' and of the towns of Judah, 'They shall be built,' and of their ruins, 'I will restore them.'"

"Tell me the key word that controls this particular passage," Breslov had said when he'd finished reading.

"Chayah," Gur remembered answering.

"And what about that word, *chayah*? What does it mean?"

"It means 'to restore.'"

"Very good," Breslov replied. "I will bring Jerusalem back to life. That is what the prophet is saying."

But Gur had questions that went much further and the answers he heard that day changed his life, turning him away from rabbinical school toward the study of history, a change that propelled him toward the life that brought him to this very day.

"Some say Jerusalem will be restored to us," he'd said to Breslov. "Some say it is being restored to us now and that the events we see happening around us are part of it. Others say the words of the prophet were spoken long ago and are no longer of any effect."

"In order to understand the text, to find its truest meaning," Breslov explained, "we must look to history. The Hebrew language gives us a choice of only perfect and imperfect: I have restored. I will restore. But history shows us Jerusalem was destroyed and restored many times. It was destroyed by the Babylonians and it was rebuilt by Nehemiah. It was destroyed by the Romans, and it was rebuilt by the Romans themselves. Others in faraway lands try to decide our fate, but God will have His way.

"Men of the world have shown they can take the city from us and from each other, but God has shown that they cannot take the city from Him. This is a holy city and no matter what men do to it, this city will always belong to God. He has restored the city in the past. He is restoring it in the present. He will restore it in the future. It will always be His city, and He will always return it to us."

Tears came to Gur's eyes as he remembered those words and as he realized that the prophecy of Isaiah had come true once more. Rabbi Breslov was no longer alive and Gur's own father was dead, too. They had longed to see Jerusalem fully restored to the Jews, an event many before them had hoped to see but few, even in all its thousands of years of existence, had lived to witness.

"This time," Gur said to himself, "I not only saw it take place, I was part of it. Blessed are you, Lord God, King of the Universe," he prayed softly, "who has granted us life, who sustained us, and enabled us to reach this occasion."

THE SIX-DAY WAR

AFTER ISRAEL'S INDEPENDENCE and rousing victory in the 1948 war, Arab neighbors continued to call for a military solution to the presence of Jews in Palestine. By 1967, those tensions reached a crescendo when Egypt moved a large portion of its army into the Sinai Peninsula and appeared on the verge of launching an attack. Israel responded by placing troops near its borders and calling up its reserves. Events soon spiraled toward war.

International pressure was meant to force Israeli leaders to refrain from action, but as tensions continued to increase, Prime Minster Eshkol and others realized that Israel was particularly vulnerable to a first strike by either of its neighbors. Rather than wait for the inevitable, Israel launched an air strike against the Egyptian air force. Over the course of the following two days, almost ninety percent of the Egyptian air force was destroyed or rendered inoperable.

At the same time, Israeli troops moved south across the border into the Sinai Peninsula and west into Gaza. Jordan countered by moving troops into the West Bank. By the sixth day, however, Israel had vanquished the armies of Jordan and Egypt and decimated the Syrian air force.

Near the end of the conflict, with international pressure mounting for a cease-fire, Israel moved against Syrian artillery positions on the Golan Heights, from where many farming settlements in Galilee had been harassed. That battle proved to be one of the most difficult of the war but Israeli forces prevailed, and by June 10, 1967, Israel occupied all of Palestine from the Syrian border southward through the Sinai Peninsula, and eastward to the Jordan River, a task completed against armies easily two and three times that of Israel.

Our novel is loosely based on a compilation of events surrounding the Six-Day War. We have attempted to portray these events as realistically as possible, but with an eye toward creating an entertaining and engaging story. Nevertheless events, locations and some of the characters in the story are the work of fiction. Our hope is that in seeing events through their lives you will be inspired to read further on the subject of the 1967 war and the continuing Arab-Israeli conflict.

ACKNOWLEDGEMENTS

My deepest gratitude and sincere thanks to my writing partner, Joe Hilley, and to my executive assistant, Lanelle Shaw-Young, both of whom work diligently to turn my story ideas into great books. And to Arlen Young, Peter Glöege, and Janna Nysewander for making the finished product look and read its best. And always, to my wife, Carolyn, whose presence makes everything better.

BOOKS BY: MIKE EVANS

Israel: America's Key to Survival

Save Jerusalem

The Return

Jerusalem D.C.

Purity and Peace of Mind

Who Cries for the Hurting?

Living Fear Free

I Shall Not Want

Let My People Go

Jerusalem Betrayed

Seven Years of Shaking: A Vision

The Nuclear Bomb of Islam

Jerusalem Prophecies

Pray For Peace of Jerusalem

America's War: The Beginning
of the End

The Jerusalem Scroll

The Prayer of David

The Unanswered Prayers of Jesus

God Wrestling

The American Prophecies

Beyond Iraq: The Next Move

The Final Move beyond Iraq

Showdown with Nuclear Iran

Jimmy Carter: The Liberal Left
and World Chaos

Atomic Iran

Cursed

Betrayed

The Light

Corrie's Reflections & Meditations
(booklet)

GAMECHANGER SERIES:
GameChanger
Samson Option
The Four Horsemen

THE PROTOCOLS SERIES:
The Protocols
The Candidate

The Revolution

The Final Generation

Seven Days

The Locket

Living in the F.O.G.

Persia: The Final Jihad

Jerusalem

The History of Christian Zionism

Countdown

Ten Boom: Betsie, Promise of God

Commanded Blessing

Born Again: 1948
Born Again: 1967

Presidents in Prophecy

Stand with Israel
